COURTS AND MEDIATION: NEW PATHS FOR JUSTICE

SELECTED PAPERS FROM THE SYMPOSIUM
ON COURTS AND MEDIATION,
GEMME-CATALAN WHITE BOOK ON MEDIATION,
COSMOCAIXA, BARCELONA,
JUNE, 18TH-19TH, 2009

Editors
Marta Poblet, Sílvia Gabarró, Núria Galera, Emma Teodoro

EUROPEAN PRESS ACADEMIC PUBLISHING

ISBN 978-88-8398-067-1

Copyright ©2011 by European Press Academic Publishing
Florence, Italy
www.e-p-a-p.com
www.europeanpress.eu

PRINTED IN

ITALY, USA, UK

Contents

II. Short Papers: Practices and Experiences in Mediation

2.1. Restorative Justice

Preface

Building a model to regulate, favour and promote mediation as an alternative system to solve disputes is not a task that can be improvised. The Spanish division of GEMME (European Association of Judges for Mediation) was engaged in collaborating with the authorities whose responsibility is to promote the projects of legislative reform in Catalonia. From the beginning, in spring 2007, GEMME's role was to contribute to the pre-legislative debate with its judicial experience in this field. This experience was to be offered not only on the Spanish case, but about the European and pro-European environment, as it is GEMME's identity sign.

The Catalan Government (Generalitat de Catalunya) was facing the challenge of taking a step forward to introduce this methodology in the justice system. This challenge was represented by the research project "White Book on Mediation in Catalonia" and GEMME Spain decided to devote its 2009 annual assembly to attract Spanish and European experts in mediation and present them the work that was being carried out to be the basis of the research project. Therefore, in parallel with the annual meeting of the judges, prosecutors, judicial secretaries and judicial mediators, GEMME contributed to organize a macro event gathering more than six hundred people. Fourteen research groups presented the work done throughout the first semester of the project in several workshops.

Contrary to those apparently rigorous approaches asking for top-down legislation as the mechanism to introduce and promote mediation (without bringing real life into the picture), we have always believed that to lay the foundations of the model a previous study was required. Consequently, GEMME fully endorsed the White Book from its very inception.

The introduction of mediation in a justice system such as the Spanish one, strongly anchored in litigation as the sole legal channel to solve a dispute, cannot be improvised. The lack of a professional collective of mediators with an acceptable level of training and the incomplete knowledge of the reality where the model has to be embedded could result in the utmost reject of relevant groups of professionals such as the lawyers or the judges, whose collaboration is essential to move forward in an effective way.

The symposium lasted for two days and hosted discussions on the research proposals between judges and jurists from more than twelve European. This volume includes the most relevant papers presented there. The volume would not have been possible without the collaboration of the UAB Institute of Law and Technology and the entities that supported the event: the Catalan Department of Justice, the Spanish Judicial School and the two private foundations: *Fundació La Caixa* and *Fundación Carmen y María José Godó*.

Pascual Ortuño
Director of the Spanish Judicial School

Foreword: Assembling Professional Experiences

At the moment of writing this Foreword, the Catalan White Book on Mediation has been officially presented (http://www.llibreblancmediacio.com). The White Book is the final result of a long research depending from the Department of Justice of the Catalan Government, generously funded by the Obra Social La Caixa, and involving nearly all the Catalan institutions, sixteen research teams, and about one-hundred researchers.

However, some time ago, at the moment of celebrating the Symposium *New Paths for Justice* (June 18th-19th 2009), its results were not as clear as they are today. We were still struggling to produce fresh data, and trying to understand the way in which mediation as institution was being constructed within the Catalan society.

We suspected that mediation was not only a "new" procedural way to deal with conflicts or a simple device to avoid heavy caseloads and high litigation rates. We intended to show that in a country of 7.5 million people, with 16% of immigrant population growth in the last ten years (about one million people), ADR, dialogue and mediation in all its forms sustained the regulatory way in which Catalan institutions, professionals and the civil society were reacting to the adjustment problems, conflicts, integration strategies and policies produced is this unattended and new situation.

Therefore, we distinguished between the *mediation system* —concerning all the actions, interventions and preventive or restorative processes required in potentially active conflicts— and *mediation as institution*, the procedural way to reach an agreement with social, political and eventually legal effects.

In this restrictive second meaning of mediation, Courts and the coordinated behaviour of professional mediators, lawyers, judges and magistrates are crucial. It corresponds to the top of the pyramid, in the axe of different lines that guide to the production of agreements. But the basis is most important as well. In several markets, consumer agencies, hospitals and health units, prisons and detention units, primary and high schools, neighborhoods and cities, and family and community centers, mediators behave as mediators *and* facilitators at the same time. As a result, there is a dynamic interactive flow between the mediation system —in the broad sense— and the institution of mediation (as procedural and legal device). The mediation system shapes the kind of mediation that is needed for each domain.

The joint GEMME-White Book Symposium intended to explore this interactive space. Judges, magistrates, lawyers and mediators shared their professional experience with researchers from several related disciplines (namely, criminology, psychology, anthropology, political science, sociology and law).

I think that the selected papers contained in this volume have to be read from this dynamic approach, and doing so, perhaps the reader will soon realize that mediation is not only a kind of *alternative* legal procedure, but a *joint process of governance and law* in which citizens —within the nation-states and in the wide global world as well— assume dialogue as a culture of peace and as a source of law alike.

Acknowledgments follow now. This volume would not have been possible without the intensive work of the editors. Marta Poblet, Sílvia Gabarró, Núria Galera and Emma Teodoro did a great job selecting, correcting and editing some of the papers presented at the Symposium, and first published in Catalan or Spanish in the original Proceedings (*Simposi sobre tribunals i mediació / Simposio sobre tribunals i mediació*, Huygens Ed., Barcelona, 2009). Authors had furnished the English version of their papers, but this team —and especially Sílvia Gabarró— assumed the supplementary work of proofreading the final versions. Olga Baranowska, Paula Ruiz Alfaro and Cristina García Gálvez eventually provided their assistance, as they did in the organization of the Symposium (gathering almost four hundred people). It was held in the setting of Cosmocaixa, which has also given the image for the cover of this volume.

Finally, this edition, as well as the complementary logistics of GEMME-White Book, falls under the Projects ONTOMEDIA (CSO-2008-05536-SOCI; I+D TSI-020501-2008), and IDT SGR- 688.

Pompeu Casanovas
IDT Director
Chair of the Symposium

Introduction

Marta Poblet,[1] Sílvia Gabarró,[2] Núria Galera,[2] Emma Teodoro[2]
[1]ICREA, UAB Institute of Law and Technology
[2] UAB Institute of Law and Technology

1. Introduction

Alternative Dispute Resolution (ADR) and the mediation movement in particular have long-established practices with a venerable tradition behind them. While the Pound Conference of 1976 is frequently quoted as the foundational moment of ADR in the US, the preceding decades witness a number of public and private initiatives—legislation, programs, reports, etc.—steering the use of negotiation, mediation, and arbitration as prominent means of resolving conflicts. To Barret (2004), the 1888 Arbitration Act on labor conflicts in the railroad sector can be considered as the first piece of legislation on ADR in the US. Equally, the creation of the Federal Conciliation Service (1917) and, later on, the Federal Mediation and Conciliation Service (1947) endorse the institutionalization of mediation within the domain of labor conflicts.

The next wave of initiatives emerge from the convulsed decade of 1960, featured by racial disturbs and the struggle for civil rights. The US Congress passes the Civil Rights Act of 1964 and, one year after, the Community Relations Service (1965) impulses conciliation in conflicts involving civil rights. As unrest remains high, the Kerner Commission issues a report on the need to introduce social and legislative changes to face the growing cleavages of the American society (Barret 2004). It comes as no surprise, therefore, that the Ford Foundation, among other private institutions, starts financing projects on mediation for racial and community conflicts and two new institutions see daylight in 1968: the National Center for Dispute Settlement (NCDS) and the Center for Mediation and Conflict Resolution (CMCR) in Washington and Nova York, respectively. The foundation of the Society of Professionals in Dispute Resolution (SPIDR) in 1972 and, one decade after, of the Academy of Family Mediators (AFM) are therefore consonant with the zeitgeist. The 1980s and 1990s decades dwell on these achievements to consolidate ADR as a well defined alternative to the judicial resolution of conflicts. In parallel, as Baruch points out, mediation has also become "a central element in the overall case-management system of many courts, and this phenomenon continues to grow unabated." (Baruch, 2008). According to this author, there is a resulting ambivalence towards mediation than can be traced throughout these last decades:

> [T]he current ambivalence about the relationship of mediation to the courts is only the latest phase of a four-decade-long tension in this "partnership" of two very different dispute resolution processes. From the earliest beginnings of the "modern mediation field" in the late 1960s to the present, the relationship of mediation to the courts has fluctuated between two orientations. In the first, mediation has been seen and has served as a faithful "servant" of the court system, performing functions vital to the courts and to effective judicial administration. In the second, mediation has been encouraged and has sought to "break free" and establish itself as a separate and distinct conflict resolution process, performing very different functions that are vital to society but unrelated to judicial administration per se. The cycling between these two orientations is driven by the very different potentials mediation offers as a social process, as viewed through different professional eyes. These different views explain why some today are gratified by what they see as mediation's success in finding a firm place in the court system, while others are discouraged by what they see as the court system "capturing" mediation and depriving it of its real social value. (Baruch, 2004: 706)

In Europe, similar cycles can be traced with regard to the progress of mediation (Benichou, 2010). Nevertheless, since the decade of 1980 mediation in Europe has undergone a sustained impulse with the several Recommendations of the Council of Europe on alternative forms of justice (and notably the Recommendation n° R (98) 1 reinforcing recourse to mediation in family law matters; Recommendation n° R (99) 19 promoting mediation in criminal law matters; Recommendation n° R (2001) 9 supporting "alternative forms of resolution of conflicts between state officers and citizens" or Recommendation R (2002) 10 encouraging mediation in civil law matters. The European Commission contributed to this framework by opening the consultation process leading to the Green Book on ADR in Europe (EC, 2002), the general goal being the preparation of legislation in a European framework. The legislative work at the European level has crystallized in the Directive 2008/52/CE of the European Parliament and the European Council of Mai 21, 2008 "on certain aspects of mediation in civil and commercial law matters",[1] which defines mediation as a structured process in which one or several parties in a dispute try voluntarily by themselves to find an agreement for the resolution of their dispute, with the help of a mediator. The Directive is an

---

[1] http://eurlex.europa.eu/LexUriServ/LexUriServ.do?
uri=OJ:L:2008:136:0003:0008:FR:PDF

attempt to articulate mediation as a voluntary process and the formal trials held before a judge, and it proposes different mechanisms to facilitate this goal.

In a way, this book is also an attempt to transcend the quandaries of the relationship between mediation and the courts by offering some reflections on current practices and experiences that, from different domains and standpoints, aim at fostering productive relationships between mediation and the judicial system. As Barrot puts it "[t]he need for justice is often a need for mediation: resolving a conflict does not exclusively mean going to court if the situation could be equitably resolved in another way" Barrot, 2010: 11). The book gathers selected papers from the Symposium on Courts and Mediation held in Barcelona on June 18-19, 2009. The Symposium was co-organized by the Association of European Magistrates for Mediation (GEMME: Groupement Européen des Magistrats pour la Médiation)[2] and the Institute of Law and Technology of the Universitat Autònoma de Barcelona, whose director was at the time simultaneously coordinating the research activities leading to the White Book of Mediation in Catalonia. The result was a fruitful cross-fertilization of ideas, experiences, and ongoing research on mediation.

2. Structure of the volume

This volume is divided in two parts: Part I includes long papers covering the state of the art, and it is split in two different sections: "Justice, Conflicts and Courts" and "Transnational and International Trends"; and Part II comprises experiences and practices in mediation.

In the first section of Part I, Daniel Gamper provides a philosophical approach to mediation by linking the notion of tolerance to those of conflict avoidance and resolution. In this view, John Rawls' theory on liberalism and silence in ethics is compared to that of John Gray on pluralism of values and peaceful coexistence, with a final review of Michael Sandel's communitarism and search for a common ethical background.

The second paper by Josep Redorta approaches mediation from a psycho-sociological perspective and tries to reconsider our current conflict resolution mechanisms. Redorta argues that the debate between judicial and extra-judicial processes is a false one and points out at processes of dejudicialisation as channels to improve the access of citizens to justice.

Anna Mestitz and Massimo Vogliotti describe in "The Rise and Growth of Mediation in Italy" how victim-offender mediation (VOM) for the youth was introduced, how services started to run, what the outcomes were and

---

[2] Today, Gemme's membership consists of more than 350 magistrates, spread across 20 European Union countries.

which are the initiatives to implement restorative justice and mediation. The lack of a legal framework is also considered as well as the role of their Department of Juvenile Justice in comparison with other European bodies having similar roles.

Isabel Viola paper closes this section by discussing the enforceability of mediation agreements. To do so, she draws a map of the European Union position with regard to mediation, giving special attention to Directive 2008/52/EC of the European Parliament and of the Council of 21 May 2008 on certain aspects of mediation in civil and commercial matters. The issues surrounding the enforcement of documents resulting from a mediation agreement in Spain are examined taking into account the experiences of other jurisdictions in this area.

In the second section of Part I Jordi Palou notes how victims and civil society at large are beginning to play an important role in achieving a peaceful solution to violent conflict by participating in the processes of justice, whether international or transitional justice during or after the conflict as well as in international mediation and dialogue. The paper presents the experience obtained from the specific approaches to peace and justice in Central Africa featuring the involvement of civil society and truth as cornerstone of all action.

Patricia Orejudo analyses in chapter 6 the law applicable to international mediation contracts. When mediation contracts involve transnational elements, the laws of the diverse states involved could claim to be applicable. The paper therefore aims at illustrating the functioning of the present and the future instruments of private international law that solve the conflict-of-laws issue.

The final chapter of Part I examines the legal framework of the use of alternative dispute resolution (ADR) procedures to deal with consumer complaints, which enjoy a specific legal framework in the EU. Immaculada Barral also describes how online dispute resolution (ODR) procedures in this area of consumer relations are constantly being explored in an effort to bolster e-confidence.

Part II on mediation practices starts with the chapter by Ramón Alzate and the experience on restorative justice deployed by the Victim-offender Mediation Services in Bilbao and Barakaldo (Basque Country, Spain). Also within the criminal domain, Maria M. Chumillas *et al.* present a study that evaluates victims' and offenders' degree of satisfaction towards the Juvenile Mediation Program of the Catalan Department of Justice. The results show how the appraisal mediation is positive for both parties, but especially for the minor.

Juan Ramón Liébana analyses in chapter 10 the mediation procedures deployed by the English Juvenile Criminal system as a well established referent for other continental initiatives. Finally, Maria Munné *et al.* offer in Chapter 11 an overview of their experience in community mediation. By complementing professional mediation with non-formal mediation, the aim of their project consists of introducing a new role in the community: the "natural mediator", a person who facilitates citizens' communication and participation channels.

The area of family mediation is covered in two chapters. First, Núria Villanueva describes how the mediation service of the Center of Family Mediation in Barcelona handles the judiciary referrals to intra judicial mediation informative voluntary sessions.   In particular, the chapter analyzes the mediators' discourse to inform the parties about the overall process. Second, Josep Fité analyses the dynamics and special characteristics of the extrajudicial information session provided by the Legal Guidance Service of the Barcelona Bar Association, which is the main referral source for directing individual parties towards the family mediation process run by the Barcelona Mediation Guidance Service (SOM).

Finally, the last section of the book is devoted to the health domain and gathers contributions from experts in mediation within this area. Thus, Judit Esparrica *et al*. offer a theoretical review and a case study on how to create spaces for conflict management in healthcare organizations. Next, Blanca Igual *et al*. analyze the typology of mediators currently working in the Catalan health sector. And thirdly, Glòria Novel relies on the concept of "complex organization" to present a three-year research project on mediation in the Catalan healthcare system.

Acknowledgments

This volume has benefited from research funded by three different projects: (ii) The White Book of Mediation in Catalonia (Department of Justice of the Government of Catalonia and Obra Social La Caixa Foundation); (ii) ONTOMEDIA: Platform of Web Services for Online Mediation, Spanish Ministry of Industry, Tourism and Commerce (Plan AVANZA I+D, TSI-020501-2008, 2008-2010); (ii) ONTOMEDIA: Semantic Web, Ontologies and ODR: Platform of Web Services for Online Mediation (2009-2011), Spanish Ministry of Science and Innovation (CSO-2008-05536-SOCI).

References

Benichou (2010). Mediation in Europe. In *Overview of Judicial Mediation in the World: Mediation, the universal language of conflict resolution*. First International Conference on Judicial Mediation, Paris, 16-17 October 2009. Paris: L'Harmattan: 29-33.

Baruch Bush, R.A. (2008). Staying in Orbit, or Breaking Free: The Relationship of
    Mediation to the Courts over Four Decades. North Dakota Law Review, Vol.
    86: 705-768.
Breneur, B. (dir.) (2010). *Overview of Judicial Mediation in the World: Mediation,
    the universal language of conflict resolution*. First International Conference on
    Judicial Mediation, Paris, 16-17 October 2009. Paris: L'Harmattan.
Casanovas, P.; Magre, J.; Lauroba, E. (eds.) (2010). Llibre Blanc de la Mediació a
    Catalunya.   Barcelona: Generalitat   de   Catalunya.   Available   at:
    http://www.llibreblancmediació.com
European   Commission   (2002).   Green   Book   on   ADR   in   Europe,
    http://europa.eu/eur-lex/fr/com/gpr/2002/com2002_0196fr01.pdf

Conflict at the Centre of Contemporary Political Philosophy

Daniel Gamper
Universitat Autònoma de Barcelona

Abstract. The mediation of conflicts can be relevant to political philosophy in two senses: it involves a dejudicialisation of daily life, and it is also a means of promoting the kind of civic coexistence that goes beyond bare coexistence. This article aims at describing the concept of tolerance for conflict avoidance and resolution from a philosophical point of view. Therefore, John Rawls' theories on liberalism and silence on ethics are firstly explained and then those of John Gray on pluralism of values and peaceful coexistence. Finally, Michael Sandel's communitarianism and the search for a common ethical background close the series of interpretations made by the most outstanding contemporary political philosophers of this field.

Keywords: Political philosophy, Liberalism, Mediation, Democracy, Conflict, Tolerance, Dialogue, Citizenship

1. Preliminary considerations

Contemporary political philosophy and, in general, any philosophical reflection about coexistence, originates from the existence of conflicts, the disparity of opinions and more or less fundamental disagreements of different degrees of importance. These disagreements arise when deciding about distributive justice, recognition of rights or even about the correct definition of reality. Nowadays, political philosophy specially focuses on the type of disagreement among citizens to which no solution can be hoped unless coercive force is used. Particularly, it involves reasonable disagreements; in other words, those that are reasonably motivated by the affected parties and in which there is a reciprocal rejection of violent methods to resolve them. These disputes are conflictive to the extent that both parties want that their respective views find echo in public policy. Therefore, the questions raised concern issues such as abortion, euthanasia, same-sex marriages or stem cell research.

Anglo-Saxon political philosophy has particularly focused on conflicts arising from ethical discrepancies; in other words, conflicts between individuals, groups or institutions caused by different ways of understanding the meaning of good life. Political science is largely concerned with designing political institutions so that they are able to resolve socio-political conflicts in a peaceful, orderly and fair manner. However, political philosophy concerns itself much more with conflicts caused by clashes in the way the good life is understood, discrepancies among individuals or groups that are motivated by different and frequently irreconcilable conceptions of what life is, what it is for, who owns it and when it is available. These are conflicts about the ultimate justifications of existence, based on a set of beliefs and/or reasons to which citizens resort to justify their choices.

In these cases, we say that there is conflict because we cannot reasonably expect those involved to renounce to their principles or ultimate values for the sake of peaceful coexistence. We often talk about conflict in terms of tragedy for the very reason that its solution or abatement cannot satisfy both sides equally.

Therefore, the central conflicts of political philosophy are those caused by the worldviews of citizens who, either in the name of those views or based on them, insist that institutions take their requests or demands into account. For example, this is the case for members of a religion who demand to be exempted from certain civil obligations, or citizens who want their own worldview to be taken into account when a law –that should be applied to society as a whole— is passed. Political philosophy is therefore centred on the repercussions that people's reasoned preferences should have in legislation, on what the public debate itself should be like in the democratic process, on which subjects and which vocabularies are appropriate when basic laws are drawn up, and so on.

From a philosophical point of view, it is essential to question whether there is a single solution to conflicts in which there is some kind of institutional mediation and if this solution can be reached objectively. In other words, whether there is a single, objective, correct solution to conflicts motivated by ethical discrepancies. Clearly there is not such a single and correct solution for liberalism, nor are there independent criteria for the views of the participants that enable us to decide what the correct, objective solution to such a conflict should be. The only tangible objective for determining the correctness of the solution to a conflict is that it should have considered the reasons offered by the affected parties and that it should not result in the discrimination of either. While liberalism tends to be focused on the procedures used to resolve conflicts, community-based proposals are based on the assumption that there exists a substantive solution which best reflects the ways in which a certain community ought to resolve the conflicts that arise within it. What both share is the importance of avoiding situations in which external elements introduce relationships of domination and infringe the individual's negative rights.

2. Democracy and the civic virtue of tolerance

Why has political philosophy not paid enough attention to the mediation of conflicts? Perhaps its proximity to political science has led it to place too much emphasis on institutional designs, so the informal processes of collective will formation have been ignored. Nevertheless, the mediation of conflicts can be relevant to political philosophy because not only does it involve a dejudicialisation of daily life, but also a means of promoting the kind of civic coexistence that goes beyond bare coexistence. Both of these questions sway political philosophy beyond liberalism, towards models more focused on virtues, participation and civic duties.[1] Mediation of conflicts can be understood as a democratisation of civic relations, in which an explicit rejection of any recourse to traditional legal institutions is involved. While it is true that mediation in itself means adding an institutional link to civic interaction, the presence of these institutions does not mean the abandonment by citizens of their responsibilities, nor does it establish new relationships of dependency. Nevertheless, it can be seen as a civic exercise in public autonomy. Mediation gives an incentive to imagination for the solution of conflicts and promotes reciprocal knowledge, so it could be seen as a small-scale but crucial tool for the construction of citizenship as well as a guarantee of democratic wellbeing. In the same semantic field as mediation, we find words such as horizontality, citizenship, civil society, public-spiritedness and independence. The counterpoints here are democracy and liberalism, or in words of Benjamin Constant, the liberties of the ancient and the modern. The emphasis on mediation contributes to a displacement of interest towards democracy to the detriment of a conception of liberalism that is too narrow and, in that sense, individualistic.

Philosophical discourse on civic virtues arises as a criticism of liberalism. Compared with the emphasis of liberalism on individual liberties and non-interference by institutions into privacy, the discourse of virtue underlines the importance of the fact that the community using these liberties is linked by more than just the same laws. This is to say that there is a common language, a system of shared values and collective participation in the public arena.[2] A theory that is excessively centred on individuals loses sight of the need for citizens to create significant links between themselves. Therefore, they try to resolve their conflicts without systematically resorting to the legal institutions. What the discourse of virtue demands is a step forward from the paradigm of the individual to the paradigm of the citizen.

Within the context of citizenship, one of the tools that enables a more civil and horizontal approach to conflicts is tolerance. This is a controver-

---

[1] Here I am referring to the increasing importance in political philosophy of republicanism represented in its different forms by Philip Pettit, Quentin Skinner and Maurizio Viroli, not forgetting the Kantian republicanism of Jürgen Habermas.

[2] Cf. MacIntyre (1981), Camps (1991).

sial concept, as it does not express an opening up to one's fellow citizens, but rather a relationship of distancing. Moreover, tolerance tends to imply a power relationship and so it is obviously not the same to tolerate than to be tolerated. In any case, despite its inherent ambiguity, tolerance is generally considered an element that promotes peaceful coexistence, solving conflicts by eliminating their causes.

However, there has recently been a growing tendency to see tolerance not only as a negative self-limitation for the sake of peaceful coexistence, but also as a positive virtue. Tolerance is therefore referred to in terms of positive tolerance (Thiebaut, 1999), tolerance founded on reflection (Forst, 2003) or tolerance for clearly moral reasons (Garzón Valdés, 1993) to mark the distance with respect to prudential or strategic tolerance.[3] When reclassified like this, tolerance is an expression of a willingness to understand the reasoning that motivates others to act. This should really lead us to talk about respect rather than tolerance, since we are not only placing the emphasis on the reasons we have for tolerating others. Nevertheless, we are also moving towards the reasons that others have for doing what they do (things that we do not like or approve and which are precisely what caused the need for tolerance in the first place). This reformulation of tolerance in terms of respect means the abandonment of the indifference and rejection contained in social relationships of bare coexistence and become a way of understanding conflict. This conflict is motivated by fierce discrepancies about the idea of the good life, as something that can be solved or deactivated thanks to an attitude of openness towards the other. In the same semantic field as respect, we also find concepts like dialogue, deliberation and citizenship. Then, we are talking about a normative conception of what civic participation of citizens should be according to which the social fabric is a space where relationships of mistrust and confrontation caused by philosophical or religious discrepancies can be overcome by the reciprocal adoption of the other's point of view, as Habermas said. However, as we shall see next, it is not an interpretation shared by the majority of contemporary political philosophers.

3. John Rawls: liberalism and silence on ethics

The first thing to highlight is John Rawls' contribution and his concept of "overlapping consensus" as the founding basis of a fair process for the mediation of conflicts shared by all. Within this concept, the main lines of his theory of justice are found, sketched out in *Political Liberalism*: the basic

---

[3] Cf. the definition proposed by Rafael del Águila: "It is a negative, pragmatic, prudential, minimalist, consequentialist and political concept that contemplates tolerance as being the lesser of two evils, possibly as a necessary evil, but never as good in its own right" (Del Águila, 2003: 365).

laws of a fair society should be subject to being accepted by all citizens. If any citizen feels that he or she cannot sincerely subscribe to the fundamental laws of society, then the content or terms in which those laws were drawn up and approved must be reviewed, as long as the reasons alleged by the citizen are reasonable (in other words, they are not the result of fundamentalist convictions that deny the exercising of fundamental rights by other citizens by virtue of arbitrary actions). Overlapping consensus means that everyone should be able to rebuild the laws of society on their own terms, without having to renounce their basic beliefs. To this end, Rawls places restrictions on the way in which laws should be justified. They must not be based on reasons or vocabularies that are incomprehensible to some citizens. Given that these citizens have not only to feel that they are subject to the law, but that they are also the authors of it. In other words, given that their adhesion to the principles of justice should be sincere and not simply strategic, it is essential that they are able to understand it, that they are able to rebuild it in their own terms and that they can find some way of linking it to their own religious or philosophical convictions. Therefore, when establishing or justifying the law, a move should be made to avoid the sectarianism and bias that divides society.

The basic laws to which everyone should subscribe find their greatest expression in the parliament. For that reason, politicians, political post holders and civil servants who have either participated in the legal drafting process or are responsible for its implementation, should maintain a certain degree of neutrality in relation to citizens' worldviews. Here we are dealing with the typical mandate of neutrality contained in liberal theories, which should guarantee the non-discrimination of citizens on ideological or religious grounds, and which also keeps the institutions open to everyone, without differentiating. Evidently, the neutrality of laws cannot be total since they fall within the framework of the specific political culture that formulates them. Nonetheless, within that framework it is important to ensure that civil servants do not tackle their specific situations of responsibility from their own worldview, but they abstract themselves from it and confine it as it was to the private ambit. This move, which is undoubtedly applicable to civil servants in liberal public institutions, should be extended, according to Rawls, to all other citizens. Rawls imposes on citizens the obligation to vote in elections or referendums on basic legal questions independently of their religious or philosophical convictions. Citizens should be reasonable; in other words, they should be able to distinguish between reasons that serve in the private ambit and those that are valid in the public sphere. Once this distinction has been made, he calls on citizens, when they are acting as such, to make public use of their reason. This is to say that they should discriminate between their reasons and only make use of those that they have good motives to believe can be shared with other citizens.

They are asked to put their strong ethical convictions to one side, filter them and bring forward only those that can be formulated in a language that is comprehensible to everyone.

In short, the political model proposed by Rawls tries to ensure that discussion motivated by serious ethical conflicts remains outside political decisions, and remains privatised, so to speak, and therefore guarantees that legislation is as neutral as possible and not marked by a specific worldview. Public debates on controversial questions should remain deactivated in order to reach sustainable agreements. The great diversity that exists in society makes it impossible to reach agreement on these issues, and it is therefore recommendable that they remain off the political agenda. It is a matter of applying the so-called 'gag rule', which keeps the most controversial issues out of the public arena, or rather outside public discussions which, at the end of the day, will affect in a substantive way all legislation on essential matters.

These conflicts can later be resolved or abated by using the principles of justice that constitute the common ground accepted by everyone. These principles should serve as a procedure for the resolution of conflicts, like the parameters that are used to establish hierarchies of values and principles which contribute to redirect serious disagreements among citizens. However, the important thing is that this procedure should not give anyone an advantaged position, so the way it is drawn up should be neutral in relation to the worldviews that exist in society. For the same reason, citizens should abstain from appearing in the public sphere with their moral and ethical convictions and limit themselves to doing so with a firm desire to achieve agreements with their fellow citizens.

4. John Gray: pluralism of values and peaceful coexistence

John Gray, inspired by the work of Isaiah Berlin, maintains that political philosophy and any possible agreements on conflicts of values should take into account value pluralism. This goes somewhat beyond the social diversity described by Rawls. Not only does it confirm that different worldviews co-exist in society and which are unable to reach agreement on questions discussed, but he goes further to maintain that it is impossible to find a meeting point of all these worldviews. From these worldviews, a procedure and legal principles could be established, and everyone may share them with nobody having to yield on fundamental aspects of their conception of good life. In his book *Two Faces of Liberalism,* Gray maintains that any form of overlapping consensus results in the discrimination of some citizens by others, the discrimination of one worldview by another. This is due to the fact that it is not possible to find a field of common argument on fundamental aspects that can be shared by everyone. It is unreasonable to expect citizens to abandon some of their convictions to adapt them to others. Therefore, instead of proposing a confluence of the different worldviews that constitutes a meeting point shared by everyone, Gray maintains that temporary agreements need to be reached on the basis of a thin agreement which he calls *modus vivendi*. The most important thing is peace not justice. The insistence on justice can have two-fold consequences: either citizens give in to each other reciprocally, where one worldview imposes itself on others, or the conflict becomes irresolvable and instead of a confluence the result is the disappearance of peaceful coexistence.

This *modus vivendi* shares certain scepticism with Rawls' model about the possibility of reaching agreements on controversial questions. The difference lies in the fact that, for Gray, the scope of what we consider to be controversial is even broader, so there are more questions that need to be removed from public debate. This is because of the impossibility of reaching agreements and the possible effect on public order that could occur as a result of an insistence on resolving all conflicts that arise. If an attempt is made to resolve all of them searching a central point on which everyone can agree, this can only lead to a situation where the liberties of some must be sacrificed for the sake of the liberties of others. The intuition that these conflicts are resolvable is due to the failure to perceive the radical incommensurability between the different worldviews that are present in society. Not only that, but conflicts can also arise if an attempt is made to apply universally recognised principles, such as human rights down to the last letter. According to Gray, the application of human rights should be adapted to the context and the needs of each situation. If human rights are still applied radically and totally, we will see that even in the writing of a single article, such as religious liberty, there are requirements that may cause serious conflicts in certain cases (Gray, 2000: chap. 4). What is required here is an adaptation of the legal requirements to specific contexts, something that could be seen as a renouncement of any theory of justice that tries to establish universal principles universally applicable.

The order of *modus vivendi* does not expect citizens to adapt their preferences to the demands of coexistence, but rather that the terms of coexistence adapt themselves to the demands of the citizens. One example of this can be seen in the recent recommendation of the Archbishop of Canterbury, Rowan Williams. He accepts Islamic law or Shariah to be considered legitimate in the United Kingdom for the resolution of conflicts among members of the Muslim faith. *Modus vivendi*, as a provisional agreement that is susceptible to revision, does not require a group of citizens to abandon their customs or their religion, but allows them to maintain them and offers them the channels to do so.

Gray bases his ideal on the concept of tolerance which, as has already been seen, is one of the terminological keys for understanding mediation in conflicts, or rather for avoiding situations in which any possible conflicts arising become irresolvable. In contrast to the monist approach to tolerance propounded by Rawls (tolerance based on agreement by all on a universal procedure), Gray proposes a pluralist-type tolerance. In his own words it is described as "an ideal for common life that is not based on common beliefs" (Gray, 2000: chap. 1). For Gray, a society is tolerant when it does not impose abusive demands on its citizens to adapt to their coexistence, where everyone can live their own lifestyles. These lifestyles must be obviously reasonable and respectful with regard to people's basic human rights but may be also considered abhorrent by the rest of the population.

5. Michael Sandel: communitarism and the search for a common ethical background

The case of Michael Sandel, a philosopher who ascribes – not without a certain reticence – to communitarianism, is different. He considers it important for societies to maintain a strong ethical cohesion. In other words, they should strengthen social links for a kind of good life that is shared by everyone. That is why it is important not to reject controversial questions in citizens' discussions on public issues. It is not just a case of reaching strong agreements that respect the liberty of the citizens, nor is it a question of undertaking negotiations that allow peaceful coexistence. It is rather one of substantive debates that illuminate the principles of justice, the ethical principles shared (or which could be shared) by all citizens. These potentially divisive principles may be introduced into the public debate, thereby going beyond reciprocal tolerance in favour of a positive form of tolerance that respects the different ways of understanding what is good and what is not. Moral discourse can and should play an important role in political and constitutional argumentation.[4] The alternative to this moralization of political discourse is liberal tolerance. If we consider the case of the decriminalisation of homosexual practices, the liberal argument holds that there is no need to question the morality or values of this kind of life. Doing so means entering into a discussion that has no predictable outcome, given that one cannot expect the parties discussing the issue to reach an agreement. It is the idea of citizen's abstinence that we encountered earlier when talking about Rawls. If it is a matter of living in peace and not seeking reciprocal knowledge between citizens. In other words, if one does not aspire to a situation in which citizens have the option of changing their opinions when pitched against the opinions of those with whom they are forced to coexist, then it is better to put the respective opinions to the test. As Sandel says:

---

[4] Cf. Sandel (2005).

"By insisting only that each individual respects the freedom of others to live the life they choose, this tolerance [liberal tolerance, D.G.] seems to promise a basis for political agreement that does not require shared moral conceptions" (Sandel, 2005: chap. 21).

There is no need for anything more than tolerance and the concomitant virtue of respect for the autonomy of others. This is precisely the case because tolerance arises from the fact that individuals deplore lifestyles that they must tolerate. As a result of this, there is a rejection to understand the reasons for their actions. In this sense, liberalism is the result of a certain anthropological pessimism related to the likelihood of people being prepared to listen to the arguments of their fellow citizens. Not only does listening mean being prepared to understand what the other is saying, but also take on the consequences of having listened, which are nothing more than the possibility that this active listening will bring with it changes in the values of each side.

When considering whether homosexual practices should be decriminalised, according to Sandel, it is not enough to say that we need to be tolerant. What we must do is to evaluate whether the decriminalised practices are admissible or desirable. Of course, this kind of evaluation could be considered paternalistic and offensive to those who demand recognition of their practices and lifestyles, and this is why the liberal solution of abstinence of judgement seems more respectful. However, the quality of the social fabric improves if, instead of recognising that people may do as they like in their own private space, which is precisely the argument given by the liberals, it is confirmed that homosexuality is a way of experiencing love. This way of experiencing love can be recognised perfectly well as such by those whose knowledge is limited to their personal experience of heterosexual relationships. In other words, those who constitute what is referred to, not without some irony, as the country's moral majority.[5] Nonetheless, it is not a case of a gracious or condescending concession by the moral majority of the right of homosexuals to live their own lifestyle. It is not a case of tolerance understood as permission.[6] What the communitarian argument tries to underline is that only by doing this can a substantive defence of a social practice and consolidation of the social fabric be offered. Sandel maintains that if the justification for decriminalisation of homosexual practices is based on their positive evaluation and not on tolerance alone, the resulting respect will be of a higher quality. This is because not only does it express that these practices may be carried out by consenting individuals in their private space (in other words, practices that result in social rejection), but it goes further to value them positively. If there is only tolerance, the arguments and opinions opposed to homosexuality will not be

---

[5] Cf. (Taylor, 1992).
[6] Cf. (Frost, 2003: 172-180).

counteracted. Nevertheless, if there is approximation to and recognition of them, then opinions that may have been gaining ground during centuries of prejudice may be abated and even (as we can see in today's society) eliminated.

6. Concluding observations

Moral and ethical conflicts, or conflicts that do not arise exclusively from opposing interests and cannot be resolved automatically by legal or parliamentary institutions, constitute one of the key elements of political philosophy. They are either seen as questions that are too divisive to be dealt with in public or judged by law, or it is considered necessary to deal with them publicly to ensure a stronger foundation of the political community. The concept of tolerance may be operative for the resolution of certain conflicts, but it should be remembered that it functions by making them disappear or silencing them. Peaceful coexistence that is free from serious disagreements can be achieved in this way. However, too broad a consideration of tolerance may result in the social majority. In other words, those that are able to practice tolerance, persisting in their silent rejection of those members of the political community who carry out practices that are socially ill considered. This means that the conflict retains its potential and social harmony is only apparent, lasting only while the cause of the specific situation of tolerance remains hidden or private.

References

Camps, V. (1991) *Virtudes públicas*, Espasa, Madrid.
Del Águila, R. (2003) "La tolerancia" in Arteta, A. *et al*. (eds.) *Teoría política: poder, moral, democracia*, Alianza, Madrid, pp. 362-383.
Frost, R. (2003) *Toleranz im Konflikt*, Suhrkamp, Frankfurt.
Garzón Valdés, E. (1993) "«No pongas tus sucias manos sobre Mozart». Algunas consideraciones sobre el concepto de tolerancia" in Garzón Valdés, E. *Derecho, ética y política*, Centro de Estudios Constitucionales, Madrid, pp. 401-415.
Gray, J. (2000) *Two Faces of Liberalism*, Polity Press, Cambridge.
MacIntyre, A. (1981) *After Virtue*, University of Notre Dame Press, Notre Dame.
Rawls, J. (1993) *Political Liberalism*, Columbia University Press, New York.
Sandel, M. (2005) *Public Philosophy. Essays on Morality in Politics*, Harvard University Press, Cambridge (Mass.).
Taylor, Ch. (1992) *The Ethics of Authenticity*, Harvard University Press, Cambridge (Mass.).
Thiebaut, C. (1999) *De la tolerancia*, Visor, Madrid.

The Future of Justice

Josep Redorta
Centre de Recerca i Estudis de Conflictologia, Universitat Oberta de Catalunya

Abstract. Ours is an age of significant social change. Change is associated with conflict, so we must reconsider the appropriateness of our current conflict resolution mechanisms. Law, order and justice are under immense pressure. The debate between judicial and extra-judicial processes is a false one and should be redefined. Dejudicialisation is both a necessity and an opportunity. New trends are beginning to emerge and there are a number of changes in judicial policy that must be urgently addressed.

Keywords: Justice, Alternative justice, ADR, Judicial process, Mediation, Dejudicialisation, Judicial policy, Social change.

1. Justice in an epoch of significant change

There is no doubt that we are undergoing a period of rapid worldwide changes, with dramatic developments that have both profound consequences and multiple causes.

Society and, of course, legal practitioners are heavily involved in this open-ended process. But we should not forget that the idea of change is deeply associated with the idea of conflict.[1] The immediate consequence is that conflicts will increase enormously in the coming years – in fact, it is a process that has already begun.

This reality forces us to reconsider whether the mechanisms currently used for resolving conflicts are those that are best suited for the present time. In Western societies, we have learned to resolve conflicts in a confrontational manner, with the judicial process playing an important role.

However, legal practitioners are increasingly frustrated at all levels, and especially in terms of personal satisfaction and self-respect. The same is true for those benefiting from the system. Litigation rates in all countries show that the current system is becoming more and more overloaded. The question is: what are we doing wrong?

---

[1] Current sociology is already well integrated with the notion that conflict may be a motor for change. For more on this subject, see Lorenzo, P.L. (2001), *Fundamentos teóricos del conflicto social* (The theoretical basis of social conflict).

The Law, as an institution, is under pressure from all sides, since its role as regulator requires prompt and effective responses for the many, increasingly diverse, social problems. Meanwhile, in all countries the Administration of justice, as an institution, is also subject to a lot of protests for change, with different degrees of ferocity and effectiveness.

The paradigm of the court ruling as the only way to put an end to a conflict resolution process is currently in crisis.[2] Generally speaking, the current judicial process, regardless of the form it takes, finds it difficult to face up to the complexity of the modern world. Whether it is specialisation by area (civil, criminal, administrative, etc.) or the pace of resolution compared with the time required or the standard of judgments given, they all fall short of the expectations of the public in an era when time is perhaps overvalued.

Meanwhile, jurists at all levels are strongly resistant to change or, more specifically, changes to their profession. It may be that this resistance comes from within, as well as without.

If we talk about endogenous difficulties, it is true that lawyers, judges and legal practitioners of all kinds are very accustomed to the application of analogous references. This is case law: the comparison of situations similar to the case in question is a firmly established doctrine.

But this practice, carried out almost automatically, on a daily basis, is a highly inadequate framework for the modern era. Instead of looking forward, case law places the conflict "in the past". When lawyers dare to look further, we look at comparative law. This is equivalent to looking sideways. In fact, it is very difficult for us to look forward. There is nothing to compare with. Lawyers are not used to looking ahead, they feel uncomfortable. This makes it difficult for them to appreciate new and emerging developments.

However, lawyers are experienced in resolving conflicts. It is just that the tools we have today are inadequate or insufficient. Our experience tells us that the court is an effective institution that deserves respect. Our experience also tells us that personal relationships are highly complex, and that solutions tend not to be easily achieved if they are to be satisfactory. Our intuition also tells us that, outside of the law - and even sometimes specialised law, we do not know much. Hence our exogenous resistance to belief in miracle cures in any way, shape or form. The lawyer is a cautious and prudent person. We are entitled not to believe in everything.

---

[2] The movement that drives the European Group of Judges for Mediation (GEMME) is clearly significant of this fact.

2. Conflicts and their regulation

History tells us that there are three main methods of resolving conflicts: force, the law and the spoken word.[3] The use of force is present in nature and in human nature and to an extent which is not necessary to discuss here. However, as the use of force requires the use of very important resources (for example, in times of war), it is the case that once a rule is legitimised and integrated into the law, it becomes much more effective regulation.

Nevertheless, in addition to the use of force and the law, all societies, throughout history, have used the power of the spoken word in various non-judicial institutions to resolve conflicts.[4] The spoken word has always existed alongside the other two systems and, at various times in history (or in specific societies), it has held sway over the other two methods. Negotiated solutions to conflicts lie at the heart of the culture of society. Furthermore, they are often high quality solutions which satisfy all parties concerned, which is not the case for imposed solutions.

The field of regulation of social conflict is intimately and epistemologically linked with the earlier study of those conflicts. Many authors[5] have argued that research should be directed at the many multidisciplinary aspects of social conflict. In short, conflict and its resolution should be jointly approached. This has led to the appearance – although still very limited - of conflictology[6] as a science and an umbrella term for all conflict phenomena and forms of resolution. One of the most important is the law.

If knowledge is central to the conflictology model, its application corresponds to the field of conflict management. This area includes mediation, in its strictest sense, along with other forms, such as facilitation, use of the ombudsman, preventive neutral evaluation, negotiation, arbitration, fact-finding, etc.[7] In this field, the conflict resolution resource is the spoken word.

Therefore, although use of the law is necessary in many cases, the idea that judicial solutions are the only way to resolve a problem represents a restrictive vision that might ignore other, more socially acceptable, solutions which could be successful and satisfactory.

---

[3] Redorta, J. (2007). *Entender el conflicto* (Understanding Conflict). pp. 196-200

[4] Mediation has been observed even in primates, with whom we share up to 98% of our genes. See Waal, F. (1989) Peacemaking among primates.

[5] For example, Pruitt, D. (1998). The Handbook of Social Psychology. Gilbert, D.T.. Fiske, S.T. and Linzey, J. (eds.). Social conflict. However, this is quite consolidated in social psychology where the theoretical principles affecting conflict are to be found.

[6] For a basic definition of conflictology, see Wikipedia.

[7] The Dictionary of Conflict Resolution (Yarn, D., 1999): This work stands alone in the field; it has 1,400 entries (which gives us an idea of the depth and wealth of this discipline).

The emergence of formalised mediation in the last few decades has initiated a strong debate in the legal field. What, in fact, is mediation? How effective is it? Does it limit the professional field for lawyers? Is it a resource for judges? Is it a more economical option for the state?

These questions require much reflection. We are faced with an important social delegitimisation of traditional justice systems. In a context of real legislative inflation that often leads to great legal uncertainty, we need to resolve problems which are increasingly interdisciplinary (the environment, new technologies, food, etc).

Mediation questions the law and, in turn, the world of the law can, and does, question mediation. In a democratic society, we should be able to distinguish between the wide range of non-imposed solutions which must be maximised wherever possible, and the field of imposed solutions which must be minimised wherever possible.

We need to find the common ground between law and mediation; those areas which allow the quality of judicial systems to be improved for the public interest. Current hurdles for the development of mediation are:

- The development of conflict management is a subject of intense debate.[8]
- A litigious culture fostered by the mass media and sometimes by the law itself.
- Many mediators have little practical experience.
- Excessive expectation due to ignorance of the difficulties of the different techniques.
- Too little expectation due to a lack of awareness of the advantages.
- A legal culture that is resistant to change.

3. Dejudicialisation

We must consider how to give institutional character to the two most basic forms of conflict resolution, the law and the spoken word; force is under state and governmental control in our societies.

This implies that the debate about the judicial/mediation process is a false one. There are some things that must be resolved within the process, and there are others that belong to the field of conflict management, with its instruments of social regulation.

We propose that access to justice by citizens must be seen as *the right of access to the appropriate means of conflict resolution,*[9] depending on the

---

[8] Mayer, D.S. (2004) *Beyond Neutrality:* provides a study of this debate. There is a Spanish version published by Gedisa.

[9] For more details, Redorta, J. (2006), *Entorno de los métodos alternativos de solución de conflictos (Environment of the alternative methods for conflict resolution)* is available on the Internet from the Americas Legal Studies Centre database, and is published in Spanish in the

circumstances of each case. This involves the development of a culture of conflict resolution linked less exclusively to litigation, and this is the responsibility of the authorities.

By way of illustration and, as far as the standard mediation technique is concerned, it can be said that, in general, out-of-court settlements tend to be more effective in the following situations when:

− Communication between the parties is poor.
− The relationship between the parties is ongoing.
− There is a need to vent feelings.
− One dispute is connected to another.
− Multiple conflicting parties.
− The problem in question is technologically complex.
− Privacy is valued.
− There is a need for swift resolution and cooperation of the parties.
− Costs must be minimised.
− Dealing with small claims.

In other situations, the best solution is judicial. For example, in:

− Cases of discrimination.
− Cases of mandatory law.
− Defence of important principles or beliefs.
− The need to set a precedent.
− Maximising or minimising economic reparations.
− Vindication.
− A neutral and public opinion.
− A different perspective of the law.
− Pressure of legal terms.

If this is true, it is necessary to articulate a political system based on the general objectives of efficiency and satisfaction of public interest and society. This implies a broader view than that of the law; it involves multidisciplinary studies and a major change to the system.

The process of linking mediation to the judicial system is essential, and this will bring with it significant regulatory problems that need to be well thought out, discussed and debated. In general, we believe that the comparison between official medicine and alternative or natural medicine is a useful metaphor for understanding what may happen in the field we are analysing.

There are four chronological stages:

1. ADR as a system is not linked to the judicial system.

   At this stage, mediation and the judicial process are two different realities, as was the case with official medicine and homeopathy.

Revista Mediación, Year 2, Vol 3, March 2009, pp. 28-37.

2. ADR has a tentative relationship with the judicial system.

At this stage, both systems cooperate. Mediation takes place in an intrajudicial environment and in Annexed Courts Programmes. In the case of medicine, this would be doctors prescribing homeopathic remedies, etc.

3. ADR enters the legal system.

At this stage, the process is more flexible and negotiated solutions in various proceedings are allowed. In medicine, for certain diseases atypical solutions are given credence (referral to health spas in Norway, the use of cannabis for therapeutic purposes, acupuncture, etc).

4. ADR takes over from the judicial system, with the latter being reserved for particularly relevant cases.

At this stage, the process is seen a last resort, as happens with conflicts in new technologies. The court and its proceedings are an exceptional, last resort option, or appropriate, depending on the nature of the case.

This assumes that society accepts and values the important work of conflict managers and that the Judiciary and the Administration of justice in general have, once again, the prestige and recognition they deserve.

4. Current trends

A number of new tendencies would seem to indicate the beginnings of a paradigm shift:

– New global concepts of Justice

Restorative Justice partially removes the state's role and transfers it to society; *Proximity Justice* is closer to the public and not disassociated from the social context; *Relational Justice*[10] develops the foundations of justice from a much more multidisciplinary perspective.

– The intensive use of new technologies

New technologies are changing the foundations of space, time and life itself.[11] The resolution of social conflicts is affected by this intense movement. Electronic signatures, videoconferencing, databases, virtual courts and other technological advances are propitiating the change of both legal and extralegal processes to adapt to this new communications reality. Platforms such as e-Negotiation, Cybersettle or the entire field of Online Dispute Resolution are clear evidence that new technologies

---

[10] For an excellent discussion of the concept, see Casanovas, P.; Poblet, M. (2009), Concepts and Fields of Relational Justice. http://idt.uab.es/llibreblanc/index.php?option=com_docman&task=cat_view&gid=15&Itemid=48 (awaiting publication).

[11] These ideas are fully developed by Castells, M. (1999) in his reference work, *La Era de la información* (The Information Age), Volume I.

are already having a small or large - but irreversible - impact on the field of conflict resolution, regardless of the method employed.

- The internationalisation of justice

  Globalisation changes the way law is practised; now the law has to operate in very different geographical areas and in diverse cultural contexts. We are experiencing the slow but insidious emergence of public and private international law. At the same time, for those that are geographically distant, proximity justice does not exist and litigation in another country is always complicated. This situation favours extrajudicial forms of conflict resolution.

- The heightened awareness of the legal profession

  Many judges, lawyers and other legal practitioners are becoming aware of the new situation (though at this stage they are probably still a minority). The experience of the GEMME group[12] in Europe illustrates this concern. Similarly, current processes for training lawyers, in both America and Europe, in communication skills, negotiation, problem-solving, etc. show that the belief that the judicial process is the only resource is beginning to change (with the exception of some specific cases).

5. The implementation of change

Having redefined law as a means of attaining justice, as a right of access to appropriate methods of particular conflict resolution, everything so far described indicates that the judicial process and extrajudicial means of conflict resolution should be at the core of any policy to address structural reform of the Administration of justice.

This involves dealing with a variety of problems. It demands intensive, effective training for all legal practitioners; training that is based more on psychology than on the law. In reality, such training would benefit the entire legal profession as personal relationships are fundamental to the operation of the law. Those that practice law must understand the importance of this point.

There must also be a shift to a culture of dejudicialisation among the public, at the same time as the effective implementation of adequate resources, so that today's extrajudicial resources are valued for the role they will play in the short term. The integration process/ADR should be carried out at all levels. The experience of the Alternative Justice Centres in Mexico can be seen as a reference. Cases arrive at these centres via a

---

[12] For more information on this powerful pressure group, see   http://www.gemme-conference.org and www.simposiummediacio.com

judicial route and by direct social demand. These and similar organisations could have a direct and central role in the transformation process.

Figure 1. Alternative Justice Centre (Sonora, Mexico).

If mediation and the range of conflict management resources are channelled through the Alternative Justice Centres, dependent on the judiciary itself, we would be producing a high level transformation, and one in line with future trends.

This means putting an end to legislative inflation,[13] the start of a review of procedural law with the aim of accommodating the different forms of conflict resolution, and the disconnection of conflict resolution resources from the judicial dynamic. However, this will not be possible without a high degree of social credibility and it must therefore be a social process, undertaken in a controlled manner and in a reasonable time. Cultural changes have never been easy to bring to fruition.

Legal, psychological and conflictology research must be coordinated via multidisciplinary national plans that highlight the costs, indicators, benchmarks and validation of this process of converging justice reform. Nothing is more economical than justice functioning effectively, since this is the mechanism that allows and ensures that the rest of the society's services function correctly. The concept of relational justice must be developed and put into practice in the interests of a better society.

Currently, and in the immediate future, it seems that for legal practitioners, training in new technologies, languages, knowledge of conflict resolution and resources (other than those that may be considered

---

[13] In Spain, the *Boletin Oficial del Estado* (Official State Bulletin) publishes every year about 2000 legal provisions of every type.

as 'classical' in a legal sense) will be as essential as training in civil law or criminal law. In fact, negotiation is already central to the practice of law. What has been outlined here is an extension of this idea, but the potential is much more than we are able imagine at this juncture.

6. Conclusions

The Administration of justice will be affected by the present social changes. The legal professions are not ready for the change yet and the aspects which are more linked to human relationships should be renewed instead of the law. Mediation is on the base of the new tendencies that will build a more flexible extrajudicial process. Such names as Restorative Justice, Proximity Justice or Relational Justice are creating new trends. The future of new justice has arrived.

References

Casanovas, P.; Poblet, M. (2008) "Concepts and Fields of Relational Justice" in Casanovas, P. et al. *Computable Models of the Law*, LNAI 4884, Springer Verlag Berlin, Heidelberg, 2008, pp. 323-329.

Castells, M. (1999) *La era de la información*, vol. 1, Alianza Editorial, Madrid.

Lorenzo, P.L. (2001) *Fundamentos teóricos del conflicto social*, Siglo veintiuno de España Editores, Madrid.

Mayer, B. S. (2004) *Beyond neutrality*, Jossey-Bass, San Francisco, CA.

Morin, E. (2001) *La mente bien ordenada*, Seix y Barral, Barcelona.

Pruitt, D. (1998) "Social conflict" in Gilbert, D.T.; Fiske, S.T.; Lindzey, J. (eds.) *The handbook of Social Psychology*. Mc Graw Hill, New York, pp. 420-502.

Redorta, J. (2006) *Entorno de los métodos alternativos de solución de conflictos*, Centro de Estudios de Justicia de las Americas, available at: http://www.cejamericas.org/doc/documentos/entornometodosalternativos_Redo rta.pdf (accessed 3 March 2009).

Redorta, J. (2007) *Entender el conflicto*, Paidós, Barcelona.

Waal, F. (1989) *Peacemaking among primates*, Harvard University Press, London.

Yarn, D. (1999) *Dictionary of Conflict Resolution*, Jossey-Bass, San Francisco, CA.

The Rise and Growth of Mediation in Italy

Anna Mestitz[1], Massimo Vogliotti[2]
[1]Research Institute on Judicial Systems of the National Research Council (IRSIG-CNR), Bologna
[2]Law Faculty, Univerità del Piemonte Orientale "Amedeo Avogrado"

Abstract. Italy has been reluctant to mediation and to the restorative paradigm for years. Victim-offender mediation (VOM) for the youth was introduced in the nineties thanks to the promotion and support of juvenile prosecutors, lay judges, magistrates and social workers. This paper aims at explaining how VOM services started to run and where, what the outcomes were and which were the initiatives to implement restorative justice and mediation. However, there is still a lack of a legal framework for VOM, that is why this practice is still considered experimental, sometimes due to the culture, values and ideology of the country. Finally, the performance of the Department of Juvenile Justice with regard to VOM services is described and compared to that of other European agencies having similar roles.

Keywords: Restorative Justice, Mediation, Young offenders, Reparation, Victim-Offender Mediation (VOM), Alternative Dispute Resolution (ADR), Juvenile Court Social Services.

1. Cultural resistance

Over the last twenty years the movement for Restorative Justice in Western democracies has gained more and more attention among citizens, legal professionals and scholars, mainly by means of articles and books (Christie, 1977; Braithwaite, 1989; Zehr, 1990), and across a variety of continents and cultures.[1]

Italy is one of the European nations where mediation and, more generally, the restorative paradigm and practices have found it most difficult to develop. Many factors caused this delay (not least of all the corporative interests of the lawyers), but probably the most important has been cultural resistance. Indeed, the majority of the Italian legal community has long shared an "internal juridical culture" (Friedman, 1975) including

---

[1] For an exhaustive comparative overview see Morris and Maxwell (2001). For a guide to practice and research see Umbreit (2001).

theories, ideologies and beliefs, deeply rooted in the legalistic and formalistic tradition. Such a culture provides logics, a "grammar" and a system of values which prevents the acceptance of the different principles, values and methods underlying mediation. This is particularly true in the criminal area – the focus of this contribution – where, for centuries, the procedure followed the inquisitorial model where private victims were totally emarginated. The aim of this model was the search of truth, the leading role was played by public prosecutors and judges and punishment was its unavoidable and ultimate goal. According to such a paradigm – historically imposed by modern State principles – the victim was the State, the *Reppublica*, and the real victim damaged by the crime was disregarded.[2] This approach is the exact contrary of that of mediation, where the victim and the offender have the leading roles in the procedure, where the aim is conciliation and reparation is the means by which the offender is made accountable, and where the agreement with the victim is facilitated.[3]

Last but not least, the cultural resistance of the Italian criminal law community in accepting restorative practices can also be explained by the principle of mandatory criminal initiative (*obbligatorietà dell'azione penale*) included in the Constitution of 1948. The principle is considered to be untouchable, much like a taboo. Moreover, for a long time mainly the maximalist interpretation of it provided by the legal doctrine prevented Italian jurists from imagining alternative responses to crime.

In recent years, however, the criminal law community has become more conscious of the fact that the application of the principle of *obbligatorietà* is not feasible. Indeed, after the publication in 1979 of an important collection of essays edited by Giovanni Conso, the empirical impossibility of prosecuting all crimes and the consequent inevitability of establishing priorities in the exercise of criminal action became increasingly clear.[4] This realisation might represent a first, crucial, step in overcoming deep-set cultural constraints and in moving both legal doctrine and professionals of criminal law forward to a greater commitment to mediation and restorative justice.

Instead, in the non-criminal field, where there is greater leeway for individual autonomy, it is undeniable that significant steps have been made

---

[2] See Sbriccoli (2002) about the birth of this new paradigm which progressively replaced the criminal justice model used in the medieval Italian city-states.

[3] The code of criminal procedure of 1988 (inspired by the adversary model but saving relevant traces of the ancient inquisitorial paradigm) has not significantly changed the victim position inside the trial.

[4] More than twenty years ago Giuseppe Di Federico - the first Italian legal scholar to carry out empirical research on criminal initiative - argued that it is in fact based on the unavoidable personal choices made by each prosecutor (Di Federico, 1991 and 1998). On the same issues see also Vogliotti (2004: 465-476) who shows the efforts made by the Higher Council of the Magistracy and by some Italian prosecutors in order to make criminal initiative transparent and reasonable.

in Alternative Dispute Resolution (ADR). Starting from the 1990s, informal experiments and specific acts (commercial, company, labour and family acts)[5] have been implemented with the aim to reduce the civil justice workload[6] by using the traditional institute of "conciliation". Notwithstanding these efforts, however, the majority of legal professionals maintained their traditional lack of interest in ADR, thus preventing in fact a real "launching" of mediation. On the other hand, the habit of the legislator to use the old term "conciliation" [7] instead of "mediation" represents a clear indicator of the Italian cultural resistance.

Although mediation and conciliation share common values, the two notions must be well differentiated: mediation refers to a method, while conciliation is an objective. The first is carried out by an impartial third person (different from the judge) and must take place outside the court in order to underline its autonomy. The second can be carried out by a judge. The word "mediation" entered the Italian legislation only in 1997 with art. 4 of the Act n. 285 of August 28, which provides for the creation of mediation services for the family, with the aim of helping to solve difficult relationships inside the family itself. Although mediation is conceived as an autonomous procedure of dispute resolution, the mediation services provided for by the act are generally used only during the separation or divorce conflicts, or in cases of litigation between children and parents before a judge.

Evident here is one of the constant features of the Italian experience: the close interweaving of mediation and trial, two opposite worlds which should remain separate. The first, with an eye to the future, seeking new family or social arrangements to facilitate the pacification; the second, rooted in the past, seeking to manage the conflict and restore violated rights by declaring winners and losers.[8]

Only in recent years have the topics of mediation and restorative justice gained the attention of the Italian legal community, partly thanks to requests brought by the Council of Europe and the European Union. We can mention that in the implementation of the EU directive of May 21, 2008, the Italian legislator established the obligation to attempt conciliation in some areas before going to court (*condizione di procedibilità*). This obligation represents a crucial step forward in the diffusion of the culture

---

[5] For an overview see Comba (2005).

[6] As is well known, Italian civil justice is one of the slowest in Europe.

[7] The "conciliator judge" of the past was substituted by the justice of peace.

[8] See Occhiogrosso (2008: 163). The interweaving has been reconfirmed by the Act n. 54 of February 8, 2006 which provides for new regulations in divorce disputes about shared child custody (*affidamento condiviso*). Regarding this proposal Maglietta (2008) stressed the scarce application of mediation by judges.

and practice of mediation in Italy and, moreover, succeeded in separating the two phases of mediation and trial.[9]

2. The "discovery" of mediation with young offenders

Similarly to what happened in other continents and countries, the "discovery" of mediation in Italy took place in the juvenile criminal justice system, which functioned as an experimental laboratory. Then, with time, the institute was also adopted with adult offenders.[10] In Italy, in the mid 1990s, the introduction of victim-offender mediation (VOM) in the juvenile criminal justice system was facilitated by the reform of juvenile criminal procedure, implemented in 1989, which included the new institute of probation (art. 28 DPR 448/88) allowing the judge to refer the case to the Court Social Service with the aims of "reparation" and "conciliation". In this regard, it must be noted that the Italian institute of probation differs substantially from similar institutes in other countries. Instead of being a real sentence, it results in the suspension of the trial until a later time when a sentence will be given. During the time of suspension, the young offenders may participate in programs or projects aimed at rehabilitating them and/or favoring a positive outcome of the probation. At the time of the sentence, if the outcome of the probation is positive, the judge may proceed by dismissing the case or giving judicial pardon.

Results of a longitudinal analysis of the application of probation in the period 1991-96 carried out in Bari showed that restorative justice practices had arisen spontaneously before the formal birth of VOM services in 1995 (Mestitz and Colamussi, 2000). This research significantly showed that such strategies were part of the probation projects for the large majority (81.1%) of the sample (190 probation cases). Mainly restorative prescriptions entailed the reparation of those damages caused by the crime (either materially or symbolically) and/or the reconciliation with the victim.

---

[9] It is the new legislative decree n. 28 of March 4, 2010 (which puts into effect article 6 of the Act n. 69 of June 18, 2009). The main novelties established by this act are:

a) Before going to court the lawyer *must* inform the client about the possibility to engage in mediation. It will be operated by permanent and independent professional bodies which can be created by the lawyers' councils in the tribunals.

b) The Ministry of Justice will keep a register of these mediation bodies establishing by decree the criteria for their inclusion.

c) The law grants tax facilities to the parties showing the legislator's favour for this alternative dispute resolution which can give an important contribution to the improvement of the efficiency and quality of our civil justice.

[10] In Italy victim-offender mediation with adult offenders was introduced in 2000 by the legislative decree n. 274 of August 28. This decree only concerns the victim's action under the justice of peace's jurisdiction and a few petty offences ("*reati perseguibili a querela della persona offesa*"). In this case, there is also the principle of *obbligatorietà dell'azione penale* that represented an insurmountable obstacle to a broader application of mediation in a kind of justice which (at least in name) was inspired by the idea of pacification.

Direct mediation through victim-offender meetings had already begun to be applied (9.1% cases) even if, in most cases, mediation was formal and indirect.[11]

The introduction of these practices demonstrates the attention paid to alternative procedures inspired by restorative justice in the Italian juvenile justice context. Such attention ultimately led to the establishment of VOM groups promoted by juvenile prosecutors and judges, and supported by social workers and/or lay judges, some of whom were directly involved in mediation. In fact a small group of juvenile magistrates[12] of Turin was the main promoter of VOM in Italy. They were directly influenced by the new approach to juvenile crime which was originated in the wave of the introduction of the *médiation pénale*[13] in France (Bouchard and Mierolo, 2000).

Namely, some articles published in the period 1992-1994 were crucial for the implementation of VOM, opening a new scenario in the juvenile criminal justice. In particular two articles, published in the same issue of the official journal of the juvenile and family magistrates association,[14] had the most remarkable impact. One of these (Bouchard, 1994) pointed out that "restorative practices as mediation had quickly developed in Eastern European countries, and lamented that Italy had remained substantially resistant and unavailable for the experimentation". The other one, by Bouchard and his colleagues, magistrates of the Juvenile Court and Prosecution Office of Turin, was published under the unusual collective label "Juvenile magistrates of Turin" (1994).[15] Not only did it propose the guidelines and the norms to be used in applying restorative justice strategies, but it also declared the creation of a new "mediation section"[16] inside the juvenile prosecution office in Turin. Taking into account the journal where this article was published, the absence of the authors' names and the fact that at that time the authors were probably the most representative and authoritative group in the juvenile justice arena, the

---

[11] According to Mestitz and Colamussi (2000), the two main restorative practices were: symbolic financial compensation to charity and welfare institutions, churches (51.3%) and writing formal letters of apology to the victim (35.7%).

[12] Should it be noted that, like in France, the Italian word *magistrati* includes both judges and public prosecutors who share the same bureaucratic recruitment (by means of national competitions), training and career. Consequently when we use the term "magistrates" in this article, we refer to both roles according to the Italian style.

[13] Like in Spanish and French, the Italian translation of VOM is *mediazione penale*.

[14] The quarterly *Minori giustizia*.

[15] The names were replaced by this meaningful premise: "We present a document prepared by the magistrates of the juvenile court and prosecution office of Turin. It proposes a new path for the juvenile criminal process through the so-called victim-offender mediation and the reparation of damage caused by the crime" (Juvenile magistrates of Turin, 1994: 26).

[16] In Italian: *Uffici di mediazione*.

article may be considered as a true *manifesto* for the application of restorative justice and VOM in Italy.

Significantly, juvenile magistrates from Turin had creatively found a new normative anchorage to legalize the case referrals to VOM services.[17] They proposed that prosecutors and judges of the preliminary investigation rely on the article providing for "personality assessment" (article 9 DPR 448/88), which entails an investigation of the family and social background of young offenders. The idea behind this was that probation occurs in an advanced phase of the procedure providing a coercive context that is not suitable for the mediation activity (the reparation of the damage and the attempt of conciliation are imposed on the minor). For this reason, the promoters suggested that VOM was applied during the investigative phase of the criminal process.

According to this interpretation, after the referral, Juvenile Court Social Services may autonomously carry out mediation in the legal framework of art. 9, or may refer the case to a mediation service (where existing) as a part of the "assessment". This norm (art. 9) does not include any provision concerned with VOM, but its wide use in the practice fully confirms again what Lemert argued many years ago (1986): Italian juvenile magistrates rely on the available norms and extend their use to implement measures not covered by current legislation.[18]

Prosecutors cannot themselves dismiss cases but must ask the judge to do so. Thus once mediation is concluded, the case is sent again to the prosecutor who asks the judge to drop the case if the VOM has ended successfully with an agreement between victim and offender;[19] if such was not reached, the case follows the normal judicial path.

Three independent studies converge on the finding that public prosecutors refer the large majority of cases (73-75%) during the investigative phase of the criminal proceeding.[20] Notwithstanding the absence of norms, it is interesting to note that Italian magistrates follow the same trend of the majority of EU countries, where VOM is mainly applied by prosecutors and/or by other agencies in the first phases of the criminal

---

[17] For an overview of the legislation concerned with VOM see Patané (2004).

[18] According to Lemert (1986), Italian juvenile magistrates "*in most aspects achieved only the form but not the substance of juvenile justice... the explanation for such a development lies in a much more profound and articulated sensitivity to the inconsistencies and ambiguities of law and in the religio-familistic values that influence its expression and administration*".

[19] The judges drop the case through judicial pardon or article 27 DPR 448/88 (the case can be dismissed when the crime is negligible).

[20] According to the directors of mediation centres, 74% of cases are referred by public prosecutors (Mestitz, 2004b); according to court social workers and mediators, the percentage of cases referred by public prosecutors is 73% (Mastropasqua and Ciuffo, 2004); finally, according to magistrates' perceptions, public prosecutors deal with twice as many cases as judges (Ghetti, 2004).

proceeding (Mestitz and Ghetti, 2005). In other words, in Italy the main path to refer cases to VOM is by means of art. 9 DPR 448/88, while art. 28 (which provides for probation) is frequently used only in some juvenile courts (or exclusively, as in Bari).

3. The spontaneous rise of local mediation services and their difficulties

Given these premises, it comes as no surprise that the first Italian VOM service was founded in Turin in 1995 (one year after the aforementioned *manifesto*), and temporarily located inside the same juvenile prosecution office. It began its activity in full collaboration with the Juvenile Court Social Service and the Interregional Centre of the Ministry of Justice located in Piedmont and in the Aosta Valley.[21] Subsequently, VOM was spontaneously adopted elsewhere and new VOM services were created in other cities: in 1996 in Bari, Trento, Catanzaro and Rome, in 1998 in Milan, in 1999 in Sassari, in 2000 in Cagliari and Foggia. In the following years, the VOM service in Rome was closed but other services sprang up spontaneously elsewhere.

The creation of local VOM services in Italy was actively organized by juvenile professional magistrates and lay judges. Indeed, the first four local mediation services were located in the same buildings of the juvenile courts and/or prosecution offices (i.e. Turin, Bari, Trento and Milan)[22] or in the same location of the Court Social Service (i.e. Catanzaro). After receiving funding from local governments, four of these VOM services (in Turin, Bari, Trento and Catanzaro) changed their location and were founded again (see "2nd foundation" in Table 1). In Table 1, the first 10 local VOM services are listed by date of foundation and by their promoters/founders.

---

[21] The organizational units (centres) of the Department of Juvenile Justice of the Ministry of Justice are located in each region or sometimes they include two regions. The court of social services working in each Italian juvenile judicial office (including prosecution and courts) are functional units of these regional and/or interregional centres. For an overview of the organization of the Italian juvenile justice system see Mestitz (2000).

[22] For example, from January 1995 to May 2000, the VOM service in Turin was named *Ufficio Mediazione* and was located in the juvenile prosecution office. In May 2000 it was renamed *Centro mediazione penale minorile di Torino* and it became an institution of the city government. This model was also followed by the VOM service in Trento which until February 1999 was located inside the juvenile prosecution office and then became an institution of the autonomous province of Trento.

Table I. The first 10 local VOM services established in Italy by date of foundation (1995-2001).

Sites of VOM services	Dates of foundation	Promoters and founders
Turin (Northern Italy)	1st foundation 1995 2nd foundation[23] 2000	Juvenile magistrates, lay judges and Local Social Service
Bari (Southern Italy)	1st foundation 1996 2nd foundation 2001	Juvenile magistrates, lay judges and Local Social Service
Trento (Northern Italy)	1st foundation 1996 2nd foundation 1999	Juvenile magistrates, lay judges and Local Social Service
Catanzaro (Southern Italy)	1st foundation 1996 2nd foundation 2002	Juvenile magistrates, lay judges and Local Social Service
Rome (Central Italy)	1997 (closed 1999)	University professors and researchers
Milan (Northern Italy)	1998	Lay judges, researchers and university professors
Sassari (Sardinia)	1999	One lay judge
Cagliari (Sardinia)	2000	Two juvenile magistrates, one lay judge
Foggia (Southern Italy)	2000	Juvenile magistrates, lay judges and Local Social Services
Bologna (Northern Italy)	2001	One lay judge

Starting from 1998, at the establishment of a new local VOM service formal documents such as "letters of intent" (i.e. *protocolli d'intesa*) were signed by groups of local institutions, e.g. the Juvenile Court and the Prosecution Office, Court Social Service, Local Social Service, Interregional Juvenile Centres of the Ministry of Justice, municipalities, provinces and/or regions. The letters of intent were fundamental because they provided for the attribution of financial and human resources (i.e., the mediators and other personnel) by the institutions or public administrations

---

[23] We will explain later why the first four mediation services were founded twice.

which signed the letters (Ministry of Justice, municipality, province or region). This permitted mediators to carry out part-time activities in the mediation services. Such formal letters of intent have been signed in almost all mediation services and now represent the main "model" of collaboration among different institutions. Not only are they very useful to move part-time civil servants into the VOM services, but also to acquire resources such as offices, furniture, computers... and funding. For this reason, a second foundation based on the new model of collaboration was needed for the first VOM services created in Turin, Trento, Catanzaro and Bari before 1998.

The current political orientation of VOM with young offenders is to include the mediation centres/services in the framework of public services as in Spain and France. Thus VOM is carried out both by groups of social workers from the Juvenile Court Social Services and by the local mediation centres funded by local governments.

The organizational models and the funding of the VOM local services vary, but some common elements can be traced in: i) the active role of magistrates and lay judges in their foundation; ii) the mediation activity carried out by part-time mediators; iii) the funding by one or more local governments (regions, provinces and municipalities); iv) the approval and support and collaboration of the court social workers. There is only one exception: the VOM service founded in 1997 by a group of researchers at the University of Rome, which can be considered a "deviant" model. This initiative failed (notwithstanding the fact that it was totally funded by the university) and the service was closed in 1999 after three years in which only twenty cases were referred. According to the founders, the failure was the result of a silent boycotting by youth court social workers and juvenile magistrates. This seems to confirm the unwritten rule that a strong agreement between both categories and their participation in the foundation is needed to make a VOM service work in Italy.

At present, after 15 years of application of VOM, about a dozen of the above described local mediation services (based on letters of intent) and approximately another dozen groups operating inside the Juvenile Court Social Services carry out VOM.[24] Thus, more than 20 mediation groups are presently active and the situation is rapidly changing as new services and groups are emerging. However, they are as yet insufficient to apply mediation in all of the 29 youth prosecution offices and courts on the national territory.

---

[24] Local mediation services were operating in the following cities: Turin, Milan, Bari, Cagliari, Catanzaro, Foggia, Trento, Florence, Bologna, Ancona, Sassari, Palermo and Pavia. In the same years, some court social services begin directly to manage mediation meetings in Bolzano, Salerno, Perugia, L'Aquila, Naples, Venice and Caltanissetta (Ciuffo et al., 2005).

Although the majority of local mediation services work on referrals of crimes committed by juveniles (VOM), in the second half of the 1990s mediation was also implemented to address different kinds of conflicts, such as parental disputes in divorce and separation, and conflicts among students at schools or among neighbours. Frequently, these conflicts are brought in the existing local mediation services. Recently some of them, as the one in Turin, have begun to work on litigations, which are not crimes yet, reported by schools.

Some local services are also available to practice mediation with adult offenders because – as mentioned above – since 2000 the justices of peace (lay judges) are allowed to use VOM in this way. Nevertheless, they rarely do so since mediation services have not been created in all districts[25] and/or because justices of peace are paid for each case and consequently prefer to carry out mediation themselves instead of sending cases to the services. The first local service specifically for adult offenders referred by the justice of peace was founded in Bolzano in 2004 and subsequently the mediation services in Trento, Pavia and Florence were available to deal with cases involving adults. Additionally, private - lay or religious - associations carry out some mediation activities with adults, such as the one in Turin of the *Gruppo Abele* - led by Don Luigi Ciotti - which recently opened a section to hear the victims of crime.

The main weakness of the new local mediation services (which operate VOM free of charge) is the uncertainty regarding the continuation of funding (and funding policies), generally provided by the regions, provinces and municipalities. These sources are not mutually exclusive as most services rely on multiple funding. Because VOM services depend on local governments, they receive funding according to the level of priority VOM maintains with respect to these agencies' public policies. This uncertainty prevents systematic planning and reduces the motivation of the personnel involved. Obviously the local policies vary according to the political parties participating in the local governments, so some services have had to suspend their activity for quite a while (i.e. for two years in Milan, for some months in Bari). The scarcity of funding is also the reason why VOM services can recruit only volunteers and part-time personnel (generally detached from other public administrations).

A second weakness is the mediators' training which has been left to the initiative of the individual and/or local group. Nevertheless, a strong cultural homogeneity has emerged from our research in Italy (Mestitz, 2004b; Mestitz and Ghetti, 2005), since, with few exceptions, almost all mediators underwent the same training: that proposed by Jacqueline Morineau from the *Centre de Médiation et de Formation à la Médiation* of

---

[25] For example Mazza and Caruso (2006:63) stressed that the justice of peace of the Genoa district never uses mediation because the local mediation service was never established.

Paris (Morineau, 1998). In fact, by far the great majority of Italian mediators received their training directly from Morineau either in France and/or in Italy (or were trained in turn by those who were trained by Morineau). According to this model - in Italy indicated as "the French model" - the mediator uses his/her "empathetic capacities" in order to share feelings and "to give emotions back to the parties". It is interesting to note that Morineau's model *"has not made a significant impact on the French experience"* (Milburn, 2005: 311-312). On the contrary, it has had a considerable influence in Italy, spreading by imitation from one group to another. Moreover, the practice of co-mediation, a feature of Morineau's model, has been adopted by both local mediation services and VOM groups in Juvenile Court Social Services.

4. The main steps towards the implementation of restorative justice and mediation

A short survey of the main steps forward which accompanied the implementation of VOM and restorative justice in Italy illustrates a slow but constant path. After the spontaneous birth of the local mediation services and the creation of a normative framework in the second half of the 1990s, the introduction of mediation in the adult criminal justice system in 2000, though limited to the justice of peace jurisdiction and to a few petty offences, was certainly an important development.

A further advance was the birth of a community of experts in mediation matters grouped under two different umbrellas. Firstly, in 2003, a new six-monthly review named *Mediares* (from Latin *media res*) was created to be entirely devoted to this topic. Directed by the president of the Juvenile Court of Bari, Franco Occhiogrosso, the review re-confirmed the primary role of magistrates in promoting VOM in Italy. During the course of the years, the review has become the most authoritative cultural tool to inform, communicate and promote VOM.

Secondly, on July 2nd 2004, during a meeting in Rome at the Higher Council of the Magistracy, a group of magistrates (again!) stimulated by Marco Bouchard (as mentioned above, one of the first promoters of VOM) and Maria Giuliana Civinini (a magistrate, at the time member of the Higher Council of the Magistracy) founded the Italian section of the new European Magistrates Association *GEMME (Groupement Européen des Magistrats pour la Médiation).*[26] Not only did this new professional association regroup magistrates, but also mediators, university professors

---

[26] French magistrates were the founders of GEMME in 2003. This circumstance reconfirms again the close connection between French and Italian magistrates.

and researchers[27] who shared the aim to increase VOM and mediation activities as well as by producing new knowledge. In 2006 the section organized a conference on "Good practices of mediation in Europe" in Rome at the Court of Cassation. Although GEMME is very much involved at an international level (i.e. the Symposium of Barcelona 2009), so far the Italian section has been somewhat emarginated at the national level by the main magistrates' associations such as the ANM (National Association of Magistrates) and the AIMMF (Italian Association of Family and Juvenile Magistrates). The marginalization confirms the cultural constraints and resistance to change which characterize the Italian legal community, notwithstanding the undeniable progress made in juvenile justice in the 1990s and, subsequently, in other areas such as work law, family law, commercial and company law.

A further step forward worth to be mentioned was the initiative by the Department of Penitentiary Administration of the Ministry of Justice which consisted of creating in 2002 the National Study Commission "Victim-offender mediation and restorative justice" with the aim to define the guidelines to apply a homogeneous model of restorative justice to prison inmates. The commission completed two monitoring activities revealing a highly unsatisfactory situation, and as a result prepared a series of recommendations which became compulsory by means of a departmental memorandum (dated June 14, 2006). From June 2003 to June 2004, the activity of the Commission continued under a different label: a research project (called *MEDIARE: Mutual Exchange of Data and Information About Restorative Justice*) funded by the European Commission and coordinated by a magistrate from the Department together with the research group "Transcrime" of the University of Trento. However, the aims of the project were modest: *i)* conducting a study of norms and application of mediation in three countries: Italy, Austria and France; *ii)* to exchanging visits in Austria and France in order to compare mediation practices. An outline of ideal VOM good practices emerged from the comparison at the final seminar held in Rome in June 2004 (Ministero della Giustizia, 2004).

In 2002 some early empirical research –carried out at the Research Institute on Judicial Systems of the National Research Council (IRSIG-CNR, Bologna), promoted and directed by Anna Mestitz—had aimed to widen knowledge about VOM and restorative justice in Italy and in Europe. The surveys originated from the idea to provide the most relevant leading indications to help the legislator when preparing a law reform based on knowledge of the actual practice and application of VOM. Two first studies were conducted to know both the real distribution and organizational set-up of mediation services in Italy as well as the juvenile magistrates' opinions

---

[27] Anna Mestitz was present in the event and was enrolled in the Italian section due to her research activity carried out in the area of restorative justice and VOM.

regarding VOM. Data were collected by using different questionnaires administered to all mediators (Mestitz, 2004b) and to a wide sample of magistrates (Ghetti, 2004). These studies were published in a volume (Mestitz, 2004a) which also included the first exploratory survey autonomously conducted on VOM by the Department of Juvenile Justice (DJJ) of the Ministry of Justice (Mastropasqua and Ciuffo, 2004).

The two independent studies (Mestitz, 2004b; Ghetti, 2004) showed that the diffusion of VOM was quantitatively scarce and relevant organizational problems had to be faced to extend the use of mediation in Italy. There was a general agreement among magistrates that most of the offences referred to VOM were relatively minor (Ghetti, 2004). Moreover, magistrates seem to rely on some common criteria in referring cases to mediation centres: the option "crime committed" was selected by 93% of a sample of juvenile magistrates from a list of several non-mutually exclusive possibilities (*ibidem*). When participants were asked to further elaborate on the type of crime, all of them indicated two theoretical and/or ideological criteria: *i*) crimes whose victim was a clearly identified person; *ii*) the need of a pre-existing relationship between victim and offender. These findings would appear to confirm that strong theoretical and ideological criteria affect the application of VOM (*ibidem*).

Furthermore, a presentation of the volume with the research results in a national conference was organized by the IRSIG-CNR in 2005 in Rome at the National Research Council. The most representative members of the mediation experts' national community discussed the findings and the future perspectives of VOM. The conference was sponsored by the Senate, the DJJ of the Ministry of Justice and the Italian section of Unicef, and the most relevant politicians and legislators were also invited. The proceedings of the conference were immediately published[28] in order to provide Italian legislators with the necessary information to adapt legislation regarding mediation before the deadline of March 2006 established by the EU Council.[29] Unfortunately, at this writing, no government, regardless of its political position, has accepted the challenge to prepare a bill on mediation.

Contemporaneously (2002-2004), the researchers from IRSIG-CNR had also promoted and coordinated the above mentioned international project funded by the European Commission,[30] which aimed at comparing the organization and management of VOM in 15 European countries. At the end of the project, the national reports were presented and discussed at the final seminar held at IRSIG-CNR in Bologna in September 2003. Two years later, a volume appeared including chapters widely re-written from

---

[28] The proceedings of the conference were published in a special issue of the above mentioned quarterly journal *Mediares* (Mestitz, 2005).

[29] See EU Council Framework Decision of March 15, 2001, arts. 10 and 17.

[30] By means of the Grotius II Criminal Programme (project 2002/GRP/029).

the original national reports (Mestitz and Ghetti, 2005). Some results of both of the above-mentioned research are mentioned here.

Later, perhaps also because of these initiatives, a noticeable flourishing of new articles and books on mediation were published in Italy. Although they discussed the topic from the theoretical legal perspective, they testified that the legal community had finally "discovered" VOM.

5. The persisting lack of a legal framework for victim-offender mediation

In the above illustrated situation, the lack of a specific law regulating VOM and the main features of the mediators' role (tasks, training and so on) may appear totally anachronistic considering, on the one hand, that the practice has been used for about 15 years and, on the other, that significant steps forward had been made in the implementation of the new paradigm.

But, from a comparative perspective, there is nothing new. In fact, VOM was spontaneously introduced in the majority of European countries in the absence of specific laws and mainly through pilot projects.[31] Moreover, the time interval between the first pilot projects and the implementation of specific laws generally ranges between long to very long: the mean time interval is nine years, although this varies very much from country to country. For instance, in Poland and Ireland, where it was shortest, the time was only two years, whereas in Belgium the interval was around 20 years, in Sweden 15 years, in Norway and Spain 10 years (Mestitz, 2008).

Another common feature was that the spontaneous bottom-up initiatives were actively promoted by various professional and social groups: the academy, legal professionals such as lawyers, judges, public prosecutors, social workers, etc. Everywhere these processes developed relatively easily, probably because restorative justice and VOM are based on shared values rooted in popular moral/religious beliefs and an innate sense of justice. On the other hand, in many countries, public policies - both at national/federal and/or local levels - introduced VOM practices and services based on the idea that they would be an effective tool for crime prevention and for increasing the citizen's security (*ibidem*).

As illustrated above in the first paragraph, the lack of a specific law on VOM is mainly due to widespread cultural resistance because VOM, and more in general the restorative justice paradigm, were quickly adopted by the small juvenile magistrates' group, but they had been neglected for a long time by the legal community and legal scholars. Even today, VOM is

---

[31] To the best of our knowledge, only in Portugal and Bulgaria the laws on VOM were implemented in the absence of informal experiments.

still qualified with the adjective "experimental" and no legislation has been passed. A debate currently exists between those who advocate the introduction of specific norms providing for mediation - mainly the academy (Patané, 2004) - and those who do not consider new laws necessary (mainly juvenile magistrates). Among juvenile judges and prosecutors who think that norms are not necessary to implement VOM, there are both the magistrates favourable to VOM (because they can maintain their wide discretion) and those who do not like this strategy (who without norms do not have to apply it).

One additional and important implication of the absence of norms is that it may perpetuate the limited role exerted by victims in the criminal proceeding. Thus, the introduction of new legislation can help to overcome this limitation. The victim's role is still marginal in the Italian legislation and legal culture even if some small openings have been introduced by the reform of 1988. This is particularly true in the juvenile jurisdiction in which the minors' "educational needs" always prevail over punishment. This results in a series of exceptions and guarantees. For example, criminal trials involving juveniles must be held behind "closed doors" (no public is admitted in the court room), and the victim's civil action aimed at obtaining compensation for damages cannot be brought in juvenile criminal proceedings. This provision (obviously) strongly limits the victim's participation in the juvenile trial: if there is no possible way to seek compensation for damages, there would be little interest in participating. In addition to the well-known difficulties encountered when attempting to gain the victim's assent to mediation, the negligible role of victims in our country may further discourage their participation.

One final implication of the absence of norms is the lack of specific codes or standards of ethics regarding mediation and mediators: so far neither mediators nor judges and public prosecutors have implemented such rules.

6. The influence of values, ideologies and beliefs

In Italy, public prosecutors and judges are the only gatekeepers of VOM, and their values and ideologies, based on their legal formalistic tradition, strongly influence its application. This has been confirmed by research findings. For example, juvenile magistrates agree that offences referred to VOM must be minor, that the victim must be a clearly identified person (not a school, a shop, an institution etc.), and that there must have been a pre-existing relationship between victim and offender in order to achieve the resolution of conflict through mediation (Ghetti, 2004).

A survey conducted by the research unit of the DJJ examined the characteristics of cases of young offenders who underwent mediation in 2002 (Mastropasqua and Ciuffo, 2004). This survey showed that on average about one third of the total referrals to VOM were not carried out for various reasons (e.g., the case was not suitable to be mediated, the victim and/or offender were not willing or available to meet, an agreement was reached independently by victim and offender etc.). In addition, data confirm that the majority of crimes referred to mediation are those against persons (62.3%) and those in which the victim and the offender have had a previous personal relationship. But observing the results of mediation activities, it emerges that VOM is more likely to be successful when offences are against property (71%), whereas it is less likely to be successful when the offences are against persons (20%). Thus Mestitz (2007) argued that both phenomena - the high quantity of cases not mediated and the unsuccessful mediation with crimes against persons - show that, in practice, theoretical principles and ideologies prevail over practical results. In other words, the subgroup of juveniles referred to VOM is evidently the result of the case selection process operated by magistrates on the basis of ideological factors, given that in Italy, as well as in other countries, the great majority of crimes committed by youth offenders are against property and not against persons.

It can be added that the judicial culture shared by magistrates and personnel working in the Italian juvenile justice system is rooted in the values and culture of Italian society with respect to family and children, such as: the central catholic value of the family at the cornerstone of the society, and the tolerant and paternalistic orientation toward children and adolescents which supports the idea of their lack of accountability. In particular, the core concept of restorative justice - that an adolescent must be accountable for his/her crimes - seems not yet accepted by law professionals, social service workers as well as Italian citizens. In addition, the role exerted by victims in the criminal proceeding, the other core concept of restorative justice, is very limited in the juvenile jurisdiction where the offenders' "educational needs" always prevail.

In recent years the groups of mediators have almost doubled but, surprisingly, data on the application of VOM in the juvenile jurisdiction are almost stable. The phenomenon seems to confirm again the strong influence of ideologies and cultural bonds in introducing principles of restorative justice in the slow development of VOM in Italy.

7. The role of the Department of Juvenile Justice of the Ministry of Justice

It is evident that the mediators' categories (professionals and volunteers) influence to a large extent the existence/absence of a central coordinating institution or agency. Volunteer groups cannot be organized or coordinated from the top, whereas this is easier with public servants and groups such as social service units. From an organizational point of view, the existence of a central agency which coordinates the different initiatives in the field of VOM is relevant for human and financial resources. In fact, in the large majority of European countries, there is a central agency acting as the promoter of VOM initiatives, providing guidelines or standards, sometimes coordinating and funding local services and groups, and/or providing for the training of mediators. These agencies may be departments of the State governments, often the Ministries of Justice, or other Ministries. Sometimes there is a special central organization, funded by the executive branch, which coordinates and supplies financial support to private groups and NGOs offering VOM (such as in Austria, Germany, Sweden and Poland). In the majority of nations, a central agency (a specific one or a Ministry) is considered an essential part of the organizational set-up of the network of services working in the field of VOM. Particularly, the Ministries of Justice play the role of central agencies in five nations (France, Italy, The Netherlands, Norway and Spain/Catalonia), while in five others (Austria, Belgium/Flanders, Germany, Sweden and Poland) specific central agencies have been created, funded by a Ministry or State department. They are only lacking in Finland, England and Wales, and in the French speaking areas of Belgium (Walloon and Brussels).

The Italian Department for Juvenile Justice (DJJ) of the Ministry of Justice acts, as other Ministries of Justice, promoting VOM, supplying guidelines for the legal application of VOM but, differently from other Ministries, it has no function in coordinating and/or supervising local VOM services and does not fund VOM activities. More recently the DJJ has promoted some training courses on VOM only for its own personnel (social workers and educators), but its contribution in terms of human resources is limited to a dozen groups providing for mediation inside the Juvenile Court Social Services and a few social workers who are appointed part-time in the local mediation services.

As a matter of fact, in Italy the expansion of local VOM services on the national territory has been slowed down by the limited role played by the DJJ as a central agency. This happened for several reasons. At the very beginning, the DJJ was excluded from the new bottom-up way of law elaboration by youth magistrates regarding VOM. It tried to take over the leadership and since 1996 began to encourage the diffusion of VOM firstly by means of a traditional tool: a departmental memorandum including indications for a uniform application of VOM. Later, in 1998, pursuing the same aim, the DJJ organized a national conference and published the proceedings starting a national debate on VOM (Ufficio Centrale Giustizia Minorile, 1999).

In the last decade the DJJ took further steps, on the one hand by providing for some surveys on VOM application data (though not systematic) and, on the other hand, by offering special training initiatives on mediation to its personnel working in the Juvenile Court Social Services and/or in the juvenile prisons (social workers, educators, psychologists etc.). In the meantime, the DJJ has also relied on its web site to stimulate the experimental application of VOM.[32] More recently this institution became a partner in the third European Agis project founded by the European Commission and awarded to the European Forum for Restorative Justice (EFRJ). On this occasion, the DJJ presented itself on the international stage in the official capacity of a central agency.[33]

The above-mentioned first exploratory survey by the research unit of the DJJ (Mastropasqua and Ciuffo, 2004) examined 321 cases of young offenders who underwent mediation in 2002. Results show that there is an average time lag of about one year (380 days) between the occurrence of the crime and the mediation. This long time interval may be surprising only for non-Italian readers because, for a number of years, Italy set the record of condemnations by the European Court of Human Rights for the unacceptable delays in sentencing civil and criminal cases. Thus, Italian readers would probably consider the time interval reported above quite short. Second, the vast majority of offenders undergoing VOM were Italian (97%). This result does not correspond to the national data on offences committed by minors, as 22% of minors referred to the prosecution offices in 2002 were foreign. This finding suggests that one of the selecting criteria of the VOM subgroup is Italian nationality.

In conclusion, it must be recognized that the DJJ tried to do its best by means of different initiatives in order to increasingly play the role of a central coordination body, as other Ministries play in other European countries. Unfortunately, on the one hand, it could never provide any funding and/or practical support and, on the other, it was practically impossible to coordinate the many spontaneous mediation services funded by local governments and closely connected with the local judicial offices. As a result, the Italian DJJ is able to provide general guidelines, to lead and to train its own groups of social services practicing VOM, but so far it has not been able to fully assume the role of a central agency even if on the

---

[32] See "*minori*" section on the web site of Italian Ministry of Justice, www.giustizia.it.

[33] Notable were the very large teams from the DJJ participating in the EFRJ international conferences of Lisbon in May 2007 and in Verona in 2008.

international stage it presents itself as the national coordinator of Italian VOM initiatives.

8. Concluding remarks

Without forgetting the problem of cultural resistance and other theoretical and ideological difficulties, it cannot be denied that today restorative justice measures and mediation are a reality in Italy. The process may be slow but it is in constant progress and the above-mentioned implementation of the EU directive of May 21, 2008 might help to finally overcome the cultural obstacles. On the other hand, the wide experience developed in these years of mediation with young offenders represents a reliable basis for writing - also in the criminal area - a bill concerning both the mediation application as well as indications regarding mediators' recruitment and training. In fact, the lack of norms may potentially result in unequal treatment for juvenile offenders. There is also a risk for VOM to remain a marginal practice.

In the absence of norms, the prevailing legal formalism has left to chance all practical aspects of the development of VOM: diffusion through imitation from one actor to another, planning in establishing new mediation groups, recruitment and training of mediators, ethical principles for mediators, funding and supplying resources to VOM groups, suggestions of opinion leaders, of professional press and associations and so on. For this reason, the expansion of RJ and VOM in Italy appears strongly affected by cultural and ideological factors. If the legislators were to produce a new law on mediation, many of these factors could be overcome and the bill could also provide for safeguards for equal treatment of juvenile offenders.

Certainly, more information on RJ to legal professionals and reliable data on RJ and VOM application could be very useful for stimulating the expansion of restorative measures, but training initiatives, systematic follow-up and evaluation procedures are still missing. University groups and public research units do not receive authorization by the DJJ to conduct new research projects, as at present the DJJ seems oriented to conduct any data collection inside its own research unit (recently strengthened), but systematic follow-up is not yet a current practice. The exploratory data collection on VOM initiated by the DJJ is not only non-systematic but also poorly supported by correct methodological criteria so, in our opinion, it is not reliable. The risk is that the lack of statistics and reliable research can be used instrumentally by those who do not wish to apply RJ measures or VOM. For example, one president of a Juvenile Court commented that the lack of data supporting the benefits of VOM can clearly be interpreted as meaning that VOM is useless (Ghetti, 2004).

The other side of the coin of this new trend is that independent research by university groups and public research units has been cut off. In other terms, it has become increasingly difficult to acquire the necessary authorisation of the DJJ to undertake data collection and/or to carry out interviews into the juvenile judicial system offices. Paradoxically, the DJJ collects data in the field without possessing the necessary methodological skills, it has no money to fund research, but it can efficiently prevent any other research initiative carried out independently by universities or National Research Council institutes using their own research funds.

In conclusion, on this ground we can also observe a remarkable cultural resistance because such a trend does not exist in any other European country where, on the contrary, the results of VOM programmes have been the object of independent research, frequently requested and/or stimulated by the central agencies and Ministries coordinating the programmes themselves.

References

Bouchard, M. (1994) "Dove va la delinquenza dei giovani, dove va la giustizia minorile?", *Minori giustizia*, n. 4, pp. 10-18.

Bouchard, M., and G. Mierolo (2000), *Prospettive di mediazione*, Edizioni Gruppo Abele, Torino.

Braithwaite, J. (1989) *Crime, Shame and Re-Integration*, Cambridge University Press, Cambridge MA.

Christie, N. (1977) "Conflicts as property", *British Journal of Criminology*, vol. 17, n. 1, pp.1-15.

Ciuffo, E.; Mastropasqua, I.; Pelliccia, M.T. (2005) *Rilevazione sulle attività di mediazione penale minorile. Anno 2003*, Dipartimento Giustizia Minorile, Ministero della Giustizia, Roma (unpublished report).

Comba, D. (ed.) (2005) *ADR: la negoziazione assistita nei conflitti economici. Guida alla conciliazione e al mini-trial*, Il Sole 24 ore, Milano.

Conso, G. (1979) (ed.) *Pubblico ministero e accusa penale. Problemi e prospettive di riforma*, Zanichelli, Bologna.

Di Federico, G. (1991) "Obbligatorietà dell'azione penale, coordinamento delle attività del pubblico ministero e loro rispondenza alle aspettative della comunità" in Gaito, A. (ed.), *Accusa penale e ruolo del pubblico ministero*, Jovene, Napoli, pp. 170-208.

Di Federico, G. (1998) "Prosecutorial independence and the democratic requirement of accountability in Italy. Analysis of a deviant case in a comparative perspective", *British Journal of Criminology*, vol. 38, n. 3, pp. 371-387.

Friedman, L. M. (1975) *The legal system. A social science perspective*, Russel Sage Foundation, New York.

Ghetti, S. (2004) "Cosa pensano i magistrati minorili della mediazione penale?" in Mestitz, A. (ed.) *Mediazione penale: chi, dove, come e quando*, Carocci, Roma, pp. 89-109.

Ghetti, S.; Mestitz, A. (2007) "Victim-Offender Mediation with juvenile offenders" in Cutler, B. (ed.) *Encyclopedia of Psychology and Law*, vol. 2, Sage Publications, Thousand Oaks, CA, pp. 837-840.

Juvenile Magistrates of Turin (1994) "Proposta per una risposta penale riparatoria", *Minori giustizia*, n. 4, pp. 26-33.

Lemert, E. M. (1986) "Juvenile justice Italian style", *Law & Society Review*, vol. 20, n. 4, pp. 509-543.

Maglietta, M. (2008) "Sulla mediazione familiare prevale la tendenza a un'applicazione «blanda»", *Guida al diritto. Famiglia e minori*, n. 4, pp. 13-15.

Mastropasqua, I.; Ciuffo, E. (2004) "L'esperienza della mediazione penale nei servizi della Giustizia Minorile. Indagine su un anno di attività" in Mestitz, A. (ed.), *Mediazione penale: chi, dove, come e quando*, Carocci, Roma, pp. 111-134.

Mazza, F. A; Caruso, R. (2006) "Giudice penale di pace protagonista fra conciliazione e giurisdizione", *Diritto e Giustizia*, n. 1, pp. 58-76.

Mestitz A. (2000) "Managing juvenile criminal justice in Italy" in Fabri, M.; Langbroek, P. (eds.) *The Challenge of Change for Judicial Systems*, IOS Press, Amsterdam, pp. 221-234.

Mestitz, A. (ed.) (2004a) *Mediazione penale: chi, dove, come e quando*, Carocci, Roma.

Mestitz, A. (2004b) "I centri locali per la mediazione penale" in Mestitz, A. (ed.) *Mediazione penale: chi, dove, come e quando*, Carocci, Roma, pp. 45-88.

Mestitz, A. (ed.) (2005) "Prospettive di mediazione penale", *Mediares*, n. 6 (special issue).

Mestitz, A. (2007) "Perché la mediazione penale stenta a decollare?", *Minori giustizia*, n. 3, pp. 121-143.

Mestitz, A. (2008) "Organisational features of victim-offender mediation with youth offenders in Europe", *British Journal of Community Justice*, vol. 6, n. 2, pp. 29-42.

Mestitz, A.; Colamussi, M. (2000) "Messa alla prova e restorative justice", *Minori giustizia*, n. 2, pp. 223-288.

Mestitz, A.; Ghetti, S. (eds) (2005) *Victim-Offender Mediation with Youth Offenders in Europe. An Overview and Comparison of 15 countries*, Springer, Dordrecht.

Milburn, P. (2005) "Mediation and reparation for young offenders in France: an overview" in Mestitz, A.; Ghetti, S. (eds) *Victim-Offender Mediation with Youth Offenders in Europe. An Overview and Comparison of 15 countries*, Springer, Dordrecht, pp. 311-319.

Ministero della Giustizia, Dipartimento Amministrazione Penitenziaria (2004) *M.E.D.I.A.Re. verso il futuro. Atti del seminario transnazionale conclusivo del progetto M.E.D.I.A.Re.* (Roma: ISSP).

Morineau, J. (1998) *L'esprit de la médiation*, Erès trajets, Ramonville Saint-Agne.

Morris, A.; Maxwell, G. (eds.) (2001) *Restorative Justice for Juveniles. Conferencing, Mediation and Circles*, Hart Publishing, Oxford.

Occhiogrosso, F.P. (2008) "La mediazione nella giustizia minorile", *Minori giustizia*, n. 1, pp. 161-191.

Patanè, V. (2004) "Ambiti di attuazione di una giustizia conciliativa alternativa a quella penale: la mediazione" in Mestitz, A. (ed.) *Mediazione penale: chi, dove, come e quando*, Carocci, Roma, pp. 19-43.

Sbriccoli, M. (2002) "Giustizia criminale" in Fioravanti, M. (ed.) *Lo Stato moderno in Europa. Istituzioni e diritto*, Laterza, Roma-Bari, pp. 163-205.

Ufficio Centrale Giustizia Minorile (ed.) (1999) *La mediazione penale in ambito minorile: applicazioni e prospettive*, Franco Angeli, Milano.

Umbreit, M.S. (2001) *The Handbook of Victim-Offender Mediation*, Jossey-Bass, San Francisco, CA.

Vogliotti, M. (2004) "Les relations police-parquet en Italie : un équilibre menacé?", *Droit et Société*, n. 58, pp. 453-504.

Zehr, H. (1990) *Changing Lenses: A New Focus for Crime and Justice*, Herald Press, Waterloo.

Enforceability of Agreements Resulting from Mediation

Isabel Viola Demestre
University of Barcelona

Abstract. In less than two years, Member States must bring into force the laws, regulations and administrative provisions necessary to comply with the Directive 2008/52/EC of the European Parliament and of the Council of 21 May 2008 on certain aspects of mediation in civil and commercial matters, with one exception, namely article 10 of the Directive. In fact, the Commission will make publicly available, by whatever means it deems appropriate, the information provided by Member States on the courts or other authorities which are competent to receive a request for the enforcement of written agreements resulting from mediation (articles 12.1, 10 and 6 of Directive 2008/52/EC). This information must have been submitted to the Commission by 21 November 2010 at the latest. This study aims at briefly examining some of the issues surrounding the enforcement in Spain and to assess the possibilities of introducing new ways of granting enforceability to documents resulting from a mediation agreement, given the experiences of other jurisdictions in this area.

Keywords: Enforceable document, Judicial approval, Out of court settlement, deeds.

1. Introduction

Mediation is an autocompositive way of solving disputes. Although a third party, the mediator, is involved in the process of resolving the conflict between two or more parties, it is known that ultimately the solution is reached by the will the parties. It is not the mediator who brings the solution, as occurs with heterocompositive methods (such as court proceedings or arbitration) where the judge or arbitrator impose an outcome in favour of either party. In mediation, conflict resolution is achieved as a result of agreements reached by the parties. The task of the mediator is restricted to creating the optimal space to enable the parties to talk and communicate in a manner sufficient to reach such agreements.

If the parties comply with these agreements (voluntary performance) the conflict will be resolved definitively. However, if one fails to comply with the agreements or with part of it, how can the other party force performance? To whom may he or she address its claims? Quite possibly, the party will contact the mediator again, to inform about this situation. However, the mediator does not have the ability to solve the problem, if the party who has complied with the agreement seeks to enforce it again the other. Regardless of whether the parties agree to undertake a new mediation process (bearing in mind that applicable provisions may require a certain lapse of time between both processes), in the event that one of them is simply searching compliance with the previous agreement reached through mediation, the mediator has no authority to forcibly enforce it upon the parties.

For this purpose, i.e. for the enforcement of the agreements reached in mediation, the parties have to go to court. Under section 117.3 of the Spanish Constitution (SC) and Article 2 of the Judicature Act (*Ley Orgánica del Poder Judicial* LJ), enforcement is reserved to the courts. Literally, the provision of Article 2 LJ proclaims the principle of exclusivity of jurisdiction for enforcement, saying that:

> "Judicial power in judging and enforcing judgements lies exclusively in the courts and tribunals as set down by the laws and international treaties".[1]

The justification for such exclusivity could be found in the fact that enforcement implies interfering in the debtor's sphere and, therefore, the monopoly of the exercise or coercion by the State is particularly relevant in the area of enforcement. The same applies to other forms of what is traditionally known as alternative dispute resolution such as arbitration: although the State recognizes the effectiveness of the autonomy of the parties as long as *ordre public* considerations do not apply – and allows them to submit the resolution of their dispute to arbitration—, the enforcement or compliance in any case is reserved to the State (Article 44 of the Spanish Arbitration Act).

Therefore, the judiciary has exclusive powers to enforce the agreements reached (with the exception of the power of the Public Administration to enforce their own decisions). For this purpose the procedure governing enforcement is provided for in the Civil Procedure Act, articles 517 seq.

When seeking enforcement, two prerequisites apply: on the one hand, that there has been a failure to perform and, on the other, that the petition of

---

[1] The wording of Article 2 LJ concerns the enforcement of judgments. Regarding agreements resulting from mediation, as in any negotiation, there has been no judgement, so the question arises as to whether agreements reached by parties to end a conflict could be enforced using alternatives to the judicial system or if the power or coercion lies exclusively in the State thus preventing other procedure, in the light of the fact that court procedures ensure the parties' right to a fair process.

enforcement is based on a title that grants this possibility, i.e. it is a prerequisite that the agreements reached in mediation have been laid down in a document that entails enforceability. These documents are described for commercial and civil matters (covered by Directive 52/2008/EC) in article 517 and following of the Civil Procedure Act.

2. Enforceable titles according to the Spanish Civil Procedure Act

The 2008/52/EC Directive provides in its article 6, paragraph 2, that the content of the agreement may be made enforceable by a court or other competent authority in a judgment or decision or in an authentic instrument in accordance with the law of the Member State where the request is made. There are two exceptions to this general rule of enforceability of mediation agreements: when it is contrary to the law of that Member State where the request was made or when the law of that Member State does not provide for its enforceability.

In the event that the mediation agreements have not been included in any of the documents or resolutions referred to in Article 517 CPA, the only possible alternative is to resort to the relevant court proceedings which will end with judgement granting specific performance, and once it becomes final, it will entail enforceability.

On the other hand, if the agreement is laid down in one of the documents that entail enforceability, there is no need for a previous plenary procedure before the courts to obtain a judgement granting specific performance. The parties can seek enforcement from courts directly.

The justification for the enforceability of such titles draws from their two main characters: their indisputable nature and the fact that it states the imposition of a duty. Regarding the first aspect, the indisputable character of the title draws from the fact that both the identity of the parties, creditor and debtor, as well as the content of the obligation are included acts that involve authoritative statements. While differences between the procedure for enforcing judicial titles (from courts or arbitration) and that for enforcing out of court titles, since in the latter ground for opposition are wider, the enforceability of out of the court titles is based on the idea that when someone states the will to become bound, in a deed or in a certain commercial titles (article 517.2 (6) and (7) of the Civil Procedure Act, which we will come back later), it is because that party has engaged to comply with an obligation because that party must do so. The obligation stated in the title that is not disputable, more precisely, it does not require a previous declaration of its existence, validity and enforceability. Notwithstanding, academics that specialize in procedural law consider that the debtor's position is not the same when faced with a final judgement laid down by a court or an arbitration award as when an out of court title is being enforced against him. The judicial title (including the arbitration award for these purposes) is preceded by a plenary phase where the final decision ends the dispute for good. This is why the procedure for the enforcement of out of court titles allows a wider range of grounds for opposition, whether based on facts that preceded the titles or on facts that occurred simultaneously or after it was drafted, since in this case the indisputable nature is not so strong because it is based on appearances.

As far as the second character of enforceable titles is concerned, that is, the imposition of a duty, the procedural doctrine agrees with the need to reflect an obligation, whether determined or determinable, whatever its content, as described by article 1088 of the Spanish Civil Code: to give, to do or not do something.

Once we have established the characters of enforceable titles, it is time to move on and discuss which of those enforceable titles recognized in the Spanish legislation are apt to embody a mediation agreement according to article 517 of the Spanish Civil Procedure Act, and bearing in mind that they are *numerus clausus*. We will classify them according to their judicial or non judicial nature.

2.1. JUDICIAL ENFORCEABLE TITLES

Judicial enforceable titles are described in article 517.2 (1), (2) and (3) of the Spanish Civil Procedure Act. That is to say that judicial decisions following the relevant plenary procedure, arbitration awards (considered equivalent to judgements) and settlements approved by the court, as well as agreements reached by the parties during the procedure and that the court approves.

2.1.1. *Judgements*
The final judgement of a court granting specific performance or compensation is the enforceable title *par excellance* (article 517.2 (1) Spanish Civil Procedure Act). This type of judgment is not only considered to impose a certain performance, but also to close the dispute for good. Constitutive and declaratory judgments lead to the enforcement procedure provided for in Articles 521 and 522 CPA.

Matrimonial causes end with this kind of final judgement. Marriage is a civil status of the person, an issue of public policy. Thus, excluding the parties' power to decide, which means that to obtain a declaration of separation, divorce or nullity, a judgement is required. Therefore, agreements reached through mediation are included in the marital settlement agreement that must accompany the main petition when the proceeding is amicable or that may be produced during the proceedings so that a contested separation or divorce turns into an amicable one. In any case, the proceedings will end with a judgment, approving (or not) the parties' agreements.

Thus, the agreements reached in mediation are included in the marital settlement; its clauses will be included in the judgment, which will be enforceable. If the court does not approve the settlement, it will retain *inter partes* effects but it will not be directly enforceable.

2.1.2. *Judicially Approved Agreements*

The parties may resort to judicial approval of agreements reached in accordance with paragraph 3 of Article 517.2 of the Civil Procedure Act. This is in strict conformity with article 1816 of the Civil Code (CC), regarding the so called judicial settlements. In the Spanish Civil Code, settlements are configured as a contract whereby the parties, by mutual concessions, end the dispute between them, whether judicial proceedings are underway or not. According to case law (Supreme Court's decision, December 20, 2000):

> "The delivery of mutual benefits is not an essential requirement of the settlement, since sometimes the wish to put an end to litigation, to avoid arguments and to forget about facts occurred in the past, drives the parties to accept agreements where conditions are not equal (...) there may be moral sacrifices and they need not have an economic nature".

Judicial settlements have the authority of *res judicata* for the parties, i. e. they cannot return to this issue in a judicial proceeding because the conflict has been solved. If any of the parties presents a claim court on the same subject of controversy, the other party could oppose the exemption of settlement completed, according to the provisions of Article 1816 CC. However, settlements approved by the court are needed to obtain this enforceability. The settlement will have the judicial consideration if the court issued a resolution that would reflect the adoption of the agreements settled by the parties, by themselves or as a result of a mediation process in accordance with the relevant legal formalities. It occurs in two cases depending on whether or not the process has been initiated. In the first case, the settlement will be judicial if the procedure ends with a court order which includes the agreements that the parties have reached. In the second case, when there is not any process, the parties could obtain the enforceability of the settlement through the approval of the court, within a procedure of voluntary jurisdiction, as provided in Articles 1811 seq. the CPA, 1881.

2.2. NON JUDICIAL ENFORCEABLE TITLES

Enforceability can also be based on the titles specified in items (4) to (8) of Article 517.2 CPA, i. e. "genuine enforceable, instruments that have certain characteristics to allow the rights to base reasonable certainty of a debt" (at the beginning of the Civil Procedure Act).

In some concrete cases, it is allowed the process of enforceability of those titles whose existence has not previously been declared by a judicial decision. As stated above, these non-judicial enforceable titles are listed in Article 517.2, (4), (5), (6), (7) and (8) of the Spanish Civil Procedure Act, which are the deed, some commercial contracts with the legal requirements and, finally, the court order setting the maximum amount claimed as compensation, covered by the Compulsory Liability Insurance in circulation of motor vehicles, which we address below.

2.2.1. *Deed*

Another way through which the parties may have agreed the enforceability is the deed with the requirements of Article 517, paragraph 2, point 4 CPA. Among different documents made by notary (deeds, policy intervention, the minutes and any document that authorizes the notary - Article 144, paragraph 1 of the Notarial Regulation -), the CPA recognizes only enforceable to the deed, i.e. the document authorized by the notary according to the parties' will, the acts involving the provision of consent, contracts and legal settlements of all kinds (Article 144, paragraph 2 of Notarial Regulation).

This deed must meet the requirements of Article 517.2. 4 CPA: it must be the first copy of it, or if it is given a second one under a court order. The target of this rule seems to be avoiding duplication of executions of the same title, which could occur if infinity copies of deeds are allowed.

Therefore, the parties could agree that the mediation agreements can be sustained in deed by the notary.

2.2.2. *In the commercial field, some specific commercial contracts, are considered an enforceable title as well, according to the requirements of article 517, paragraph 2, (5), (6) and (7) of the CPA*

It is important to point out a remarkable difference between the judicial and non judicial title under Article 520 CPA. According to this provision, non judicial enforceable titles can only be referred to an economic issue. Additionally, some features are required: the claim has to be for more than 300 euros in cash and in foreign currency convertible or in something computable in money or kind.

We question the possibility of obtaining an enforceable title that includes the non judicial settlements resulting from mediation when the agreements consists of something different than giving money, to do or not do something, as it is, for instance, in family matters. The enforceability of this agreements resulting from mediation is restricted to judicial enforceable titles.

2.2.3. *Court order of maximum*

This title has its origin in Article 10, 632/1968, of November 21, which according to the Eighth Additional Provision of Law 30/1995, of November 8, management and supervision of private insurance is called Act on civil liability and insurance on the motor.

2.3. THE RESIDUAL CLAUSE OF ARTICLE 517.2 CPA

Finally, Article 517.2, number 9, in the CPA recognizes enforceability to the titles indicated in this particular Act or some other law. The last paragraph of Article 517. 2 CPA is considered as a residual clause of the enforceable titles. It is the law that indicates which title is enforceable because it allows acting in the estate of the debtor so that the legislator is the only one who can establish what titles may lead to such consequences, excluding therefore the will of the parties. The law may be national as well as the coming from the European Union, for example, the regulations established by Regulation 805/2004 of April 21, laying down a European enforcement order for uncontested claims.

According to this Spanish Article 517.2 (9) CPA, it would be possible to admit enforceability to a title performed by some particular person or organism, if the law says so. This is an interesting point because it opens the door to new forms of enforceability of agreements resulting from mediation if these agreements are settled in a certain form or legal document. In this sense, we can provide lessons for other jurisdictions. For instance, we may find some legal systems in which mediation agreement may be enforceable in accordance with the procedure laid down in relevant procedural law (like in Argentina). In some other systems, the final document of mediation process is considered as an enforceable title (Article 18 of the Act Conciliation No. 26872, 1997, from Peru; article 32 of the Mediation and Conciliation Act in the Mexican state of Aguascalientes published in the official newspaper of the state December 27, 2004, amended on October 27, 2008) or there is also the possibility to consider enforceability to the agreement ratified by the parties before the director of the mediation centre.

We emphasize this latter case. According to Article 32 of Act 112, 2005, corresponding to Mexican State of Durango, the state director of the mediation centre as well as the deputy director general of the district will have the ability of certificate and give enforceability to the ratification that parties do about the agreement resulting from mediation. For its part, Article 71 of the Act states that:

"Immediately after the signed agreement, the parties and experts involved in the case will appear before the director general or deputy director of the Centre of the Central District if necessary, so that they ratify its contents and recognize the signatures. (...) The agreements will be approved only if they are not against moral, public policy provisions and do not affect inherent rights, or infringes the principle of equity harmful to one party (...)".

3. Conclusion

In conclusion, according to Article 12 in conjunction with Article 6 and 10 of Directive 2008/52/EC, Member States shall inform the Commission of the courts or other authorities competent to receive requests in order to ensure that it is possible for the parties, or for one of them with the explicit consent of the others, to request that the content of a written agreement resulting from mediation is made enforceable. We have analysed the enforceable titles according to the Spanish legislation in civil and commercial matters and we think that it is time to study the possibility of including in the appropriate act some other non judicial enforceable titles, as it happens in countries such as Peru (the final document of mediation process) or Mexico (the ratification by the parties about the agreements resulting from mediation).

References

Alonso-Cuevillas Sayrol, J. (coord.) (2000) *Instituciones del nuevo proceso civil: comentarios sistemáticos a la Ley 1/2000,* Economist&Jurist, Barcelona.
Flores Prada, I. (2005) *El procedimiento de apremio en la ejecución,* Tirant, monografías, Valencia.
Garberí Llobregat, J. (2003) *El proceso de ejecución forzosa en la nueva Ley de enjuiciamiento civil: comentarios y jurisprudencia Libro III ("de la ejecución forzosa") de la Ley 1/2000, de 7 de enero, de enjuiciamiento civil,* Editorial Bosch, Barcelona.
Ramos Méndez, F. (2000) *Guía para una transición ordenada a la LEC,* J. M. Bosch Editor, Barcelona.
Suárez Robledano, J. M. (coord.) (2003) *Ley de Enjuiciamiento civil 1/2000, textos legales, comentarios, jurisprudencia y formularios,* Dijusa, Madrid.
Xiol Ríos, J. A. (2008) *Enjuiciamiento civil: comentarios y jurisprudencia. Ley 1/2000, de 7 de enero,* Sepín Editorial Jurídica, Madrid.

Mediation and Transitional Justice: Global Approaches Aimed at Establishing Harmony and Featuring the Involvement of Victims and Civil Society

Jordi Palou-Loverdos
Palou-Rognoni Advocats Associats

Abstract. Even if tensions between the paths of justice and those of international peace-building are undeniable, a global approach to violent conflicts is becoming increasingly necessary. Within this context, we must take into account that victims and civil society are beginning to play an important role in achieving a peaceful solution to violent conflict; in participating, to a greater or lesser degree, in the process called for by the path of justice, - whether international or transitional justice during or after the conflict – as well as by international mediation and dialogue. This paper presents the experience obtained from the specific approaches to peace and justice in Central Africa featuring the involvement of civil society and truth as cornerstone of all action. To conclude, the paper argues that it is necessary to make a strong and ample financial investment in global peace processes and in the creation of a Global Centre for Peace and International Conflict Mediation.

Keywords: Justice processes, Peace processes, Civil society, Victims, International Criminal Court, Universal justice, Violent or armed conflict, Mediators, Peace-builders, Peacemakers, Rule of law, Transitional justice, Rwanda, Democratic Republic of Congo, Fighting impunity, Facilitating dialogue, Investing in peace, Global Centre for Peace and International Conflict Mediation.

1. Introduction

Several studies are known to state – either explicitly or in a veiled manner – that the path of the Administration of justice stands at odds or is even incompatible with peace-building venues. In fact, this situation is very often regarded as a dilemma. Aware of the strain that can possibly arise, not just from the differences between these two ways, but first and foremost among the different players and professionals involved in the latter, this short paper aims at contributing elements that can integrate both approaches. The paper argues – forcibly in a short and incomplete manner– how the system of observance of human rights in place for the last sixty

years, and the recent emergence of victims as international players -
together with other individual and collective players from civil society and
ethnic groups-, can offer more integrative approaches to reconcile both
paths under the common umbrella of non-violent conflict resolution.

Above and beyond the decisive involvement of governmental players
and of international, regional and universal institutions, a crucial question
arises: what role do non-governmental players have? What role do the latter
play – not only in generating, fostering, channelling, neutralizing or
perpetuating violent conflicts of today's day and age, but also in
preventing, handling, solving or transforming them in a non-violent way?
We refer here to national and transnational civil societies, to victims both
as individuals or collectively, to ethnic groups and people, or even to
multinational companies, some of which hold more power, more resources
and more leverage and influence than many nations in the planet. What role
do victims play or should play, both in the processes of justice as well as in
peace-building processes? Should they be involved? And if so, how should
they and to what extent? Regarding processes of justice, what role do
victims play or should play in investigating or revealing hidden truths or
truths that have been concealed about the violent conflict and in the fight
against impunity? What role, more specifically, in investigating, producing
and/or enabling evidence; in pressing direct or indirect charges for
international crimes or systematic human rights violations, in indictments
in application of current international law – or the rising ability to improve
or create new concepts of international law? What role should victims play
in matters dealing with moral and/or material compensation or damages,
among others? All of the above refers to their potential involvement in
universal and/or international justice processes which apply international
law to the more serious international crimes, such as genocide crimes,
crimes against humanity, war crimes – including gender crimes and large-
scale pillage of natural resources -, torture, etc.

When it comes to peacemaking and peace-building, what role do
victims play – or could play – in the following areas: in national and
international negotiations, in mediation and reconciliation related to violent
conflict; in processes of multilateral dialogue at varying levels; in other
peacemaking or peace-building processes in a general sense; in initiatives
known as preventive of future violent conflict; in the process of
transformation of existing violent conflict; in moral and/or material
compensation and damages; in post-conflict or post-war rehabilitation; in
security systems and systems of protection of human rights; civil
diplomacy; historical memory; processes of truth, forgiveness and
reconciliation; in the restatement of the Rule of Law; in the political
system, the security and defence systems and in humanitarian crises, among
others?

These questions could broaden to include the potential involvement of other non-governmental players, especially that of national and international civil society. Clearly, the answers to these questions will affect, in fundamental ways, both the processes of justice and/or peace-building themselves as well as the outcome of their outcome.

2. Civil societies, victims, justice processes and peace processes

2.1. CIVIL SOCIETY, VICTIMS AND JUSTICE PROCESSES

Undoubtedly, civil society at large, and victims in particular, have gone from being mere spectators falling prey to violent and/or armed conflict to getting actively involved at varying lengths in processes of justice and/or peace. Their participation has also extended to exerting an increasing influence on political and democratic processes related to armed or diplomatic intervention in armed or violent conflicts, both at the national and international levels. Many governmental players, formal diplomacies, as well as national and international organisations have not concealed their misgivings as they watched these developments, often perceiving them as invasive of a turf which 'does not belong' to victims or civil society, but rather only to those "with the knowledge and expertise" and those "who count." On the other hand, many other governmental players, formal diplomacies, as well as national and international organisations follow this process with careful attention and even foster this development within the periods of time and frameworks that institutions and civil society have agreed on.

It is not my intent to be exhaustive, but with regard to Spain[1] and other countries with Roman-Germanic or continental justice systems which to varying degrees allow victims to participate and be legally represented in processes of justice, it is worth highlighting the decisive involvement and intervention shown by Argentina's 'Madres y Abuelas de la Plaza de Mayo'; by Spanish, Argentine and Chilean victims; Spanish and Guatemalan Maya victims; Catalonian, Spanish, Rwandan and Congolese victims; Tibetan victims; Palestinian victims, etc. – all of them with regard to their roles in articulating, presenting, investigating – and even filing formal charges – in processes of universal justice in application of current international law. In turn, given the practices of the Nuremberg and Tokyo Trials, or of *ad-hoc* Courts for the former Yugoslavia and Rwanda, or of

---

[1] See Articles 101 and 270 of the Criminal Procedures Act in agreement with Article 234 of Spain's Organic Law of the Judiciary (L.O.P.J.) concerning international crimes mentioned there. For a more detailed analysis of the established rule and of universal justice trials featuring the involvement of victims in different countries; see Martínez, 2008, pp. 10-11; as well as Palou-Loverdos, 2007, pp. 60- 63.

other mixed courts, most of which were inspired on the Anglo-Saxon system of justice where the intervention or legal representation of victims is deemed unthinkable, the new International Criminal Court has created a new system of justice. A hybrid between the Continental and Anglo-Saxon systems, this new system marks the first time ever that an international court offers victims[2] the real possibility of participating and having legal representation –albeit in a more restricted way than in continental national systems of justice.

2.2. CIVIL SOCIETY, VICTIMS AND PEACE PROCESSES

Likewise, it is worth noting the increasing involvement which representatives of civil society – including victims and relatives of victims – are having in peace processes, as well as the impact that their participation can make on the latter. Several different scholars investigating these processes have underlined in their empirical studies that participation of civil society in peace negotiations makes it easier for agreements to be more feasible and sustainable.[3] There is no shortage of examples showing that representatives of civil society have made important contributions to formal peace talks in countries as diverse as Sierra Leone, Liberia, Burundi, Aceh or Uganda. In these cases, they have varying degrees: strengthened the content of the agreement, expanded and reinforced their legitimacy, as well as created conciliatory and integrative dynamics between the parties more reluctant to reach an agreement.[4] This paper gives below a brief account of processes in Rwanda and in the Democratic Republic of Congo.

3. Hunger and thirst for justice and peace: do the goddesses struggle or cooperate?

We hear it again and again everywhere on our planet. Literally and figuratively, the world starves and thirsts for justice and peace. In past papers I have talked about notions of law and mediation, looked at their etymological roots and principles, and delved into the symbols linked to

---

[2] See Articles 68, 69 and concordant articles of the Statute of Rome of the International Criminal Court and Rules 63, 85 and concordant rules of the Rules of Procedure and Evidence of the ICC, as well as Article 42 and concordants of the Regulation of the Trust Fund for Victims (http://www2.icc-cpi.int/NR/rdonlyres/0CE5967F-EADC-44C9-8CCA-A7E9AC89C30/140126/ICCASP432Res3_English.pdf) (June 4 2009 search). 108 countries have signed the ICC's Statute of Rome, 30 of them are African nations, 14 are from Asia, 16 from Eastern Europe, 23 nations are from Latin America and the Caribbean, and 25 nations are from Western Europe and elsewhere.

[3] Pfaffenholz, 2006.

mythological characters mentioned from time immemorial.[5] Both Goddess Ma'at and Goddess Themis stand for the Administration of justice among clashing parties and hold a sword as their major symbol. On other hand, Goddess Nefertem or the Goddess of Temperance, who stand for mediation and enabling peace-building among opposing parties, feature water as their main symbol. Whether acting as ruling judge or as facilitator/restorer, this third middle character standing between the two adversary parties who represent the duality of the conflict makes use of tools and symbols which are at the same time analogous and different. Since past times, human beings have satisfied their hunger by resorting to sharp and cutting linear elements, such as the flint, teeth or knives – tools which find their equivalent in the sword that rules justice between the two weighing pans of a scale. To quench thirst, human beings have used flexible, round elements, such as their hands, a leaf or a bowl, to contain water - element akin to the liquid that flows between the two amphorae of Temperance.

Justice and law experts, on the one hand, and experts in mediation and peace-building, on the other, often claim their respective venues and methods to be the most efficient when it comes to tackling or managing, solving or transforming violent conflicts. When mediators, negotiators and facilitators of peace processes step in, legal professionals frequently regard them to be meddling with the evidence or sentences they have had a hard time securing. This is particularly the case when there is talk of possible peace agreements that would allow partial or total amnesties or impunities. In turn, once they have reached an agreement with one or many key players in an armed or violent conflict, peace-builders or peacemakers perceive any arrest warrants, trial orders or sentences resulting from legal proceedings held in application of international law to be an outright attack to the peace process or to their hard-won agreements. Such tensions do not merely arise between these two fields which seem to start apart in terms of their methodology, principles and dynamics. They also appear within a same field, for example, between retributive and restorative justice; or between those which advocate abiding by the guidelines of the Rule of Law or those which focus on the range of measures known as Transitional Justice[6] which comprises a useful mix of judicial and non-judicial measures focusing on the responsibility for international crimes of the past. This approach includes initiatives for criminal accountability; truth commissions, reparations programs; reform of the security and judiciary sectors; demobilization and integration of ex-combatants and community-based justice initiatives,[7] among others. Legal professionals are well aware that,

---

[4] Hayner, 2009, pp. 12-13.
[5] Palou-Loverdos, 1999, pp. 88-109; and Palou-Loverdos, 2006.
[6] See Lekha, 2009, pp. 3-4.
[7] See, op.cit. *Negotiating justice: guidance for mediators*, pp. 11-12.

during the course of the legal proceedings,[8] they sometimes need to replace the sword with the water. Peace-builders, in turn, know that they more often than not have to brandish the sword when negotiating, mediating or facilitating among opposing parties,[9] for the benefit of the two parties involved, the process itself and the actual outcome. There is increasing agreement that mediators should not validate an agreement between the parties which grants amnesty to the perpetrators of the most serious international crimes,[10] since this would prove unacceptable to both the international community and the United Nations system.

Some authors point to these tensions or alleged dilemmas and conclude, through various arguments, that we are better off saying that the systems complement each other. They argue that establishing one single model applicable on a universal scope is ill-advised. It is preferable, they continue, to devise a distinct, custom-tailored approach to suit each individual territory, taking into account the historical cross-roads, the potential players, as well as the content, magnitude and degree of the violent conflict at stake, while at the same time bearing in mind certain principles or guidelines derived from past experience.[11] Although there does not appear to be consensus on this approach yet, it would seem advisable for the two goddesses to work with each other in a joint effort to alleviate –as much as possible – humankind's hunger and thirst in body and soul. In their endeavour, these deities should make available their complementary venues of peaceful justice[12] and just peace,[13] placing truth as the cornerstone and backbone of all other principles, interests and needs.

---

[8] Specially in the case of protected witnesses or particularly traumatized victims.

[9] Mediators or facilitators must occasionally resort to 'sharp tools' in order to maintain the balance between the parties, ensure one party's capacity of self-determination, preserve respect towards both parties' dignity and face and react to issues of responsibility for serious international crimes, among other similar situations.

[10] See op.cit. Priscilla Hayner, Pages 6-7; and Mónica Martinez, 13-14.

[11] Op.cit., Monica Martinez, 2008, pp. 12-13 and 15-17, Priscilla Hayner, 2009 pp. 5-6 and 20-22, ; Chandra Lekha Sriram-Olga Martin Ortega and Johana Herman, 2009, pp. 2-6. Pp. 12-13 and 15-17, 5-6 and 20-22, 2-6.

[12] That is, justice processes not centred on repression, punishment or revenge, (while not disregarding applicable sentences) but carried out by adversarial means, with all due guarantees and respect for fundamental human rights. These justice processes establish an internationally accepted criterion to determine responsibility and put an end to the impunity of perpetrators of serious international crimes- all along taking the utmost care to address the basic needs of the people and adhere to the truth of the facts.

[13] That is, peace-building processes that do not aim at securing partial and provisional agreements that may only make so. Rather, those processes which strongly observe the principles of mediation, reconciliation or the facilitation of dialogue, while at the same time not leaving out issues of social justice and formal justice in order to merely reach a visible agreement (particularly issues that address the granting of amnesties and the establishment of some kind of accountability for the most serious international crimes). Likewise, these approaches take great care to address the basic needs of the people and adhere to the truth of historical processes.

4. Rwanda/Democratic Republic of Congo: a two-track approach combining the mechanisms of transnational justice

This paper does not attempt to make even a brief analysis of the large scope of the conflict which has raged in Rwanda and in the Democratic Republic of Congo,[14] nor of the number of peace processes conducted and/or stalled there.[15] Nor, for that matter, it can look at the various interventions which international justice venues (International Criminal Court for Rwanda) undertook to investigate the countless international crimes perpetrated in Central Africa. Causing the death of almost 8 million people - Rwandan, Congolese, Burundian, Spanish, Canadian, Belgian and British victims, among others – this conflict has claimed the lives of more civilians than any other conflict since the Second World War.[16]

This paper merely looks at a modest but forceful example of a joint initiative where civil society and the victims of this conflict[17] have come together to create a mixed approach which combines the path of justice with that of peace[18] in an attempt to transform the conflict by non-violent

---

[14] For more information on the alleged war crimes and a factual and judicial analysis, see: Palou Loverdos, 2007.

[15] Although a wide range of violent incidents have continued to occur in Rwanda since October 1, 1990, the UN and many international NGOs consider there are not any violent conflicts or systematic violations of human rights which deserve special attention; in addition, most peace experts do not mention the Arusha Peace Agreement in their papers. The Arusha Agreement had been subsequently frustrated by several episodes, especially by the April 6, 1994 assassination of the presidents of Rwanda and Burundi that unleashed the infamous genocide in Rwanda as well as the chain of ongoing serious international crimes in this country and in the Democratic Republic of Congo which have only recently been subject to formal investigation.

[16] For a condensed analysis of the conflict and the two strategic paths used to transform it through the impetus given by civil society and victim: http://www.veritasrwandaforum.org/material/sintesi_en.pdf

[17] Since the need to invest in peace will briefly be discussed later on, we make here a preliminary mention of the fact that the annual budget of this transitional justice project has ranged from Euro 60,000 to 120,000 for the last eight years. By contrast, see Point Nr. 5 of this paper.

[18] To cite another example, in Colombia, institutional bodies have opted for using transitional justice mechanisms even though many experts believe this is happening at a time when the conflict is still alive (and hence talk of transition and post-conflict proves difficult). In this case, it is the government and its branches that hold this commitment, basing it on the Law of Justice and Peace passed in 2005 which the Colombian Constitutional Court reinterpreted in a resolution the following year. To this effect, see Felipe Gómez Isa, *Paramilitary Demobilization in Colombia: Between Peace and Justice.* Working Paper Nr. 57, April 2008. Rwanda and the Democratic Republic of Congo are both at different phases; it is difficult to speak of post-conflict situations in their case as well. Especially in Rwanda; no process of transition has taken place. The two-path initiative explained in this section thus applies mechanisms of transitional justice to a situation of conflict where there is in fact an absence of transition. In contrast to Colombia, the initiative originates in the involvement civil society has had and coordinated at the national and

means and achieve its resolution for the benefit of current and future generations in Central Africa. The initiatives, as we will see, do not aim at becoming a universal model to be applied on a global scale. Rather, they represent an example of how the venues of justice, on the one hand, and those of dialogue, on the other, can enhance and reinforce each other in order to reconstruct the social, political and economic fabric of a society devastated by armed conflict.

4.1. THE JUSTICE APPROACH AND THE STRUGGLE AGAINST IMPUNITY FOR INTERNATIONAL CRIMES IN CENTRAL AFRICA

At the end of the nineties a number of prominent personalities, victims, relatives of Spanish, Rwandan and Congolese victims, national and international non-governmental organizations and some public institutions – all of whom constitute the organization International Forum for Truth and Justice in the African Great Lakes Region – joined forces and resources. Their aim was to initiate an international process to investigate major international crimes perpetrated in Rwanda and the Democratic Republic of Congo between October 1990 and July 2002[19] (start of the International Criminal Court's temporal competence). These crimes had not been subject to investigation by any national or international jurisdictional body. In 2005, after years collecting information and documentary evidence and gathering witnesses, these parties filed a lawsuit at the Spanish courts in application of the principle of universal justice. On February 6, 2008, after years conducting their formal investigative proceedings, the Spanish courts issued a Bill of Indictment and international arrest warrants against 40 top officials of Rwanda's [20] incumbent political-military helm. They were charged with international crimes of genocide, crimes against humanity and war crimes, among others, which had allegedly been perpetrated during the afore-mentioned period in Rwanda and the Democratic Republic of Congo.[21]

---

international levels.

[19] For more information: http://www.veritasrwandaforum.org/querella.htm. (June 4 2009 search).

[20] At least 9 of them are away from Rwanda, holding important positions, even within the UN organization: 4 of them work for the hybrid peace-keeping forces in Sudan (UNAMID), including a Rwandan army general who is the second commander of such forces. A fifth one serves at the demobilization arm of the UN Development Program (UNDP) in Nepal. Several public institutions have formally requested the UN to destitute them and turn them over to justice (see all at: http://www.veritasrwandaforum.org/dosier/resol_Ban_Ki_Moon_es.pdf.). (June 4 2009 search).

[21] See judicial resolution:
http://www.veritasrwandaforum.org/dosier/resol_auto_esp_06022008.pdf ;
see summary of judicial action and bill of indictment: http://www.veritasrwandaforum.org/material/press_release_080208_eng.pdf (June 4 2009

4.2. THE CHANNEL OF DIALOGUE AMONG MEMBERS OF RWANDAN SOCIETY

Aware that the justice approach represented an important yet insufficient step towards transforming the Rwandan conflict, preventing further violent incidents and overcoming the tragedy of the two former decades, a group of prominent members of Rwandan civil society living abroad set out to start a dialogue from exile. Two persons initiated the dialogue: the Hutu president of a victims' association who lived in Brussels and the Tutsi former plenipotentiary ambassador of the current Rwandan government to the United Nations who lived in New York.

In 2004 ten Rwandan men and women of the diaspora met for the first time at a meeting organized by international facilitators in Mallorca (Spain). The Rwandans, both Tutsi and Hutu, were able to ascertain the different ways in which they each understood Rwandan history and the past according to their own personal, family and community experiences. At the same time, they also discovered the extent to which they agreed on constructive proposals for the future. In 2006, after two years in the works, a second encounter by then referred to as the Intra-Rwandan Dialogue took place in Barcelona (Spain), giving rise to the International Network for Truth and Reconciliation in Central Africa. Twenty Rwandan nationals, both Hutu and Tutsi from the diaspora and the Rwandan heartlands, took part in this event. The meeting was organized with the sponsorship of Nobel Peace Prize nominee/candidate Juan Carrero and the support of both Nobel Peace Laureate Adolfo Pérez Esquivel, present at the meeting, and of the President of Senegal, Abdoulaye Wade. The protocol of findings of the 2006 event, which called for a more inclusive Inter-Rwandan Dialogue– served as the foundation for the talks held at five subsequent meetings entitled Dialogue Platforms in 2007 and 2008.[22] These five events took place in:

- Washington DC for 20 participants from the USA and Canada;
- Amsterdam for 20 participants from Holland, Belgium and Germany;
- Orléans (France) for 20 participants from France and Italy;
- Barcelona, where the Platform for Rwandan women was held; and
- Kinshasa (Democratic Republic of Congo) where a special *ad hoc* platform was organized for Congolese participants coming from the eastern region of this country bordering with Rwanda.

---

search). See also mistrust of Rwanda and African Union related to universal and international justice initiatives, (Martin Vidal, 2008), pags 3-6

[22] With the support of, among others, Nobel Peace Laureate Adolfo Perez Esquivel; and of Federico Mayor-Zaragoza, former UNESCO Secretary General (1987-1999), President of "Cultura de Paz" and co-chairman of a top level UN group of Alliance of Civilizations.

In 2007 the Spanish Parliament extended its support to this initiative and passed a resolution where all political parties unanimously agreed to offer technical, legal, diplomatic and political support and urged to take it to an international[23] level.

In early 2009, the eighth Dialogue held in Mallorca (Spain) featured the participation of thirty Rwandan men and women from all Rwandan ethnic groups- Hutu, Tutsi and Twa-, as well as two Congolese, who had come from Africa, Europe and North America. Celebrating five years since the dialogue started, they agreed to formally ask a Central African government to hold a Highly Inclusive Inter-Rwandan Dialogue, and request institutional and financial support from the international community.[24] During the course of these five years, almost 150 Rwandan leaders have participated in the process. Among them, it is worth noting the involvement of two former prime ministers, various former cabinet ministers, former ambassadors, political leaders, representatives from civil society, from victims' as well as human rights organisations, and from institutions devoted to peace and economic research. All of the above have set their eyes on the future and on carrying on this inter-Rwandan dialogue as the legitimate foundation upon which to build a new Rwanda that can be widely accepted by all political, ethnic, social and economic groups as well as by the international community.

5. Investing in global peace processes

Numerous studies study and analyze military expenditures worldwide. Military spending for 2007 alone, for example, reached 1,339 trillion dollars.[25] That same year, 61 "peace operations" were carried out worldwide (41% of them in Africa), deploying a total of 169,467 people in missions which were almost entirely military: 119 countries sent troops, military observers or police officers totalling 150,651 people, a stark contrast to the 18,816 civilians[26] overall.

---

[23] See original Proposal of Non-Legislative Motion of support to Intra-Rwandan Dialogue dated April 25 2007:
http://www.veritasrwandaforum.org/dosier/congreso_diputados_eng.pdf (June 4 2009 search).
[24] All documents with Findings and Proposals of the eight Intra-Rwandan Dialogue sessions to date (2004-2009) are available in several languages at: http://www.veritasrwandaforum.org/dialogo.htm (June 4 2009 search).
[25] See Stockholm International Peace Research Institute, *SIPRI Yearbook 2008*, Catalan translation, Fundació per la Pau 2008, -Petter Stalenheim, Catalina Perdomo e Elisabetk Sköns- page 10. This organization notes that military spending increased by 6% in 2007 compared to 2006, and by 45% since 2008, and that it accounted for 2.5% of the Global Gross Domestic Product, or US$ 202 per capita worldwide. Spain ranks 15th in terms of military spending, with military expenditures of 14.6 billion dollars that constitute 1% of the total amount spend worldwide.

There is no knowledge about the existence of studies that look at the amount spent worldwide on national and international processes of justice. Yet, if we want to have a rough idea of the huge disparity between military spending and expenditures on justice, we only need to point out the annual budget of the world's leading international court: in 2009, the International Criminal Court, which is currently investigating four major situations in the Democratic Republic of Congo, in Uganda, in the Central African Republic and in Sudan, has a total budget of Euro 101,229,900.[27] Compared to military spending, this amount is clearly a drop in the bucket - even if we compare it to military spending in Spain which accounts for 1% of military expenditures worldwide.[28]

Many scholars and experts on peace and peaceful conflict resolution continue urging for an increase and restructuring of private and public investment in favour of peace.[29] Investing in global peace processes is imperative. There are no studies which look at how much has been invested in theoretical analysis, research,[30] infrastructure and the practical

[26] Op.cit., Sharon Wiharta, pp. 7-8. There is no information about the cost of the 61 afore-mentioned peace processes which were primarily carried out by military parties. Furthermore, it is sometimes difficult to tell whether these operations were aimed at maintaining peace or at securing geostrategic military objectives. While serving in Sudan for the UNAMID, four Rwandan military officials were prosecuted in February 2008 (see footnote Nr. 20). Some months later, on September 3, 2008 the US Department of State made a donation of military equipment worth US$ 20 million to the Rwandan defence force led by one of the above-mentioned prosecuted officials, whose UN appointment in Sudan was, in fact, ratified by UN Secretary General a few weeks later and extended for an irrevocable 6-month period until March 2009. (See official information from the US Embassy in Rwanda: http://rwanda.usembassy.gov/u.s._embassy_donates_equipment_to_the_rwanda_defense_fo rces).

[27] See Report of the Assembly of Member States of the International Criminal Court ICC-ASP/8/5 dated May 13 2009, http://www2.icc-cpi.int/iccdocs/asp_docs/ASP8/ICC-ASP-8-5-ENG.pdf (June 4 2009 search).

[28] This amount pales when compared even to weapon sales figures of leading North American weapon manufacturer Boeing which had a turnover of 30.69 billion dollars in 2006. Op. Cit, SIPRI, p. 12. See another example: African Union-United Nations Hybrid Operation in Darfur (UNAMID) approved budget for $1, 569.26 million (A/C.5/62/30) for financing that mission from July 2007 to June 2008 (see: http://www.un.org/Depts/dpko/missions/unamid/facts.html, June 4 2009 search). UNAMID was established by the Security Council, in resolution 1769 (2007) for an initial period of 12 months, to help achieve a lasting political solution and sustained security in Darfur. This budget provides for the deployment of 240 military observers, 19,315 military contingent, 3,772 United Nations police, 2,660 formed police units, 1,542 international staff, 3,452 national staff, 548 United Nations Volunteers and 6 Government-provided personnel. In addition, the budget includes 55 international and 30 national staff under general temporary service (see http://www.un.org/News/Press/docs/2007/gaab3828.doc.htm, June 4 2009 search).

[29] See, as example, Anatol Rappoport, 1989.

[30] See Escola de Cultura de Pau, 2008, p. 13. This study shows that most Spanish research centres do not reveal their budgets, but notes that the budget of four centres totalled 6 million euros.

implementation of the different venues for peace-building worldwide. It took ages before a global criminal Court was created, and even now, it still needs to grow, become stronger and spread out around the world. We need to roll up our sleeves to establish a true Global Centre for Peace and International Conflict Mediation. This centre should be the outcome of an international agreement between the different countries of the world, have an adequate and sufficiently-endowed budget,[31] and operate in a concerted effort with regional and global institutions, governments, public and private entities. It should be authorized to intervene within the framework of accredited international experts – governmental, non-governmental and independent- work on the basis of multidisciplinary teams comprising people from different geographical, social, racial, ethnic, religious and intellectual backgrounds and viewpoints, and focus on preventing violent conflict and on solving and transforming conflict by peaceful means. We cannot wait for ages, we cannot even wait for decades. We are jointly responsible for making it happen in the next decade -for the sake of the earth and all present and future generations.

References

Escola de Cultura de Pau (2008) *La investigación sobre la paz en España*, working paper n. 2, Oficina de Promoció de la Pau i dels Drets Humans (Generalitat de Catalunya), October.

Gómez Isa, F. (2008) *Paramilitary Demobilization in Colombia: Between Peace and Justice,* Fundación para las Relaciones Internacionales y el Diálogo Exterior (FRIDE), Working Paper n. 57 available at: http://www.fride.org/expert/72/felipe-gomez-isa (accessed 5 July 2010)

Hayner, P. (2009) *Negotiating justice: guidance for mediators*, February report, Centre for Humanitarian Dialogue and International Center for Transitional Justice.

Lekha Sriram, C.; Martin-Ortega, O.; Herman, J. (2009) *Just Peace? Peacebuilding and rule of law in Africa*, Centre on Human Rights in Conflict. University of East London, Policy Paper n. 1, January.

Martin, V. (2008) *African mistrust of "Northern Justice"*, Fundación para las Relaciones Internacionales y el Diálogo Exterior (FRIDE), available at: http://www.fride.org/publication/539/african-mistrust-of- (accessed 5 July 2010)

Martinez, M. (2008) *Making Justice Work: accountability and complementarity between courts*, Fundación para las Relaciones Internacionales y el Diálogo Exterior (FRIDE), Working Paper n. 60, September.

Palou-Loverdos, J. (1999) "Mediació i Justicia", *Revista Perspectiva Social,* n. 42.

---

[31] To set it in motion, it would suffice that all countries contribute 0.1% of what they presently allot to military spending and earmark it to establish and authorize the first annual budget of this Global Center.

Palou-Loverdos, J. (2006) "Mediación en conflictos: hacia un bumerán armónico", *Revista Polis*, n. 14, Universidad Bolivariana de Santiago de Chile.

Palou-Loverdos, J. (2007) "Esperanzas para la justicia universal", *Abogados*, Revista del Consejo General de la Abogacía Española, n. 42, February.

Palou Loverdos, J. (2007) "Crímenes de guerra contra españoles, ruandeses y congoleses en África central (1990-2006): El conflicto de los grandes lagos desde la perspectiva de los derechos humanos y el derecho internacional humanitario", *Revista Electrónica de Estudios Internacionales,* n. 13.

Pfaffenholz, T.; Kew, D.; Wanis, A. (2006) "Civil society and peace negotiations: why, whether and how they could be involved", *Oslo Forum 2006*, www.osloforum.org (accessed 5 July 2010)

Rapoport, A. (1989) *The origins of violence. Approaches to study of conflict*, World Peace Academy.

Stalenheim, P.; Perdomo, C.; Sköns, E. (2008) *SIPRI Yearbook 2008,* Stockholm International Peace Research Institute.

The Law Applicable to International Mediation Contracts

Patricia Orejudo Prieto de los Mozos
University of Oviedo

Abstract. Mediation entails the provision of the services of a professional, the mediator, who holds a legal relationship with the disputants: the mediation contract. Where there are transnational elements in the mediation process, the contract is of an international character. In such a situation, the laws of the diverse states involved could claim to be applicable to the same contract. The determination of the (only) law applicable is of upmost interest in spite of the high degree of standardization of the obligations of both parties in the mediation contract. First, the law establishes the limits of the freedom of the contracting parties for such a *lex contractus*. And second, there are important matters that the parties do not usually tackle within the wording of mediation contracts and that model rules and standards do not either regulate. The present paper aims at illustrating the functioning of the present and the future instruments of private international law that solve the conflict-of-laws issue: Rome Convention and Rome I Regulation.

Keywords: International mediation, Contracts, Conflicts-of-laws, Rome Convention, Rome I Regulation.

1. Introduction: main features of international mediation contracts

Mediation is, by definition, a structured process whereby two or more parties to a dispute attempt by themselves, on a voluntary basis, to reach an agreement on the settlement of their dispute with the assistance of the mediator, who is the third person asked to conduct the mediation in an effective, impartial and competent way.[1] Thus, the mediator simply helps the disputants to solve the conflict by agreement without adjudication. But this task is far from being a simple one. On the contrary, for a mediation process to get to a good end, it is compulsory that the *facilitator* is acquainted with certain procedures, techniques and skills that he/she has to use (Fiadjoe, 2004: 58). In short: mediators need to be professionals.

---

[1] See these definitions (of "mediation" and "mediator") in Article 3 of Directive 2008/52/EC of the European Parliament and of the Council of 21 May 2008 on certain aspects of mediation in civil and commercial matters, *Official Journal of the European Union* (*OJEU*) L 136, 24/05/2008.

Mediation is therefore also a job: mediators do provide services on a commercial basis. As a result, there is a legal relationship between the mediator and the disputant parties. Both oblige themselves to the performance of certain acts: in order to give and receive the services of mediation, the disputants and the mediator conclude a contract.[2]

1.1. MEDIATION CONTRACTS

A mediation contract is, first of all, a *contract for the provision of services*. The mediator's performance is the one which characterizes the contract,[3] and it is a services' provision. As pointed out before, the mediator undertakes to use her/his best efforts to channel the communication between the disputants, so that they may conclude with their own arrangement on the conflict. On their part, the disputants are obliged to pay for the services rendered, even if the fees may be assumed by third parties, namely the State[4] or charities[5], notwithstanding the fact that mediation expenses may also be considered a part of legal aid.[6] The mediation contract is, as a result, an *onerous contract* and it has a *synallagmatic character*.

In addition, it is important to draw attention to the fact that this contract *has always a plurality of parties*, at least in one of the contractual positions,

---

[2] The mediation contract is usually known as mediation agreement; but I will use the term "contract" to differentiate if from the agreement that the disputants may reach at the end of the mediation process.

[3] The determination of the performance which is characteristic from the contract could be fundamental for the determination of the law applicable to the mediation contract in absence of choice. Such performance is said to be the performance that reveals the legal and economic function of the contract, i.e., the one that "gives a name" to the contract -habitually the non-pecuniary one, as the payment of a prize is common to the majority of the contracts (Carrillo, 1994: 121-129; Virgós, 1996: 5291-5297). If Rome I Regulation applies (see *infra*, note 17), it will not be necessary to resort to this notion for this particular contract.

[4] Although mediation services are normally provided free, the number of private mediators is increasing in most countries. See Walker, 2000: 30-31.

[5] For instance, mediation in cases of international parental child abduction was offered under the frame of the reunite Mediation Pilot Scheme. In this situation, mediation is supported by the Nuffield Foundation. See reunite, 2006: 10.

[6] Indeed, Council Directive 2002/8/CE of 27 January 2003 to improve access to justice in cross-border disputes by establishing minimum common rules relating to legal aid for such disputes, *Official Journal of the European Communities* (*OJEC*) L 26, 31/1/2003 establishes that "legal aid is to be granted on the same terms both for conventional legal proceedings and for out-of-court procedures such as mediation, where recourse to them is required by the law, or ordered by the court" (for further information see Cuartero, 2007: 51-52).

i.e., the disputants' position. In fact, it is likely that both parties are composed by two or more persons, and it is also possible that the process is conducted by a body of mediators (see *infra*).

Finally, it is also worthy to reveal that the existence of legal regulations specially enacted for this contract varies to a great extent. It is *nominated and regulated in some legal systems,*[7] *whilst it lacks any specific rules –it is innominated– in others.* But, whatever may be the case, the main sources for the determination of the most fundamental parties' obligations, and of the mediator's duties in particular, are to be found both in the standards of conduct to which these professionals are often voluntarily bound, and in the deontological rules of a compulsory nature given by the institutions or associations to which mediators belong. Just to mention a couple of examples of the voluntary rules, there is a "European Code of Conduct for Mediators"[8] to which the European Union has given express support,[9] and a set of "Model Standards of Conduct for Mediators", adopted in 2005 under the auspice of the American Arbitration Association.[10] As far as the obligatory norms concern, the illustrations can be found both in the International Chamber of Commerce (ICC) ADR Rules of 2001[11] and in the set of rules elaborated by the *Nederlands Mediation Instituut.*[12] Other associations such as GEMME (European Group of Judges for Mediation), remit in their model contracts[13] to the above mentioned rules. The widespread employment of auto-regulatory standards and rules, together with the extensive use of model contracts or model agreements,[14] contribute to a *vast standardization of the basic regulation of mediation contracts.* The obligations that are most intrinsically related to the mediation process

---

[7] For instance, the Act of the Balearic Islands No. 16/2006, of 22 November 2006, of Family Mediation (*Ley 18/2006, de 22 de noviembre de Mediación Familiar*), BOE 303, 20.12.2006 contains a whole title completely devoted to the regulation of the mediation contract (See Title I: articles 3 to 24). For further information concerning this regulation, see De La Torre, 2007.

[8] See http://ec.europa.eu/civiljustice/adr/adr_ec_code_conduct_en.pdf (accessed 5 June 2009).

[9] Paragraph 17 of the Preamble of the Mediation Directive asserts that "Mediators should be made aware of the existence of the European Code of Conduct for Mediators which should also be made available to the general public on the Internet". The Code is available on the web site of the European Union (see previous note).

[10] See http://www.abanet.org/dispute/documents/model_standards_conduct_april2007.pdf (accessed 5 June 2009).

[11] http://www.iccwbo.org/uploadedFiles/Court/Arbitration/other/adr_rules.pdf (accessed 5 July 2009).

[12] Netherlands Mediation Institute (NMI) Rules of 2008: http://www.nmi-mediation.nl (accessed 5 July 2009).

[13] In GEMME's "Mediation Agreement Draft", available at http://www.gemme.eu/en/article/mediation-agreement (accessed 5 July 2009).

[14] The NMI also has a Model Mediation Agreement, dated 2004, available in its web site: http://www.nmi-mediation.nl (accessed 5 July 2009).

are instituted in every set of rules with a high degree of similarity. Voluntariness, confidentiality, privacy and neutrality on the part of the mediator; right to any party's withdrawal from the process; obligation to pay the agreed mediation's fees on the part of the disputants, and so on, are some of the ever-present elements. For this reason, should the (state) law applicable to the contract have a specific regulation for mediation contracts, the duties it would establish will not essentially differ to those set up in the above mentioned sets of rules.

However, regardless of the high degree of standardization, the determination of the law applicable to the mediation contract in international situations is of utmost interest, for two main reasons. The first one is that *lex contractus* establishes the limits of the freedom of the contracting parties. The validity of all the terms of the contract would always be examined in the light of this law. The second reason is that there are important matters that the parties do not tackle habitually within the wording of mediation contracts and that model rules and standards do not either regulate. For instance, the type of obligation of the plural debtors (i.e. of the disputants in every mediation, and sometimes, of the mediators, where there are more than one). Let us imagine that the mediator, who has accomplished her/his part of the business, is not fully satisfied with the amount that the disputants have paid. The mediator needs to know whether she/he has to ask each party only for that debtor's part, or she/he may rather require it from any one of them until the full amount has been received. In short, the mediator would need to know whether the disputants' obligation is separate or solidary (*joint and several*) (respectively).[15] The answer is to be found in the law applicable to the contract.

1.2. INTERNATIONALITY OF MEDIATION CONTRACTS

The need to determine the law applicable to a contract appears where there is a choice to make between the laws of different countries or territories; i.e. where such a contract has an international character or where the contract is connected with more than one law of regional character.[16] In this paper, I will commit myself to the analysis of the international situations.[17] These situations are ruled, at the present time, by a conventional

---

[15] For a definition of these terms, see Article 10:101 of the Principles of European Contract Law (PECL).

[16] In Spain there is still no state law regulating mediation, but Andalucía, Asturias, Baleares, Canarias, Castilla-León, Castilla-La Mancha, Cataluña, Galicia, Madrid and Valencia, i.e., more than the half of the *Comunidades Autónomas*, have passed their own law.

[17] The solution for the conflict of laws issue of an interregional character could be different to the international one, as both RC and RRI (Article 19 RC and Article 22 RIR; see next note) establish the possibility of not to apply their own rules to the former.

instrument, the so-called "Rome Convention". Nevertheless, in the near future, the Rome Convention will be substituted by a European Community law instrument: Rome I Regulation.[18]

A mediation contract is to be considered international when it involves one or more elements alien to the internal social system of a given country. For example, one or all the parties to the contract are foreigners or national persons habitually resident abroad; the contract is signed abroad; or the obligations of the parties need to be performed in a foreign country.[19] In all these cases, mediation will have cross-border implications that pose particular problems.[20] However, what is important to consider here is that internationality cannot be "forced" by means of creating an inter-state conflict-of-laws issue through the introduction of a choice-of-law clause in the contract. In other words: parties in a mediation contract cannot choose a foreign law where all the elements relevant to the situation[21] at the time of the choice are connected with a country other than the country whose law has been chosen. Article 3.3 RIR states that, in that case, "the choice of the parties shall not prejudice the application of provisions of the law of that other country which cannot be derogated from by agreement".

In order to cope with the maximum range of situations concerning international mediation contracts, I will work, in the following epigraph, with three different study-cases of an international dimension. In all cases, the law applicable, as I explained before, would let the mediator know, among other aspects, whether she/he may require the totality from any of the disputants; or, on the contrary, whether she/he has to to require from each of the parties only that debtor's part (see *supra*).

---

[18] Convention on the law applicable to contractual obligations, opened for signature in Rome on 19 June 1980, *OJEC* L 226, 9/10/1980 (quoted as Rome Convention or RC); Regulation (EC) No. 593/2008 of the European Parliament and of the Council of 17 June 2008 on the law applicable to contractual obligations (Rome I), *OJEU* L177, 4/7/2008 (quoted as Rome I Regulation or RIR). Both instruments are of a universal scope: the law specified by any of them shall be applied whether or not it is the law of a contracting or a Member State (see Articles 2 RC and 2 RIR). RC is temporarily applicable where the contract has been concluded after date the RC came into effect, and RIR will replace the RC from the moment it will applicable, i.e. where the contract is concluded after 17 December 2009 (see Articles 24 and 28 RRI).

[19] See Giuliano & Lagarde, 1980.

[20] For an overview of the specific problems of family international mediation in Spanish private international law, see G. Palao Moreno, 2003.

[21] The reference is made to the "situation" and not to the "contract" itself. For an explanation of the reasons and consequences, see Forner, 2009: 61.

2. The law applicable to international mediation contracts

1.3. COMMERCIAL MEDIATION

The first of the situations announced involves two undertakings that decide to refer an international commercial dispute to mediation. Let us suppose that one of the undertakings is domiciled in the United Kingdom and the other one in Germany. As they look for an impartial, neutral and competent mediator, and they expect him/her to have a good knowledge of both English and German, they decide to turn to the *Nederlands Mediation Instituut* (NMI). [22]

Should the mediation contract lack a choice-of-law clause, the law applicable to the contract would be Dutch law. Indeed, Article 4.1 of RC establishes that the applicable law in the absence of choice is the "law of the country with which it (the contract) is most closely connected"; and Article 4.2 RC adds that "(...) it shall be presumed that the contract is most closely connected with the country where the party who is to effect the performance which is characteristic of the contract has, at the time of conclusion of the contract, his habitual residence, or, in the case of a body corporate or unincorporate, its central administration (...)". Subsequently, as the performance which is characteristic of the contract is the provision of the mediation's services (see *supra*), the applicable law is the law of the central administration of the NMI. In this case such law would coincide with the law applicable under RIR, even if its Article 4.1 has introduced a great novelty, by setting up a rigid conflict-of-laws rule. [23] According to this rule "a contract for the provision of services shall be governed by the law of the country where the service provider has his habitual residence". [24] Therefore, the law of The Netherlands would also apply, and, in consequence, the mediator would have to recover from each of the disputants the part of the debt corresponding to that party: the British undertaking and the German undertaking are separate debtors according to the general presumption established by Dutch law. [25]

In this "easy case" it is still worthy to pay attention to three particulars. The first one concerns the utilization of the "exception clause", which

---

[22] A basic assumption in international mediation is that parties will choose, when possible, a mediator from a third country; and, to this extent, the knowledge of the languages of the parties would be decisive for the election: Jagtenberg, 2001: 91-92.

[23] Garcimartín, 2008: 9-10; Bonomi, 2008: 173-176; Ubertazzi, 2008: 67-78. Forner, 2009: 77, refers to an "attenuated rigidity" (*rigidez amortiguada*), due to the possibility of employing the "exception clause" set by Article 4.3 RIR.

[24] RIR has introduced another relevant change: the determination of the habitual residence of legal persons for the purposes of the Regulation is regulated in Article 19. See Font, 2009.

[25] See Article 6.1 of Book VI of the Civil Code of the Netherlands. The presumption would fall if the parties agree on the contrary, i.e., on the introduction of a solidarity clause in the

would allow applying another law, where it is clear from all the circumstances of the case that the contract is manifestly more closely connected with another country, under any of the applicable instruments (see Articles 4.5 RC and 4.3 RIR). In the given case, such use is little plausible, for nothing in the circumstances described leads us to conclude that other law different to Dutch law is more closely connected with the mediation contract.

A second point is that the "model agreement" (model contract) currently used by the NMI[26] does hold a choice-of-law clause (Article 11), according to which "This agreement shall be exclusively governed by Dutch law". Thus, in a real case that the one proposed, the law applicable would definitely be Dutch law, not only because there is no possible use of the "exception clause" against the will of the parties, but also because an express choice of law by the parties would be valid under Articles 3 RC and 3 RIR, and is not limited here. Where disputants are legal or natural persons performing tasks in the exercise of their respective trade or profession, mediation contracts cannot be considered consumer contracts (it happens otherwise in next study-case, *infra*). Therefore, the only possible limit to the will of the parties would apply if Rome I Regulation applies, the law chosen is the law of a third country, there are Community law rules that cannot be derogated from by agreement and all the relevant elements to the situation at the time of the choice are located in one or more Member States.[27]

The last issue concerns the possibility of incorporating by reference a non-State body of law. Such possibility is expressly mentioned in Rome I Regulation (Recital 13) in order to make it clear that this instrument, following Rome Convention and contrary to the Proposal for the Regulation[28], does not permit the election of such body as *lex contractus*.[29] The (allowed) incorporation of any of the currently existing "bodies" that have a specific regulation of plurality of parties, i.e., the European Code of Contracts, the Lando Principles and the Common Frame of Reference would have led to a substantive solution opposite to the solution given by Dutch law. The debt will not be considered separate, given that, according

---

contract.

[26] See supra, note 14.

[27] For Article 3.4 of RIR (RC lacks a rule like this one) establishes that such choice of a "law other than that of a Member State shall not prejudice the application of provisions of Community law, where appropriate as implemented in the Member State of the forum, which cannot be derogated from by agreement". In favour of this provision, see Bonomi, 2008: 171-173; more critic, Garcimartín, 2008: 8.

[28]See Proposal for a Regulation of the European Parliament and the Council on the Law Applicable to Contractual Obligations (Rome I), COM (2005) 650 final. Greeting the introduction of such possibility, see, among others, Lando and Nielsen, 2007: 30-34.

[29] For an explanation of the withdrawal of the novelty in the final wording of RRI, see Garcimartín, 2008: 6. See also Heiss, 2009: 9-12.

to any of the above mentioned instruments, plural debts are presumed to be *solidary*.[30]

1.4. FAMILY MEDIATION – "ORDINARY ISSUE"

In the second situation, a British national and a German national that live together in Germany decide to separate and go to family mediation in order to reach agreements concerning their children. The couple has the same reasons as the undertakings to turn to the NMI: they want someone *truly* neutral and they want the mediator to speak both languages fluently. But in this case the determination of the *lex contractus*, even if both CR and RRI would still be applicable,[31] is a little more difficult.

1.4.1. *Consumer contract*

To start with, the family mediation contract might be a consumer contract. Be it the case, the law applicable, in the absence of a choice, would be the law of the habitual residence of the consumers (Articles 5.1 RC and 6.1 RRI). German law would apply, given that the couple has its habitual residence in Germany. According to German law, the mediator would be able to recover the whole of the sum debited from any of the disputants, since the presumption set in that law favours solidarity in plural debts. [32]

For the contract to be considered a consumer contract, both under RC and RIR, it must have been concluded by a person for a purpose which can be regarded as being outside her/his trade or profession, the consumer,[33] with another person, the professional, acting in the exercise of her/his trade or profession. This is the case in the contract signed by the members of the family and the mediator of the NMI. But it would also be necessary, according to Rome Convention, (1) that the NMI addresses the family advertising or a specific invitation to the conclusion of the contract, which must take place in Germany;[34] and (2) that the services of mediation are not

---

[30] See Article 88.1 European Code of Contracts; Article 10:102 PECL; Article III.4:103(2) CFR.

[31] Articles 1.2 of both instruments exclude their application to "rights and duties arising out of a family relationship, parentage, marriage or affinity (…). As a result, neither of them regulates the law applicable to the agreements eventually reached by the disputants in a family mediation. For further information about the enforceability of such agreements in the EU, see Palao Moreno, 2005. But the nature of the dispute (commercial or familiar) does not condition the application of RC or RIR to the mediation contract itself, since it does not change its character of contract for the provision of services.

[32] See § 427 BGB.

[33] RRI demands that this person is a natural person (see Article 6.1 RIR); however, under RC it could be a legal person, given that it does not contract in the frame of the trade or profession (see Article 5.1 RC). See Ragno, 2009.

[34] The other possibilities given in Article 5.2 of RC are not very likely to happen in the case.

supplied exclusively in The Netherlands.[35] When Rome I Regulation applies, a higher number of contracts will fall under the protection of the rule on consumer contracts: however, it will also be necessary that at least a part of the services is provided in Germany,[36] the disputants would be considered "consumers" even if they do not conclude the contract in the country of their habitual residence.[37] In our case, should the couple have travelled to Rotterdam to conclude the contract in the premises of the *Instituut*, the consideration of the contract as a consumer's contract would not be altered. What Rome I Regulation demands is that the professional "pursues his commercial or professional activities in the country where the consumer has his habitual residence, or by any means directs such activities to that country or to several countries, including that country, and the contract falls within the scope of such activities" (See Article 6.1 RIR).[38]

If the mentioned requirements are met, the election of any law different from the law of the habitual residence of the consumer (German law, in this case) shall not have the result of depriving the consumer of the protection afforded by the mandatory rules of the law of her/his habitual residence. Thus, all the mandatory rules of German law that aim at the protection of consumers would be applied, notwithstanding the fact that the choice-of-law clause in the NMI "model agreement" sets forth the application of Dutch law.[39] Paradoxically, in this case, the disputants would be more protected if Dutch law was applicable, for solidarity (Dutch solution) entails a greater protection to the creditor (the mediator) against the debtors (each of the members of the couple),[40] but the regulation of plural debts cannot be consider mandatory, in my opinion, unless the rules expressly declare so.[41]

---

[35] Article 5.4 establishes that Article 5 "shall not apply to (...) b) a contract for the supply of services where the services are to be supplied to the consumer exclusively in a country other than that in which he has his habitual residence".

[36] Article 6.4 a) of RIR holds the same exception to the application of the Article itself than Article 5.4 of RC. For an explanation of the reasons, see Giuliano & Lagarde, 1980.

[37] It has been said that by abandoning this requirement, RIR closes a gap and avoids a hole in the consumer's legal armour: see Mankowski, 2008: 138-139.

[38] For further information, see among others Mankowski, 2008; Ragno, 2009.

[39] See *supra*.

[40] See Mignot, 2007.

[41] The provisions that regulate the type of a plural obligation that are applicable when an explicit mention lacks in the contract are to be considered mandatory rules for the protection of consumers when this end is explicitly declared in the law. For instance, Article 1122 of the Draft Proposal of Law for the Amendment of the Spanish Civil Code presented by the *Comisión General de Codificación* (see in the Special *Boletín de Información del Ministerio de Justicia* of January 2009) establishes that plural debtors are supposed to be solidary debtors, except if they became obliged by the means of a contract concluded with a professional and the former acted as consumers. This provision would be a *contracts-*mandatory rule, applicable where the consumer has his/her habitual residence in Spain, notwithstanding the choice of law made in the contract in favour of the law of another

1.4.2. *Non-consumer contract*

If any of the requirements for the contract to be considered a consumer contract under the relevant instrument (RC or RIR) are not met (*ad ex.*, the mediator has never travelled to Germany to conduct the mediation), it will be necessary to turn to the general rule. Therefore, in the absence of a choice by the parties of the applicable law[42], the law of The Netherlands will be the *lex contractus*, as it is the law of the country where the service provider has its habitual residence (Articles 4.1 and 4.2 RC and Article 4.1 b RIR).

1.5. FAMILY MEDIATION – "SPECIAL ISSUE": MEDIATION IN INTERNATIONAL PARENTAL CHILD ABDUCTION

The third case concerns the employment of mediation in a situation of international abduction.[43] Let us suppose that an international couple, resident in New York, decide to separate. Both agree that the mother, a German national, will be the primary carer of the children they have in common. When the fortnight that the mother and children have spent in Germany has gone by, the mother decides not to come back to NY. The father, who has not given his permission for them to stay, makes an application for the return of the children under the Hague Convention 1980.[44] If both the father and the mother agree, a special mediation program existing between Germany and the USA comes into action. The program consists of a specific co-mediation: one of the mediators is a woman and the other one a man; one of them has a psycho-social or educational background, and the other has a legal education; one of them is a German, and the other one is a US national, and, where possible, the German will be living in the USA and the North-American in Germany.[45] The most neutral space is therefore created: any special connection to just one of the countries involved is expressly avoided. As a result, the determination of the applicable law will be much more intricate.

---

country. See, in relation with Rome Convention, Wojeboda 2000: 200-201.

[42] Remember that Article 11 of the NIM model agreement does contain a choice-of-law provision in favour of Dutch law (cit. *supra*). This election of a given state law is not restricted for this contract in RC, and according to RIR it has a single limitation: the above mentioned limitation laid down in Article 3.4 (see *supra*, note 19).

[43] For further information concerning this subject, see, among others, Moneger, 2004; Ganancia, 2004; Vigers, 2006; Paul & Walker, 2008; Orejudo, 2009.

[44] Hague Convention of 25 October 1980 on the Civil Aspects of International Child Abduction: http://hcch.e-vision.nl/index_en.php?act=conventions.pdf&cid=24 (accessed 6 July 2009).

[45] At least, both may have a great knowledge of both parent's cultural background. See Paul & Walker, 2008 and Vigers, 2006.

1.5.1. *Consumer contract*

The first complicatedness relates to the determination of disputants' habitual residence, which –if the contract is a consumer contract—is the key to ascertain the *lex contractus* (see *supra*). Neither Rome Convention nor Rome I Regulation offer a definition for habitual residence of non-professionals[46], and the resort to the criteria used in other community instruments appears to be clearly inconvenient.[47] In this case, the main purpose of the application of Article 5 RC and Article 6 RIR is, undoubtedly, the protection of consumers –the applicable law would be the law of their habitual residence–, so it would be adequate to consider the *real* or *actual* habitual residence of each of the disputants at the time of the conclusion of the mediation contract. Therefore, even if the above-mentioned requirements for a contract to be a consumer contract are met in this situation, the consumers lack a single habitual residence.

A reasonable general solution to the problem where there is a plurality of parties on the consumers' side, and they reside habitually in different countries, would be allowing them to make a choice between the law of the countries where they have their habitual residences.[48] In this particular case, this possibility would only happen if the mediation is conducted in Germany and in NY simultaneously,[49] for the contract would only be a consumer contract if the mediation is not accomplished exclusively out of the country of the consumer's habitual residence [Articles 5.4.b) RC and 6.4 b) RIR]. Should the father travel to Germany to attend the mediation sessions,[50] the contract would only be considered a consumer contract if it

---

[46] See Article 19 RIR for legal persons and professional natural persons.

[47] The fundamental reason is that private international law instruments enacted by the EC institutions have different objectives and goals. For instance, according to Brussels II *bis* Regulation [Council Regulation (EC) No 2201/2003 concerning jurisdiction and the recognition and enforcement of judgments in matrimonial matters and in matters of parental responsibility, repealing Regulation (EC) No 1347/2000, *OJEC* L338, 23/12/2003] the family would still be US resident, for habitual residence not only expresses a geographical and material proximity, linked to the procedural aspects, but also aims at protecting minor children, through the requirement of an effective integration of them in the country of their habitual residence. The protection of minors is not a goal of the consumers' protection rules applicable (or not) in our study-case.

[48] This is the solution that F.J. Garcimartín proposed to the problem in the Meeting on "La ley aplicable a las obligaciones contractuales y extracontractuales: continuidad e innovación", that took place in Palma de Mallorca on 7 May 2009.

[49] NY law would be applicable (and the presumption will favour separateness of the obligations), even if it is the law of a non-Member State: RIR has not retained the wording of the Proposal, according to which the consumer had to be a resident of a Member State. See Quiñones, 2006; Añoveros, 2006; Ragno, 2009.

[50] This is frequent practice within the programs or schemes that have been settled to cope with international abduction situations: the left-behind parent travels to the country where the retention or the removal has taken place, where a block co-mediation (over a weekend or a 2-day period) is conducted. See reunite, 2006:11; Vigers, 2006:9-10.

is the German habitual residence of the mother that is (exclusively) taken into consideration. As has been said before, if the mediation contract is deemed to be a consumer contract, the contractually imperative rules of the law of the habitual residence of the consumer would be applicable even if another law has been chosen as *lex contractus*.

1.5.2. *Non-consumer contract*

If the contract cannot be regarded as a consumer contract (for instance, because habitual residence is declared to be in the US and mediation is exclusively conducted in Germany), another complicatedness arises where co-mediation is carried out by two or more mediators, if such mediators do not live in the same country. Remember that the general rule sets for that the law applicable is the law of the country where the provider of the services (i.e., the mediator) has his/her habitual residence [see Articles 4.1 and 4.2 RC and 4.1 b) RIR]. In such a case, it would be necessary to turn to the default rule, according to which the *lex contractus* is the law of the country with which the contract is most closely connected (Articles 4.5 RC and 4.4 RIR). The complexity here comes from the already revealed fact that a great effort has been made to keep mediation –and the contract– equidistant with regard to the countries with which the situation has relevant connections (the USA and Germany). The complication could lessen if the whole mediation is in fact carried out in a single state (for instance, Germany), but where a direct mediation is conducted using video or teleconferencing facilities or communication over Internet, or where an indirect mediation with both mediators and parents in their respective states takes place; it would be extremely difficult to decide which is the "most closely connected" law.[51] The advisability of a choice-of-law clause needs, for these situations, no further explanation.

Acknowledgements

This work is part of the research project SEJ2006-1394/JURI, "Integración europea y globalización: el principio de reconocimiento mutuo en su proyección a los documentos y a las resoluciones judiciales" ("European integration and globalisation: the principle of mutual recognition as it applies to judicial documents and decisions"), financed by the Spanish Ministry of Education and Science and the FEDER. Main researcher: Dr. Pilar Rodríguez Mateos. A slightly shorter version can be found in Casanovas, P.; Galera, N.; Poblet, M. (eds.), *Simposi sobre Tribunals i Mediació. Nous camins per a la Justícia*, Barcelona, 2009, pp. 37-46.

---

[51] Both possibilities, described by Vigers, 2006, pp. 14-15, are in fact used within the German/US mediation.

References

Añoveros Terradas, B. (2006) "Consumidor residente en la Unión europea vs. Consumidor residente en un Estado tercero: a propósito de la propuesta de reglamento Roma I", *Anuario Español de Derecho Internacional Privado*, vol. 6, pp. 379-401.

Bonomi, A. (2008) "The Rome I Regulation on the Law Applicable to Contractual Obligations. Some General Remarks", *Yearbook of Private International Law*, vol. 10, pp. 165-176.

Carrillo Pozo, L.F. (1994) *El contrato internacional: la prestación característica*, Publicaciones del Real Colegio de España, Bolonia.

Cuartero Rubio, M.V. (2007) *La justicia gratuita en los litigios transfronterizos (Estudio de la Directiva 2003/8/CE y de su transposición al Derecho español)*, Iustel, Madrid.

De La Torre Olid, F. (2007) "El contrato de mediación familiar. Aspectos relevantes desde su positivización por la Ley Balear 18/2006", *Diario La Ley* No. 6765, 27 July, pp. 1-21. Available at: www.laley.net (accessed 6 June 2010)

Fiadjoe, A. (2004) *Alternative Dispute Resolution: A Developing World Perspective*, Cavendish Publishing Ltd., London/Sydney/Portland.

Font i Mas, M. (2009) "La noción de la "residencia habitual" de las sociedades, asociaciones o personas jurídicas en el Roma I y la ausencia de coordinación con el Reglamento Bruselas I" in Bosch Capdevila, E.; Decanato del Colegio de Registradores de Cataluña (eds.) *Derecho contractual europeo*, Editorial Bosch, Barcelona, pp. 133-148.

Forner Delaygua, J. J. (2009) "La ley aplicable a los contratos internacionales" in Bosch Capdevila, E.; Decanato del Colegio de Registradores de Cataluña (eds.) *Derecho contractual europeo*, Editorial Bosch, Barcelona, pp. 51-84.

Ganancia, D. (2004) "La médiation familiale internationale: une solution d'avenir aux conflits familiaux transfrontaliers?" in Fulchiron, H. *Les enlèvements d'enfants à travers les frontiers*, Bruylant, Brussels, pp. 325-335.

Garcimartín Alférez, F. J. (2008) "El Reglamento «Roma I» sobre ley aplicable a las obligaciones contractuales: ¿Cuánto ha cambiado el Convenio de Roma de 1980?", *La Ley*, No. 6957, 30 May 2008, pp. 1-23. Available at: www.laley.net.

Giuliano, R.; Lagarde, P. (1980) "Report on the Convention on the law applicable to contractual obligations", *Official Journal of the European Communities*, C 282, 31/10/1980, pp. 1-50.

Heiss, H. (2009), "Party Autonomy" in Ferrary, F.; Leible, S. (eds.) *Rome I Regulation. The Law Applicable to Contractual Obligations in Europe*, Sellier, Munich, pp. 1-16.

Jagtenberg, R. W. (2001) "Cross-Border Mediation in Europe: Prospects and Pitfalls", *Creating an European Judicial Space. Prospects for Judicial Cooperation in Civil Matters in the European Union*, vol. 30, Academy of European Law Trier, Bundesanzeiger Verlages, Köln.

Lando, O.; Nielsen, P.A. (2007) "The Rome I Proposal", *Journal of Private International Law*, vol. 3, n. 1, pp. 29-51.

Mignot, M. (2007) *Contrats et obligations. Obligations conjointes et solidaires. Solidarité passive*, JurisClasseur Civil Code.

Mankowski, P. (2008) "Consumer contracts under Article 6 of the Rome I Regulation" in Cashin Ritaine, E.; Bonomi, A. (eds.) *Le nouveau règlement européen «Rome I» relatif à la loi applicable aux obligations contractuelle*, Publications de l'Institut Suisse de Droit Comparé, Schulthess, Genève/Zurich/Bâle, pp. 121-160.

Moneger, F. (2004) La médiation dans le cadre des enlèvements d'enfants in Fulchiron, H. *Les enlèvements d'enfants à travers les frontières*, Bruylant, Brussels, pp. 317-323.

Orejudo Prieto de los Mozos, P. (2009) *Mediación y sustracción internacional de menores* (in press).

Paul, C.C.; Walker, J. (2008) "Family mediation in International Child Custody Conflicts: the Role of the Consulting Attorneys", *American Journal of Family Law*, vol. 22, n. 1, pp. 42-45.

Palao Moreno, G. (2003) "La mediación familiar internacional", *Estudios sobre la Ley Valenciana de Mediación Familiar,* Editorial Práctica de Derecho, Valencia, pp. 61-88.

Palao Moreno, G. (2005) "La libre circulación de acuerdos de mediación familiar en Europa" in Cano Bazaga, E. (dir.) *La libre circulación de resoluciones judiciales en la Unión Europea,* Centro de Documentación Europea de la Universidad de Sevilla, Sevilla, pp. 231-241.

reunite International Child Abduction Center (2006) *Mediation in International Parental Child Abduction*, available at: http://www.reunite.org (accessed 7 June 2009).

Quiñones Escámez, A. (2006) "Ley aplicable a los contratos internacionales en la Propuesta de Reglamento «Roma I» de 15.12.2005", Indret, n. 3, available at: www.indret.com (accessed 8 June 2009).

Ragno, F. (2009) "The Law Applicable to Consumer Contracts under the Rome I Regulation" in Ferrary, F.; Leible, S. (eds.) *Rome I Regulation. The Law Applicable to Contractual Obligations in Europe*, Sellier, Munich, pp. 129-170.

Ubertazzi, B. (2008) *Il regolamento Roma I sulla legge applicabile alle obbligazioni contrattuali*, Giuffrè, Milan.

Vigers, S. (2006) *Note on the Development of mediation, conciliation and similar means to facilitate agreed solutions in transfrontier family disputes concerning children especially in the context of the Hague Convention of 1980*, http://hcch.net (accessed 6 June 2009).

Virgós Soriano, M. (1996) "La ley aplicable a los contratos internacionales: la regla de los vínculos más estrechos y la presunción basada en la prestación característica del contrato", *Estudios Jurídicos en Homenaje al Profesor Aurelio Menéndez, tomo IV (Derecho civil y Derecho público)*, Civitas, Madrid, pp. 5289-5309.

Walker, J. (2000) "Introduction to family mediation in Europe and its special characteristics and advantages. Report", *Family Mediation in Europe. Proceedings of the 4th European Conference on Family Law*, Council of Europe Publishing, Strasbourgh, pp. 21-38.

Wojeboda, M. (2000) "Mandatory Rues in Private International Law", *Journal of European and Comparative Law*, vol. 7, 2, Maastricht, pp. 183-213.

Consumer Complaints, Access to Justice and e-Confidence: From ADR to ODR

Immaculada Barral
Universitat de Barcelona

Abstract. The use of alternative dispute resolution (ADR) procedures to deal with consumer complaints enjoys a specific legal framework in the EU because of the particular features of such disputes: the imbalanced nature of the relationship between the consumer and business; the small financial amounts that they typically involve; and the increasing number of cross-border conflicts – especially those involving online transactions, which makes the use of ADR particularly helpful in facilitating consumer redress. Therefore, ADR is today considered fundamental for generating confidence in e-commerce and EU consumer policy has adopted ADR as its main instrument in safeguarding the "access to justice of consumers". In parallel to this, online dispute resolution (ODR) procedures in this area of consumer relations are constantly being explored in an effort to bolster e-confidence. ODR aims to achieve optimal results by providing modern communication technologies for resolving a dispute, with or without the intervention of a third party, and both within and outside the business organisation.

Keywords: ADR, ODR, Consumer complaints, Imbalance, Small claims, e-Commerce, Automated negotiation, e-Mediation, Impartiality, Negotiation/mediation systems.

1. Why a special legal framework for consumer ADR?

The regulation of alternative dispute resolution (ADR) mechanisms to deal with consumer complaints is an important effort to avoid lengthy and costly legal proceedings. Generally speaking, the EU has validated independent and third-party mediation services, providing them with a parallel authority to that of Directive 2008/52/EC which regulates mediation in civil and commercial matters. Spain anticipated these European instruments by adopting the Regulation 636/3 May 1993 that governs arbitration practices in consumer affairs and provides a system in two distinct stages - mediation and arbitration. An analysis of these two legal texts leads to a number of interesting issues that we discuss below.

1.1. A SPECIFIC LEGAL FRAMEWORK IN THE EU

Methods of ADR for consumer complaints are bound by a specific legal system which predates the general regulation of mediation within the EU in civil and commercial matters. However, the system is based on the same principles. Indeed, point 11 of the preamble of EU Directive 2008/52/EC specifically states that consumer complaints lie outside its scope of application, together with other types of negotiation and processes. Thus, it is clearly stated that the directive should not apply to "consumer complaint schemes", i.e. any conflict resolution mechanism involving or not mediation, for this specific area of application, that is, consumer complaints.

While consumer complaints are excluded in this directive, they are covered by their own general ADR system, as laid down in two sets of regulations at the Community level:

1. Commission Recommendation of 30 March 1998 on the principles applicable to the bodies responsible for out-of-court settlement of consumer disputes (Official Journal of the EU L 115, 17.4.1998, p31), which regulated ADRs involving the intervention of a third party who might propose or impose a solution. It did not include the procedures defined in Article 1 of the Recommendation, which simply seek to bring the parties concerned together so as to promote an amicable settlement of their dispute (being the essence of mediation).[1]

2. Commission Recommendation 2001/310/CE of 4 April on the principles for out-of-court bodies involved in the consensual resolution of consumer disputes, which applies to bodies responsible for all those procedures that, "no matter what they are called, attempt to resolve a dispute by bringing the parties together to convince them to find a solution by common consent" (article 1). In the case of Spain, these procedures are legally described as "mediation" services within the "consumer arbitration system" as established by Regulation 231/2008, and they are seen as constituting an initial stage in the overall procedure (articles 37 and 38), albeit that a certain degree of conceptual independence exists.

The exclusion of "consumer complaint schemes" from the EU Directive 2008/52/EC has at times meant that certain dispute resolution systems for consumer affairs have not been considered within the traditional mechanisms of ADR. While it might well be that the methods for mediating in the case of a family or community dispute with their added problems of interculturality will differ radically from those adopted to resolve a consumer complaint, the latter mechanisms are perfectly adaptable to the scheme that D 52/2008/EC outlines for general mediation

---

[1] Cf. point 1 of the preamble to the Recommendation.

services, in terms of the quality of mediation (art. 4), the principle of confidentiality (art. 7) and the need to ensure that the content of the mediation is subsequently enforced (art. 6). The question seems to be why in the field of consumer affairs, with priority even over matters of private law, the legislator has opted unreservedly for ADR. The answer would seem to be connected to better consumer access to justice.

1.2. THE "ACCESS TO JUSTICE OF CONSUMERS": THE REASON UNDERPINNING THE LEGAL FRAMEWORK FOR ADR IN CONSUMER DISPUTES

The specific legislative approach outlined above with respect to the ADRs for consumer complaints can be traced to steps initiated with the publication of the Green Paper on "consumer access to justice in the internal market" in 1993,[2] which sought to establish a legal framework in which mechanisms might be developed to safeguard the effectiveness of the legal framework providing consumer protection. The paper, which describes the situation as it was among the Member States, notes the proliferation of ADRs in these states for dealing with consumer disputes. This proliferation, under many different guises, responded to the need for swifter and cheaper procedures than those provided by the courts. But the approach adopted is a global one, since together with the conclusions that affect the development of ADRs and, in particular, consumer arbitration and mediation, proposals are made for the protection of collective interests, and the provision of legal aid. However, the value of this initial text lies in its attempts at highlighting the existence of ADRs in a number of countries, including Spain, based on the adoption of arbitration strategies.[3]

Thus, the development of ADRs for consumer complaints was linked to consumer access to justice and to the set of actions that aimed to strengthen possibilities of redress in cases of dispute. This led to the presentation of a communication by the Commission on 14 February 1996 entitled "Action plan on consumer access to justice and the settlement of consumer disputes in the internal market - COM(96) 13 Final, which represented a clear step in favour of the use of ADRs.[4] This communication affirmed that "consumer access to justice" was being achieved with a variety of

---

[2] Commission's Green Paper, 16 November 1993, on access of consumers to justice and the settlement of consumer disputes in the single market - COM(93) 576 Final, p. 76

[3] Point 5 in the conclusion has a direct bearing on ADRs: "Closer contacts between different consumer arbitration bodies with a view to exchanging experiences on this subject; in this context, we recommend exploring in greater detail the role of certain bodies (such as chambers of commerce and industry) in the creation of voluntary arbitration systems, either at sectoral or regional level (see chapters concerning the Out-of-Court procedures in Germany, Spain and Portugal). On consumer arbitration in Spain, see section 1.3.

instruments, but it concluded with some force that this access did not always mean access to the courts and that it was possible that this access might involve alternative extra-judicial procedures. Yet, this access was considered desirable and as such the development of ADRs was promoted to deal with consumer complaints,[5] which is made evident in the Communication by the Commission on 4 April 2001 on the widening of consumer access to alternative dispute resolution - COM(2001) 161 Final. This affirms that ADRs for resolving disputes have a key role to play in improving access to justice for individual consumers.[6]

Interestingly, Communication 161/2001 clearly promotes ADRs because of the nature of their proceedings as well as favours linking the development of these instruments to two key concepts promoting their expansion: the fostering of confidence and their link to new technologies. From this point on, the development of ADRs in the EU framework was to serve these two ideas. However, before analysing this in greater detail, it is necessary to look at how ADRs for consumer disputes are organised in Spain, that is, the organisation of the state's "consumer arbitration system".

1.3. SPAIN'S "CONSUMER ARBITRATION SYSTEM"

The arbitration of consumer affairs in Spain, as discussed in Communication 2001/161, predates the ADR measures introduced by the EU legislation. The General Act 22/19 July 1984 for the protection of consumers and users led to the creation of a dispute resolution system with the decision being "final and binding on both parties". As Maluquer de Motes points out,[7] this precept falls within art. 51 EC which calls for "effective procedures" for the protection of consumers that safeguard their health, safety and the defence of their rights. Finally, Regulation 636/1993 ratifies this matter by opting for a system of institutional arbitration in a

---

[4] Similarly, the Commission Recommendation of 30 March 1998 on the out-of-court settlement of consumer disputes - COM(1998) 198 Final sought to find a standard among the different types of ADR that the Member States had created over the years. It highlighted the difference between the Scandinavian preference for an ombudsman, typically of a private character and whose impartiality might be questioned, and Spain's consumer arbitration scheme with a third-party arbitrator. Finally, as we have seen in the section above, a system of regulation was chosen based on two distinct instruments of the third-party and the party-appointed arbitrator.

[5] For more on this concept of consumer complaints, see Busto Lago, J. M.; Álvarez Lata, N.; Peña López, F. *Reclamaciones de consumo*, Thomson-Aranzadi, Cizur Menor, 2008.

[6] Cf. Com 161/2001, p. 2 of the text: "Several Community instruments do provide consumers with a set of basic rights. However, if such rights are to have practical value, mechanisms must exist to ensure their effective exercise."

[7] Maluquer de Motes Bernet, C.J. "Comentario al art. 1" in Guilarte Gutiérrez, V. (dir.) *Comentarios prácticos a la Ley de arbitraje*, Valladolid, 224, p. 56.

process that combines consecutive phases of mediation and arbitration and which, therefore, brings together both own party and third-party appointed processes of arbitration.[8] This issue is even more evident in the most recent legislation in the field, Regulation 231/2008, which regulates the "consumer arbitration system", in which mediation is seen as the first phase in the process (arts. 37 and 38); but with sufficient conceptual independence, and capable of imposing an agreement between the two parties.

Thus, the ADRs for consumer affairs in Spain involve mediation and arbitration, as well as a series of other characteristics that give them a special profile. First, as we have already seen, it is a government organised system, which means it has been institutionalised. Second, it should be noted that consumer arbitration is unidirectional. Indeed, it only resolves a consumer dispute with a business and, moreover, only the consumer can initiate consumer arbitration proceedings (art. 33.1 and 34.1).

The options available to an individual interested in initiating an ADR for a consumer complaint are therefore clear. However, we have yet to examine the characteristics of consumer complaints that make them suitable for this type of process. Here we can identify two features: they are typically concerned with small claims and involve cross-border disputes. We examine these two features below.

2. Standard consumer complaints: small claims and cross-border disputes

The two sets of regulations describe a set of circumstances that call for a specific approach to the out-of-court resolution of consumer disputes. These circumstances relate to two separate areas.

One area concerns the main defining characteristic of consumer disputes, namely the so-called "condition" for dealing with consumer claims. The other area sits at an intersection and is concerned with the joint treatment that, at many levels within the EU, is given to consumer contracts and to what is known as e-procurement, above all via websites. Three additional elements characterise the ADR system for consumer complaints within these two areas taken as a whole.

First, there is its strong legal basis, and indeed claims of this type always fall under what we might call a relationship governed by consumer law. Consumer law presupposes a relationship – a contract or any other type of instrument accepted by law – between a business and a consumer. It

---

[8] On the fact and consequences of a consumer arbitration system organised by the state, see Maluquer de Motes, C. J. "El arbitraje de consumo como instrumento de calidad al servicio del consumidor y del empresario" in Florensa Tomás, C. E. *El arbitraje de consumo*, Tirant Monografías, Valencia, 2004.

is, as such, based on a very well-established legal concept, since only a person who acts outside the framework of his profession can be considered a consumer. This means that this branch of the law normally involves the application of its own framework of regulations. Furthermore, it is taken for granted in consumer relationships that there is a clear imbalance between the parties - the consumer, on the one hand, and the business, on the other. In such a context, it is clear that the business is in a position of pre-eminence since it is this party that usually dictates the terms of the contract in accordance with the general contracting conditions. In addition, the business seeks the maximum number of clients without necessarily taking their personal characteristics very much into account.

Second, an important practical point to bear in mind is the fact that most consumer disputes fall into the category of "small claims", i.e. the consumer's claim does not have a great economic value. Two consequences arise from this: on the one hand, if there is no swift, cheap mechanism of resolution, these claims are unlikely to reach the courts;[9] and, on the other hand, although the redress sought by each separate consumer may be of little value, there might be a very large sum involved if all the consumers are considered together. Take, for example – at the EU level – the SANCO (Directorate-General for Health and Consumers) study into commercial practices relating to the sale of flight tickets via the Internet, which led to the drawing up of a list of good and bad practices.[10] This sector is, therefore, one in which disputes will only be settled if this mechanism of resolution is chosen.

The third element is also of a practical nature, stemming as it does from the fact that the EU is especially concerned for cross-border consumer contracts, since this is a clear embodiment of the internal market that is the main objective of EU consumer legislation. For this reason, it quickly becomes apparent that "cross-border" by its very nature refers to an area created without frontiers, via the Internet for example, and therefore the primary concern is to provide the new practices of e-commerce with alternative methods for dealing with disputes. It is this shift in practices that is instigating the change from ADRs to ODRs.

Indeed this coming together of ADRs as a tool for protecting consumers and the possibility of using ODRs has been stressed in the Commission's Communication dealing with «widening consumer access to alternative dispute resolution mechanisms» (p. 3), and is seen as playing a pivotal role

---

[9] Point 2 of preamble to R 98: most consumer disputes, by their nature, are characterized by a disproportion between the economic value at stake and the cost of its judicial settlement; the difficulties that court procedures may involve may discourage consumers from exercising their rights in practice, especially in the case of cross-border conflicts.

[10] See the website of the Directorate-General for Health and Consumers: http://ec.europa.eu/consumers/enforcement/sweep/index_en.htm

in developing what is known as e-confidence. And this requires the development of new schemes underpinned by new technology as the system can only grow if consumers, in the broadest sense, have confidence in it.

3. Building e-confidence

For some time now, the EU has been especially interested in creating a climate of confidence in the web as far as consumers and small and medium-sized businesses are concerned, because the EU is aware that these are the pillars upon which the real development of e-commerce for the internal market must be built. At present this process is still in its early stages.[11] Confidence in online transactions is the key to achieve the complete immersion of the European consumers in the internal market. After the introduction of the euro, this could be the second major factor in creating a definitive EU single market, involving large enough turnover figures to justify the efforts made.

Confidence in the web is measured in terms of security: consumers will only be able to evaluate the advantages that e-commerce offers over traditional methods if they are familiar with the medium and understand how it works, and so it is of the utmost importance to provide the consumer with the necessary tools to avoid or resolve possible disputes that may arise from electronic transactions, especially if they are cross-border.[12] Therefore, tools need to be developed for the use of consumers in case they have to make a claim, since only fast, simple, inexpensive methods will persuade consumers to assume the risk of a business failing to carry out its promises or failing to fulfil them satisfactorily.[13]

For this reason, the legal procedures for ODRs are not the same as those for mediation in disputes in which the economic value may be unknown –

---

[11] Communication from the Commission to the European Parliament, the Council, the Economic and Social Committee and the Committee of the Regions on the strategy on consumer policy (2002-2006), on May 7, 2002 (LCEur 2002, 1282). pg. 12. The consumer confidence is a basic bet because it is considered an essential element of the development of electronic commerce and, by extension, the real single market.

[12] Point 1 of preamble to R 98: one of the interests of the DH Health and Consumers is "... to boost consumer confidence in the functioning of the internal market and consumers' scope for taking full advantage of the possibilities offered by the internal market, including the possibility for consumers to settle disputes in an efficient and appropriate manner through out-of-court or other comparable procedures".

[13] This question has been repeated in documents on e-commerce since the e-Europe 2002 action plan. The most recent is the Report on cross-border e-commerce in the EU, SEC(2009) 283 Final, March 2009, compiled by the Commission Working Group. This reports that 21% of individuals do not use the internet for shopping because they are worried about problems in the way complaints may be handled or failures on the part of the businesses.

family disputes, intercultural disputes – or those in which the essence of the process lies in the fact that the two parties to the dispute meet face to face. The true value of consumer ODRs lies in the system's efficiency.

4. ODRs: new categories

This search for efficiency, combined with the need to keep costs low, has meant the adaptation of traditional ADRs for online use and, in recent years, much experience has been acquired with these new schemes. Thus, the same technical procedures can be used to initiate successive ADRs while the use of automated mechanisms, which do not require any human intervention, is encouraged. However, only a flexible legal framework will be able to provide a global solution and apply the regulations to all types of conflict resolution that might arise, while overcoming the problems presented by the technical system itself.

In this sense, we can distinguish between three different levels of ODR:

1. The adaptation of traditional ADRs to the new environment: the most visible in this group are methods of e-arbitration. This is the most formal type of ADR, in which the parties submit to the decision of a third party – the arbitrator. The use of e-arbitration and, therefore, initiatives such as the E-Global ADR Tribunal and e-arbitration-t are also possible. Here, software developments promote the design of online arbitration procedures using techniques such as email and videoconferencing.

2. The versatility of new technology means that mediation and negotiation procedures can be offered together online. The emphasis here is on the technical means for developing dialogue between the parties rather than on the intervention of a third party. The first step is normally a negotiation process, but if no result is obtained the next step is to assign a mediator. This is how the ECODIR (Electronic Consumer Dispute Resolution) works. It also appears in automated business systems such as eBay - Paypal.

   In this environment, ODRs therefore tend to offer technological platforms for dialogue between the parties – with or without the intervention of a third party – as consecutive procedures. On a legal level, this framework calls for the consideration of three aspects:

   a) Those directly connected to the technological processes applied: security, traceability, data protection, etc.

   b) Those connected to the specific conflict resolution technique used, i.e. negotiation, mediation, ombudsman. The use of ODRs does not exclude the application of any given conflict resolution technique.

c) Those deriving from the fact that the online environment makes it easy for the various ADRs to converge in single technical mechanism, the forms of which need to be analysed so as to provide them with a suitable legal framework.

3. New ODRs: this is the proof of what new technology can actually do when applied to conflict management on the web. Here, technology is exploited to the full, right from the start, in order to design a process equivalent to a traditional ODR - in this instance a negotiation procedure. These processes, known as "automated negotiation systems", are conducted without any human intervention. This is the great innovation of ODRs. They are used primarily for monetary claims where the only matter in dispute is the amount of compensation to be paid to the consumer. This involves providing the necessary software to enable the parties to submit offers without them knowing the amounts being offered by the other party of the dispute. When the offers from both parties reach a certain percentage ratio, agreement is established automatically as the average of the two. As can be imagined, this system is extremely fast and inexpensive, although the absence of any human intervention might mean that some of the decisions reached are not optimal. This development is a prime example of the connection between new technology and online dispute resolution.

The Green Paper on alternative methods for dispute resolution under civil and commercial law excludes these automated negotiation systems. This is not because they are automated, but rather because they lack the final characteristic of those ODRs in which a third party participates either as facilitator (mediation process) or by imposing a solution (arbitration process): namely, impartiality. Likewise the 2001 Resolution does not apply to "...customer complaint mechanisms operated by a business and concluded directly with the consumer or to such mechanisms carrying out such services operated by or on behalf of a business" (Article 1.2).

However, these regulations do not take into full account the structure of many ODRs. In fact, it is often a third party who provides this instrument for the use of the parties in dispute, while their actions are limited to overseeing the negotiations.[14] Indeed, electronic complaints centres run by businesses are mechanisms designed to help the consumer to formulate a specific complaint and to request the relevant compensation. Therefore, the

---

[14] Green paper on alternative dispute resolution in civil and commercial law, COM(2002) 196 Final: footnote 1: excluded from the scope of the document are complaint handling systems made available to consumers by professionals. These procedures are not conducted by third parties, but by one of the parties to the dispute. And "automated negotiation systems", which do not involve any human intervention, which are offered by providers of IT services. These systems are not dispute resolution procedures conducted by third parties but technical instruments designed to facilitate direct negotiations between the parties to the dispute.

existence of an online law centre is implicit if these complaints are dealt with exclusively by electronic means. It is this concept that endows them with maximum potential when they are offered by the business itself to deal with e-commerce disputes involving small amounts of money. In fact, it is more a question of offering the consumer good after-sales service rather than providing them with a means of resolving disputes, because in general terms the body generating the transaction seeks to avoid overly complex mechanisms.

Automated negotiation systems run by businesses and online complaints centres both lack the impartiality that is typically assumed when third parties intervene in the dispute resolution process. However, when complaints are dealt with appropriately and they receive a satisfactory response, this can enhance e-confidence just as if mediation procedures were adopted. Herein lays the paradox. ODRs conform to the parameters of efficiency, speed and low cost, and schemes that combine these characteristics will survive and prosper. Therefore, a legal framework regulating them needs to be developed, especially if ODRs do not conform to the traditional categories of face-to-face ADRs.

5. "Electronic arbitration" in the system of consumer arbitration

Since 2008, Spain has opted to regulate a specific type of ODR: that is, consumer arbitration understood as a system that combines procedures of mediation and arbitration keeping the description provided above. In fact, the regulation of electronic consumer arbitration is presented in the Preamble to Regulation 231/2008 as its principal novelty.[15] This innovation represents the development of a system that combines the use of ICTs for consumer arbitration and mediation and the building of on-line platforms for ODR in such matters, whose main aim is to make the procedure swifter and to eliminate costs.[16]

The regulation lays down, in a number of precepts, the procedures for electronic consumer arbitration. Here, a clear distinction is drawn between electronic arbitration and "procedural steps taken on-line" as part of a conventional arbitration process (art. 3.3). Following this distinction, in both instances it deems applicable Act 11/22 June 2007 (insofar as this is not provided for in Regulation 231/2008), governing a citizen's electronic access to public services. This reference can be attributed to the fact that consumer arbitration is of an institutional nature which means that it is

---

[15] The importance of this approach had previously been identified in the *Libro Blanco sobre Mecanismos Extrajudiciales de Solución de Conflictos en España*, op. cit., p. 97.

[16] For further discussion, see Montesinos García, A. (2008) "*El arbitraje de consumo virtual*" in Cotino Hueso, L. (coord.) *Consumidores y usuarios ante las nuevas tecnologías*, Valencia, p. 264

subject to the authority of administrative law as regards the use of electronic media for giving legal notice and for other effects.

All in all, Regulation 231/2008 has a somewhat restrictive view of electronic arbitration since it only considers procedures that are conducted "wholly" by electronic media, although it then recognises that some steps might be completed face to face. Such an approach gives rise to problems of definition: how many face-to-face operations are necessary before the arbitration will no longer be considered electronic? Art. 45, in discussing the instruction and administration of evidence in an electronic arbitration, states that "In an electronic arbitration when the instruction and administration of evidence is agreed to be conducted face-to-face, the procedure shall be undertaken by videoconference or by any other technical means that allows identification and direct communication between parties". We can conclude from the forgoing that the use of videoconferencing constitutes a face-to-face procedural step, even though it is conducted by electronic means and, strictly speaking, it is not conducted face-to-face. As such article 45 provides a good example of what was discussed earlier: the use of videoconferencing represents an ICT application to mediation and arbitration procedures that achieves an equivalent effect to that of a face-to-face hearing based on techniques of distance communication that allow the emission of images.

However, what Regulation 231/2008 actually foresees as constituting electronic arbitration is a centralised computer application that the Ministry of Health and Consumer Affairs received the mandate to create (art. 51.2) as an equivalent system to that of conventional consumer arbitration only conducted by electronic means. In other words, it is a procedure, adapted to the provisions laid down in the Regulation, that is carried out virtually and in which the problems that have to be overcome involve determining which board of arbitration has jurisdiction (art. 52); how legal notices can be served (art. 54); where the arbitration should take place (art. 55) and how the electronic signature mechanism can be implemented so as to guarantee the identity of the parties and the integrity of the communication (art. 53).

Thus, the provisions in the Regulation move between the two categories described above, as many situations can be accommodated within these provisions, of which the following are just some examples:

– The simple use of ICTs – electronic media – in an arbitration process: such as videoconferencing in the tribunal or in the process prior to mediation.
– The electronic arbitration process conducted in an exclusively virtual format using a computer application that facilitates the agreement to go to arbitration (art. 24), the request for arbitration, communication between the parties and with the arbitrator, and the communication of the decision.

− A mixed procedure with a prior phase of electronic mediation, as in the option described above, followed by an arbitration procedure if an agreement was not reached.

In short, the commitment to ODRs for consumer complaints has a huge potential and this will undoubtedly be expanded in the near future.

6. Conclusions

1. Consumer complaints have three main features: the imbalanced nature of the relationship between the consumer and business; the small financial amounts that they typically involve; and the increasing number of cross-border conflicts. For these reasons, the use of ADR is particularly helpful in facilitating consumer redress. So, ADR is today considered fundamental for generating confidence in e-commerce and EU consumer policy has adopted ADR as its main instrument in safeguarding the "access to justice of consumers".

2. On the other hand, ADR provides a high efficiency that combined with the need to keep costs low has meant the adaptation of traditional ADRs for online use. In recent years, much experience has been acquired with these new schemes from the adaptation of traditional ADRs to the new environment, for instance, automated negotiation systems that do not require human intervention. A great variety of new formulas has spread.

3. The online environment makes it easy for the various ADRs to converge in single technical mechanisms whose forms need to be analysed so as to provide them with a suitable legal framework regarding its specificity.

4. Electronic arbitration has been developed in the Spanish consumer arbitration Act in 2008. It is a system that combines the use of ICTs for consumer arbitration and mediation and the building of on-line platforms for ODR in such matters. We can consider three different degrees:

   a) The simple use of ICTs − electronic media − in an arbitration process

   b) The electronic arbitration process conducted in an exclusively virtual format using a computer application that facilitates the agreement to go to arbitration: the request for arbitration, communication between the parties and with the arbitrator, and the communication of the decision

   c)   A mixed procedure with a prior phase of electronic mediation, as in the option described above, followed by an arbitration procedure if an agreement was reached.

References

Abellan Tolosa, L. (2006) "El nuevo proyecto de arbitraje virtual para consumidores de la Comunidad Valenciana", *Revista Aranzadi de Derecho y nuevas tecnologías*, p. 367 ss.

Barral Viñals, I. (2003) "La seguridad en Internet: la firma electrónica", *La regulación del comercio electrónico,* Madrid, p. 50.

Barral Viñals, I. (2007) "Del consumidor destinatari-final al consumidor- no expert en la contractació en massa", *Revista Catalana de Dret Privat*, n. 7.

Busto Lago, J. M.; Álvarez Lata, N.; Peña López, F. (2008) *Reclamaciones de consumo*, Thomson-Aranzadi, Cizur Menor.

Encuesta del Eurobarómetro, *Informe de octubre de 2004, El acceso de los ciudadanos de la Unión europea a la justicia*, English version available at: http://ec.europa.eu/consumers/redress/reports_studies/eurobarometer_11-04_en.pdf (accessed 29 September 2009)

Gamero Casado, E.; Valero Torrijos, J. (coords.), *La Ley de la Administración Electrónica. Comentario sistemático a la Ley 11/2007, de 22 de junio, de Acceso Electrónico de los ciudadanos a los Servicios Públicos*, Thomson-Aranzadi, Cizur Menor, 2008.

Gil Nievas, R. (2008) "La Directiva 2008/52/CE del Parlamento Europeo y del Consejo, de 21 de mayo de 2008 (LCEur 2008, 803) sobre ciertos aspectos de la mediación en asuntos civiles y mercantiles", *Actualidad Jurídica Aranzadi* num. 768/2008.

Libro Blanco sobre Mecanismos Extrajudiciales de Solución de Conflictos en España, (2002), Ministerio de Ciencia y Tecnología; i+confianza.

López Sánchez, J. (2003) "Comercio electrónico y acceso de los consumidores a la Justicia", *Actualidad Jurídica Aranzadi* n. 571.

Maluquer de Motes Bernet, C. J. (2004) "Comentario al art. 1" in Guilarte Gutiérrez, V. (dir.) C*omentarios prácticos a la Ley de arbitraje,* Valladolid.

Maluquer de Motes, C. J. (2004) "El arbitraje de consumo como instrumento de calidad al servicio del consumidor y del empresario" in Forensa, C. (ed.) *El arbitraje de consumo*, Valencia.

Maluquer de Motes, C. J. (2003) "La solución extrajudicial de conflictos: Códigos de conducta y arbitraje electrónico" in Barral Viñals, I. (coord.) *La regulación del comercio electrónico*, Dykinson, Madrid, p. 113 ss.

Martín Galicia, F. (2005) "La regulación voluntaria y la defensa del consumidor", *Estudios sobre consumo*, n. 72, January.

Montesinos Garcia, A. (2008) "El arbitraje de consumo virtual" in Cotino Hueso, L. (coord.) *Consumidores y usuarios ante las nuevas tecnologías*, Valencia, p. 264.

Quintana Carlo, J.; Bonet Navarro, A. (1997) *El sistema arbitral de consumo*, Aranzadi, Pamplona.

Victim-Offender Mediation Services in Bilbao and Barakaldo. Experiences within Restorative Justice

Ramón Alzate Sáez de Heredia, Carlos Romera Antón
GEUZ University Centre for Conflict Transformation

Abstract. This paper aims at describing the activities and objectives of the two Victim-Offender Mediation Services (VOMS) currently operating in the province of Bizkaia, at the Bilbao and Barakaldo Law Courts. It also aims at providing information and a series of reflections regarding the work carried out by these services.

Keywords: Victim- offender mediation, Reparation, Restorative justice.

1. Description of activities and objectives

The Victim-Offender Mediation Services (VOMSs) are unities staffed by a multidisciplinary team, made up by lawyers, psychologists and social workers. Obviously, in addition to their formal academic background, all the staff is specialised in conflict resolution techniques and mediation.

The VOMSs depend upon the Basque Regional Government's Department of Justice and Public Administration, and are a part of the Cooperation with Justice Services, alongside the Victim Aid Service (VAS), Arrested Persons' Service (APS) and Reintegration Service (RS).

The Bilbao and Barakaldo VOMSs are currently managed by the *"GEUZ University Centre for Conflict Transformation"*. In addition to these two services, the Basque Autonomous Region also has another two Victim-Offender Mediation Services, one in the Vitoria-Gasteiz Law Courts, managed by *"IRSE – the Basque Institute for Social Reintegration"* and another one in the Donostia-San Sebastián Law Courts, managed by *"ANAME - the Navarra Association for Conflict Mediation and Pacification"*.

The decision to refer a case to mediation is always made by the judicial authorities, and the parties involved participate on a strictly voluntary basis, and are free to abandon the process at any point. In that case, their procedural rights will not be affected in any way.

Although the final decision regarding whether or not to refer a case to mediation is made by the judge, the counsel for the defence, the counsel for the private prosecution or even private individuals themselves may request to the judicial authorities referral to mediation.

As regards the objectives of the VOMSs, the main aim is to provide a mediation system in the different phases of criminal trials (pre-trial hearing, prosecution and execution), whereby both the victim of the crime and the presumed perpetrator, voluntarily and as part of a confidential process, can participate actively in the resolution or transformation of the conflict which led to the accusation and in which both are involved. The process focuses on communication, constructive dialogue and reaching negotiated agreements which aim at finding the best possible way of satisfying the personal and social needs of both parties, with the help and assistance of the team of mediators.

In short, the aim is not simply to focus on the accused, but rather to provide both the accuser and the victim with a safe space where they can express their feelings and needs, and obtain real reparation for the damage suffered. In order to verify compliance with both objectives, an external assessment is carried out by an independent academic researcher who explores the degree to which all those involved feel satisfied with the process.

Alongside this principal objective, there are also a number of other specific aims, such as the development of a model which fosters the decision making process followed by the parties involved in relation to the act committed, helping those who have harmed others to assume responsibility for their actions and ensures a greater degree of understanding for all parties involved in the criminal action throughout the whole trial. The ultimate aim is to reduce, in the short term, the recidivism rate amongst defendants participating in the mediation process. Evidently, in order to verify this result, a medium-term recidivism study (three to five years) will need to be carried out.

Other specific objectives include the consolidation of an agreed-upon mediation method throughout the criminal justice system personnel, a speeding up of legal proceedings and a decrease in the Justice Administration's workload, which in turn would help to free up the currently overburdened criminal justice system.

Since the whole process is monitored by legal professionals and the final agreement between the parties requires legal sanction, the rights of all parties are guaranteed, as is the public interest inherent to *ius puniendi*. We believe that the mediation procedure could serve to speed up legal proceedings, obtaining within less than two months an extrajudicial resolution which may then be transferred to the criminal trial by acquiescence.

Finally, the service also aims at working in collaboration with other cooperation with justice services, as well as with other organisations and social services in Bilbao and Barakaldo. The goal is to help to disseminate and raise awareness among Basque society of the importance of mediation as an effective method for resolving conflicts in the criminal justice field, through dialogue and agreement, and as a means of helping to create a social culture of peace based on integration and tolerance. In this sense, the VOMSs carry out a number of different dissemination and awareness-raising activities.

2. The mediation process: referral criteria, some results obtained and the mediation phases

The absence of specific legal regulation for the victim-offender mediation procedure (neither the Criminal Code nor the Code of Criminal Procedure mention the mediation, unlike Act 5/2000 on the Criminal Responsibility of Minors) has led to its joint, negotiated construction by diverse legal professionals working in the Basque Autonomous Region (BAR). Consequently, we believe that it is vital to ensure fluid communication between judges, public prosecutors, clerks, counsels and VOMS professionals so that reparatory victim-offender mediation proves successful as a process involving all affected parties.

Bearing this premise in mind, the goal would be not to establish a closed protocol for mediation, but rather to ensure a dynamic, open procedure which legal professionals are free to change and improve as and when they see it.

As regards to the process of referring a case to mediation, it is the law courts themselves which refer cases to VOMSs by resolution, in the form of a court order, ruling or measure of organization of procedure, specifying the referral to victim-offender mediation, setting the deadline for the end of the procedure (normally between one and two months) and, when necessary, establishing any other conditions to be fulfilled by this judicial command.

The referral of a case to the mediation process does not by itself imply the suspension or paralysis of the trial, since the agreed-upon preliminary inquiries still continue, along with any other necessary reports in order to clarify the facts, such as the obtaining of certain evidence of opinion or medical forensic reports.

With regard to the type of cases usually referred to the VOMSs by the judicial authorities, a series of different referral criteria have been established. On the one hand, the subjective condition of those who would be involved in the mediated resolution is considered, both as regards to their personal capacities and their current situation. For example, if one of the parties involved is suffering from a severe mental illness, this may severely limit the mediating process, both establishing and honouring agreements. Therefore, in addition to its legal-criminal nature, the subjective meaning of the act, or in other words, its personal component, is also a key factor in the decision to proceed (or not) with the mediation process.

It is also necessary to take certain objective conditions into consideration. For example, referral to mediation is recommended in blatant criminal actions or when there is clear evidence of criminality. In those cases in which total acquittal is seen as highly unlikely by the counsel for the defence, the idea of mediation is discarded since the participation of the accused requires a certain degree of acknowledgement of their actions, as this will in fact ensure reparation for the victim.

Mediation is recommended in cases in which the parties involved have a bitter, difficult relationship, with repeated or cross-accusations. In cases involving conflictive relations between neighbours, work colleagues or family members –in which a legal ruling is unlikely to resolve the underlying problem—, mediation is a real, effective alternative to help the parties to reach a solution.

Concerning the type of criminal cases that may be referred to mediation, given that mediation is an informal procedure located within a formal process, it is impossible to establish *a priori* and in abstract terms the types of criminal action for which mediation may be a viable option. In any case, the legal classification of the case in question as a criminal case should not be an absolutely determining factor, unless the existing legislation states otherwise or general interests are at stake. The seriousness of the crime committed as defined by the Criminal Code does not necessarily have to coincide with its subjectively perceived seriousness; neither should all serious crimes automatically be excluded, nor are all minor offences or misdemeanours suitable for mediation. Moreover, other people may also participate in the process as substitute or vicarious victims, in accordance with the individual characteristics of each case.

Bearing these premises in mind, mediation may be particularly useful in the event of crimes against property (robberies, thefts, damage, misappropriation, fraud), bodily harm, abuse, threats, slander and defamation, domestic violence or offenses against rights and family obligations.

Table I and II show the types of offenses which have been referred to the VOMSs during the first quarter of 2009.

Table I. Number of serious crimes in Barakaldo and Bilbao

Types of offence (serious crimes)	Barakaldo	Bilbao	Total	%
Bodily harm	13	17	30	39.47
Abuse	14	2	16	21.05
Damage	4	2	6	7.9
Misappropriation	2	3	5	6.57
Threats	4		4	5.26
Assault on a person in authority	1	2	3	3.95
Theft	1	1	2	2.63
Robbery and theft of a vehicle	1	1	2	2.63
Breaking and entering	1	1	2	2.63
Robbery with violence and intimidation	1		1	1.31
Slander		1	1	1.31
Failure to comply with a judicial order		1	1	1.31
Fraud	1		1	1.31
Defamation		1	1	1.31
Discovery and revelation of secrets		1	1	1.31
Total	43	33	76	100

Table II. Number of misdemeanours in Barakaldo and Bilbao

Types of offence (misdemeanours)	Barakaldo	Bilbao	Total	%
Failure to comply with family obligations	17	1	18	23.68
Injuries and physical violence	8	7	15	19.74
Threats	6	6	12	15.79
Slander	7	4	11	14.47
Damage	2	4	6	7.9
Physical violence	2	4	6	7.9
Coercion	1	2	3	3.95
Public disturbance	1	1	2	2.63
Degrading treatment	0	1	1	1.31
Disobedience	0	1	1	1.31
Defamation	0	1	1	1.31
Total	44	32	76	100

Table III. Total number of crimes and misdemeanours in Barakaldo and Bilbao

	Barakaldo	Bilbao	Total
Total crimes and misdemeanours	87	65	152

As indicated in Table I, crimes against people (bodily harm and abuse) are the ones most commonly referred to mediation by the different law courts. This trend reflects the belief which exists in the law courts that mediation is possible in cases involving personal harm and injury. Nevertheless, mediation has also been found to be effective in cases related to crimes against property or failure to comply with family obligations, as well as in other types of offences.

As regards the results of the mediation processes, the data obtained during the first quarter of 2009 indicate that in 80% of cases referred to mediation, the parties reached a satisfactory agreement. In other words, in cases in which the parties involved either met face to face or engaged in simultaneous or deferred indirect meetings, the process culminated with the signature of a reparation agreement.

Table IV. Results of the mediation processes

Result of the mediation	Barakaldo	Bilbao	Total	%
Ended in an agreement	29	21	50	81.97
Ended with no agreement being reached	5	6	11	18.03
Total	34	27	61	100

Table V also shows that the content of the agreements reached differs greatly, and does not just contemplate economic or property-based concerns; quite the opposite, in fact. Mediation processes show that on numerous occasions, the agreement reached by the parties has a much greater symbolic than pecuniary content.

Table V. Content of the agreements

Content of the Agreement	Barakaldo	Bilbao	Total	%
Renunciation of civil and criminal lawsuits	28	20	48	25.80
Commitment not to re-offend	25	15	40	21.50
Formal apology	21	18	39	20.97
Commitment to enter into dialogue	13	0	13	6.99
Mutual respect	4	8	12	6.45
Payment of compensation to the victim	4	6	10	5.38
Others (donation to charity, etc.)	2	6	8	4.30
Therapeutic treatment	5	2	7	3.76

Written thoughts on past actions	2	1	3	1.61
Community service	1	2	3	1.61
Withdrawal of the accusation	0	3	3	1.61
Total	105	81	186	100

The mediation processes can be divided into five different phases. There is an initial phase that we have termed the "Start of the process". During this phase, once the parties involved have expressed their willingness to engage in mediation, they are called to a meeting where they are told what the mediation process is about and the consequences it may have for them. At this time, the staff of the VOMS state their neutrality and impartiality very clearly, and explain the principles of voluntary participation and confidentiality upon which the process is based. If the parties wish to continue with the mediation procedure at this point, they are asked to sign an informed consent document.

The second phase is the "Welcome" phase. This phase consists of an individual interview with each party. The individuals are informed about the content and nature of the mediation process, as well as of its possible effects and influence on the legal proceedings. During these individual interviews, work is also carried out on the underlying conflicts, emotions, fears and attitudes, and the party's interest in, need for and capacity to complete the process is assessed. Having gathered this information, the mediation team decides whether or not to proceed with the meeting phase. This decision is based on an assessment of whether or not the mediation process may prove harmful to any of the parties, and whether or not the participants are truly committed to find a solution to the conflict.

The third phase is the "Meeting" phase. This phase is offered as a possibility only, since in situations of severe tension or when the victim has been deeply affected either psychologically or emotionally, the team may opt to arrange indirect meetings instead, enabling communication through its various members. The mediation team always channels any contact between the parties towards the goal of conciliation. The process may require one or several sessions, depending on the complexity of the case, the emotional situation of the parties and the number of victims.

The fourth phase is that of "Agreement", which is expressed in writing and incorporates a reparation plan. Before signing the agreements, the parties may request the advice of their legal counsel, so as to ensure that they are not signing any document which may involve the waiving or loss of any of their rights. The court will call the parties to ratify the agreement before the judge. The agreement may be awarded the status of "court settlement", with all the consequences thus established by the legal system. If the process finishes without an agreement being reached, the VOMS informs the law courts and the Public Prosecutor's Office. The confidentiality of the issues dealt with during the sessions is respected at all times.

The final phase is the "Monitoring" phase, which aims at assessing the degree to which the agreements signed are complied with. We believe this intervention phase to be especially important. The competent court may require the VOMS to present any follow-up reports it deems relevant in order to verify the compliance of the agreements signed by the parties.

3. Effects of mediation on the criminal trial

The principal legal effect of a mediation process carried out before the sentence for a criminal act is passed lies with the possibility of applying article 21.5 of the Penal Code.[1] It establishes reparation to the victim as an extenuating circumstance, to the extent (simple or highly qualified) that the judicial authority deems appropriate, bearing in mind the development of the whole process and other relevant circumstances.

Furthermore, forgiveness by the victim may also put an end to the criminal trial, since in Spanish criminal law, in the event of what are known as private offenses (slander, defamation, discovery and revelation of secrets, among others), if the victim grants his/her forgiveness, then the case can be closed.

Similarly, a mediation agreement may be reflected in the content of any plea bargain made. A plea bargain consists of the passing of a sentence agreed upon by the Public Prosecutor's Office, the counsel for the defence and the victim (if the victim is acting as a private prosecutor in the case), thus avoiding the need for a trial. The plea bargain is imposed either by the Magistrates' Court (with one third being taken off the sentence) or, when appropriate, by the Criminal Court. In addition to the sentence, the terms of the plea bargain may include the agreements reached by the parties in relation to civil liability (compensation, restitution or reparation of the damage caused) and, depending on the content of the agreement, the personal commitments made by the parties (promise not to bother or harass the victim, not to approach or communicate with them, promise to enter a treatment programme, etc.).

---

[1] Extenuating circumstances are: [...] 5ª. The guilty party having made reparation to the victim for the damage caused, or having mitigated its effects, at any moment during the procedure and prior to the oral trial.

For the defendant, it may result in the application of extenuating circumstances, with the consequent lowering of the sentence imposed, and in the case of a prison sentence, it may result in a suspended sentence (thus keeping the defendant out of prison) or even the substitution of a fine or community work.

In cases in which the victim refuses to participate in mediation or, having initiated the process voluntarily withdraws from it, the judicial authorities may take the attitude and willingness of the offender into account, along with any actions effectively carried out to make reparation for the damage (as expressed in the corresponding VOMS report) when passing sentence.

Finally, mediation carried out during the execution of the sentence may also be assessed, provided that the offender is not serving a prison sentence, and may result in an ordinary suspension of sentence or a suspension of sentence dependent on receiving treatment, as well as in a suspension during the processing of a pardon. Conciliation may also influence the decision to substitute a fine and/or community work for a prison sentence.[2] In some cases, effective reparation may be held to totally or partially satisfy the offender's civil liability, in accordance with that specified in criminal and penitentiary law in relation to serving prison sentences and prison benefits.

4. Conclusions

According to Gema Varona, the research coordinator who carried out the external assessment on the Barakaldo VOMS during the second half of 2007, the sustainability of the VOMSs depends on four factors: the legal framework, the continued and shared commitment of its creators and legal professionals (in the widest sense of the term); reasonable planning and financial support; and social support.

As regards the legal framework, it is important to have laws which provide legal cover for both the activities carried out and the mediation team themselves. These laws should be set in place as soon as possible. However, we also believe that they should allow for a certain degree of flexibility, especially with regard to not limiting mediation to misdemeanours or minor offenses. They should also contemplate the development of true restorative programmes, complete with their corresponding community components.

Nevertheless, according to Varona, we should not only consider the benefits of mediation for victims and offenders, but we should also take

---

[2] In accordance with article 88 of the Spanish Penal Code, which takes into account "... particularly the effort to make reparation for the damage caused".

into account the potential risks. In specific terms, special efforts should be made to avoid any violation of rights, both of defendants, accused, suspects, convicts and victims.

It is also important to continue working in close collaboration with both legal professionals and the social recourses available in the local environment. We should make a special effort to maintain close collaborative ties with the Basque Government Directorate for Criminal Law Enforcement, upon which the Services depend.

Another key point is the external assessments of the VOMSs carried out on a systematic, annual or biannual basis. Only in this way can we obtain sufficient data to implement improvements in the Services in both the short and long term. It would also be a good idea to carry out assessments aimed at verifying the real effects of mediation, using long term control groups.

Nonetheless, we believe that the assessment of the VOMSs should not only be carried out by external experts; we also need an ongoing self-assessment process involving all professionals working at the Services. This self-assessment may be further enriched through the exchange of information regarding experiences and best practices in victim-offender mediation both within and outside the Basque Country, with organisations responsible for running services of this kind.

Finally, and to cite Varona once again, we believe that the VOMSs should opt for a completely restorative theoretical framework. To this end, we need to think about how to gain community support and how to foster social cohesion in the administrative area, over and above any awareness-raising activities that may be carried out. This is one of the biggest challenges we will face in the coming years.

References

Aertsen, I.; Mackay, R.; Pelikan, C.; Willemsens, J.; Wright, M. (2004) *Rebuilding Community Connections—Mediation and Restorative Justice in Europe*, Council of Europe Publishing, Strasbourg.

Braithwaite, J. (1989) *Crime, Shame and Reintegration*, Cambridge University Press, New York.

Cario, R. (2005) *Justice restaurative: principes et promesses*, L'Harmattan, Paris.

Christie, N. (1977) *Conflicts as Property*, British Journal of Criminology, n. 17, pp. 1-19.

Fattah, E. (1999) *Mediation in penal matters*, report prepared for Correctional Services, Canada.

Gordillo Santana, L. F. (2007) *La Justicia Restaurativa y la mediación penal*, Iustel, Madrid.

Romera, C. (2009) *La mediación familiar, la mediación penal y el estatuto del mediador 2007-2008*, Centro de Estudios Jurídicos, Madrid.

Romera, C. (2008) "Conferencias comunitarias y justicia restaurativa" in Consejo del Poder Judicial (ed.) *La mediación civil y penal. Un año de experiencia,* Cuadernos de la Escuela Judicial del Consejo General del Poder Judicial 136/2007, Madrid.

Ríos, J. C.; Pascual, E.; Bibiano, A (2006) *Mediación penitenciaria. Reducir violencias en el sistema carcelario,* Colex, Madrid.

Varona, G. (2000) "Justicia criminal a través de procesos de mediación: una introducción" in *Las víctimas en el proceso penal,* Departamento de Justicia, Trabajo y Seguridad Social, Vitoria–Gasteiz.

Varona, G. (2008) *Evaluación externa de la actividad del Servicio de Mediación Penal de Barakaldo (julio-diciembre de 2007),* study available at: www.justizia.net and www.geuz.es (accessed 5 July 2010)

Wright, M. (1996) *Justice for Victims and Offenders: A Restorative Response to Crime,* Waterside Press, 2nd edition, Winchester.

Zehr, H. (1990) *Changing lenses. A new focus for crime and justice,* Herald Press, Scottdale, P.A.

Juvenile Penal Mediation: What Do the Parties Think?

Mª Mar Chumillas, Pepi Delgado, Mònica Díaz, Mª Pilar Fuertes, Cristina García, Rosa Mª Martínez, Anna Melero, Marian Menéndez, Lourdes Molina, Núria Mora, Rosa Mª Rué, Gemma Torra.
Servei de Mediació i Assessorament Tècnic, Generalitat de Catalunya

Abstract. The present study is an initiative of the Juvenile Penal Mediation Practices Community to evaluate victims' and offenders' degree of satisfaction in relation to the mediation program, in order to improve our intervention. For the analysis of the present study a quantitative methodology has been chosen: in particular, the completion of interviews via questionnaire in a sample of 114 minors and 95 victims, through the elaboration of a survey and a later statistical analysis with SPSS and SPAD. This study considers many dimensions and the obtained results are quite significant. Some of them are: the appraisal mediation is positive for both parties, but especially for the minor. Neither the minor nor the victim knew about the mediation program as an alternative method for conflict resolution. Other data talk about the influence of mediation on emotions manifested at the beginning and at the end of the process. Last but not least, the main motivations for the victim to participate in the program areto resolve their conflict, and also to try to avoid family suffering. The parties evaluate mediators and mediation positively. And mediation is a good alternative for resolving conflicts.

Keywords: Juvenile penal mediation, Victim, Minor, Degree of satisfaction, Emotion.

1. Introduction

The present study was initiated in the Practice Community of Juvenile Penal Mediation in the Catalan Department of Justice program Let's Share, through the Centre of Legal Studies and Specialized Training (CEJFE).

In the area of penal justice, we find that the parties in mediation are the victim and the offender, the conflict follows from the criminal act and the solutions refer to the consequences of this act. We describe penal mediation as a process in which victim and offender themselves, with the help of a neutral and impartial professional, look for solutions to their conflict. The process returns the parties the possibility to decide how they want to correct the situation and how they want the situation rectified.

The solution to the conflict has a double objective: the minor may mitigate and/or repair the damage caused to the victim; and the victim may be compensated and/or the wrong done may be corrected.

In the mediation process, when the mediator looks for an appropriate response to the offense, not only has he to consider the offenders but also the victims. With respect to the young offenders, he or she has to contribute to increase their personal and social competence, and to bolster their autonomy and personal responsibility. The aim is to stimulate a change of behaviour and facilitate the ways they face conflicts in a responsible way. The minors must be able to think about their own actions and the consequences of their acts and how to repair the damages caused to the victim. On the other hand, the victim's legitimate interest to be served and listened to must be recognized.

The goals of our practice in Mediation and Technical Advice Service (SMAT) are:
- To give justice to citizens.
- To restore and compensate the victims and the community.
- To allow voluntary and active participation of the minor and the victim in a process focused on conciliation, reparation and resolution of the conflict.
- To obtain judicial benefits that the law establishes for minors, reached through conciliation and reparation.
- To give the possibility to victims to talk about their situation, needs and anxieties in relation to the incident, to be listened to and to share while searching for suitable solutions.
- To contribute through the process of mediation, reparation and agreement to the victim's overcoming the negative consequences of the conflict.

In our intervention, we pay attention to offenders as well as victims. Because the victim in the penal system has many times been forgotten, mediation professionals are interested in how the victims view the program. It was considered that it was also important to include the offender in the study because mediation is the only viable option that offers the participation of both parties. We also pick up the characteristics of the reports, data about the process and tools used in the work.

This study allows us to contrast and confirm our intuitions, hypotheses, prejudices, doubts, beliefs and the myths that come out in our daily practice, as they relate to the three parties (offender, victim and mediator) in the mediation process.

We consider general goals to evaluate the degree of satisfaction of the victims and offenders in order to improve our intervention in mediation.

Our intention is to know the cognition and emotions of the persons who are attended directly by mediation. Consequently, inside this general goal, other more specific can be pointed out:

1. Knowing the sociodemographic and judicial characteristics of offenders and victims during mediation.
2. Specifying previous information they have about mediation and how they have obtained it.
3. Finding out which initial and final expectations victims and offenders have about mediation programs and the emotions or feelings that it generates in them.
4. Knowing the opinion of the people who have participated in the program.

2. Methodology

We have opted for a quantitative methodology to reach our objectives. In particular, the chosen method was interviews by questionnaire, through the elaboration of a closed survey. The telephone was used to administer it.

For the sample, all the mediation programs finished between January 1st and April 30th 2008 were selected. The main condition for inclusion was victim participation, both with encounter with the offender (direct mediation) or without encounter (indirect mediation). The non physical victims -like public or private entities, the Administration and the cases in which the victim is the community- and also the programs where victims and offenders have made reparation on their own initiative, have been excluded from the sample.

There were 324 minors who participated in mediation in the mentioned period. 114 of them were asked about the program. The total of victims was 317; 283 participated in mediation and 95 were asked about the program.

We have used three methodological stages to carry out the study: elaboration of the questionnaire, administration and completion of statistical analysis. The statistical analysis carried out can be described in three broad typologies. The first is the result of a frequential description of answers, especially used in the judicial sociodemographic and characteristic variables. The second is a series of statistical evidence for comparing groups (formed by variable criteria) depending on the answers given in other variables. In this case, we have used evidence of statistical inference with two variables, as they are the evidence of chi-square (relation categorical variables), the comparison of averages (evidence of T of Student-Fisher) and finally, the correlation between the variables that have been measured in the form of a scale of estimation or evaluation. The third typology is a multivaried analysis, that is, the variables are compared among themselves (in some cases, all the variables used in the study). To make this type of analysis we have used the statistical program SPAD.[1]

With reference to the questionnaire, eight dimensions are shown in the mediation process. These dimensions are:

1. Judicial data: information about characteristics of the criminal offense as well as the type of mediation program carried out.
2. Sociodemographic data on offender and victim: information about address, nationality, age and gender are reviewed.
3. Information or knowledge about mediation and evaluation of given information: this is to establish if there is previous information about the program and their opinion about explanations given by the mediator.
4. Reasons to participate in the program: it contains a series of variables in which some motivations to participate in the program are evaluated.
5. Emotions or feelings aroused during program participation: these are emotions and feelings related at the beginning and at the end of the process.
6. Image of the mediator: relation between the mediator and the parties involved.
7. Attribution of the criminal act: finding out the responsibility that offender or victim give the collectives implied.
8. Satisfaction and appraisals: this is about how the mediation process went, the agreements obtained and justice in general.

3. Results

From the mentioned dimensions, we have obtained the following results.

3.1. WITH REFERENCE TO THE CHARACTERISTICS THAT THE POLLED OFFENDERS HAVE IN COMMON

The majority of the polled offenders who have participated in mediation have the following characteristics: they are minors with only this arrest, they are accused of criminal acts against persons or property, and their acts are characterized as an offense; they live in urban areas and the offenses are usually committed in places where there is a higher concentration of population (ex. popular parties, discotheques, shopping centres...).

---

[1] Lebart, L.; Morinau, A. Fénelon, J.P. (1985) *Tratamiento estadístico de datos: métodos y programas*. Barcelona. Marcombo.
Bécue, M.B. y Valls, J.M. (2004) *Manual de introducción a los métodos factoriales y clasificación con Spad*. Service of Statistics U.A.B.
http://einstein.uab.es/_c_serv_estadistica/Manuals/manualSPAD.pdf
Sanchez Carrión, J.J. (editor) (1984) *Introducción a las técnicas de análisis multivariable aplicadas a las ciencias sociales*. Madrid. I Centro de investigaciones sociológicas.

Generally they are Spanish boys, even though girls also have a high participation in mediation processes.

3.2. WITH REFERENCE TO THE CHARACTERISTICS OF THE VICTIMS

The victims are generally adults, men (56) and women (39), they are between 20 and 45 years of age. They reside in urban zones and they are Spanish.

3.3. WITH REFERENCE TO THE CHARACTERISTICS OF THE ENCOUNTER

The parties that share a direct mediation (encounter) have a high degree of acquaintance and geographical proximity (family members, neighbours...) In general, one encounter takes place. The result can be conciliation and the injured party asks for compensation, the completion of restorative tasks or introspective writing.

3.4. WITH REFERENCE TO THE CHARACTERISTICS OF THE INFORMATION IN THE MEDIATION PROCESS

A low degree of previous knowledge about the mediation process is observed. Previous knowledge comes generally from penal field professionals (police, Public Prosecutor's Office, lawyers and technicians).

3.5. WITH REFERENCE TO THE CHARACTERISTICS OF THE MEDIATOR'S PERFORMANCE

Parties characterise the mediator as respectful, kind and also understanding and comforting. Information given about program is considered mainly useful and suitable.

There are other data that can be interpreted in this dimension: relapse is not related to information received initially; the type of offense does not determine participation in a mediation program. With regard to satisfaction, mediation is good for the parties and they would recommend it to their relatives.

3.6. WITH REFERENCE TO EMOTIONS OR FEELINGS

The feelings in this dimension are: worry, calmness, surprise, satisfaction, rage, fear and indifference. The polled participants were able to evaluate them on a 5-point scale: very little (1), little (2), medium (3), a lot (4) and quite a lot (5). From this moment we will relate positive (calmness, surprise and satisfaction) and negative (worry, rage, fear, indifference) feelings.

The young offenders demonstrated mainly negative feelings at the beginning of mediation, especially showing more worry than the victims. On the other hand, the victims, at the beginning, generally presented calmness. At the end of the process, both offenders and victims show an increase in positive feelings and a decrease in negative feelings. However, if we make a comparison at the end of the process between offenders' and victims' feelings, the minors present more worry and the victims more indifference.

If we observe the data obtained from gender, female offenders present more rage at the beginning than the males. In the case of the victims, the difference is significant with respect to calmness. At the beginning of mediation, males feel calmer than females. Females express more negative feelings like fear and worry. At the end of the process, males continue feeling calmer than females and females continue to be more worried than males.

If we analyze the data taking the age of the victim into account, the minor victims feel more indifference at the beginning and at the end of the process than adults.Concerning the differences observed in the cases with encounter, we observe that rage is more present than without any encounter. In the end, if an encounter has not been made, there is more surprise. When we consider the crime, there is more final satisfaction if the crime is a felony and more indifference when it is a misdemeanour.

In general, the offender as well as the victim would recommend mediation to relatives, especially the ones that have shown satisfaction at the end. Those who predominantly feel indifference at the end would recommend it less.

3.7. WITH REFERENCE TO THE ATTRIBUTION OF THE CRIMINAL ACT

The total population of study focuses on the assignment of responsibility, first of all to the minor, and later, to his or her friends. Victims consider other people also responsible, in this order: parents, the justice system, friends and school. If we take the age of the victims, we observe that adult victims especially assign responsibility for the offenses to parents and friends. Minor victims consider themselves to have a large degree of responsibility.Concerning the offender's gender, boys consider themselves more responsible than girls. Girls attribute responsibility to other groups.

3.8. WITH REFERENCE TO MOTIVATION AND SATISFACTION

The expectations and main motivations of offenders and victims to participate in mediation are the resolution of the conflict and the avoidance of family suffering. The females participate more to avoid family suffering than the males do. In our investigation, avoidance of family suffering was the only motivation that was not attained.

As to the crime, we observe that victim and offender recommend mediation more often and attain their expectations more often when the crime is characterized as a felony. Moreover, they recommend mediation more often when they have participated in an indirect way. The satisfaction with the agreements is related to the satisfaction with the process and with the recommendation of mediation to other relatives and acquaintances. Offenders and victims considered mediation more valid than a court proceeding. For offenders, mediation has allowed them to resolve the conflict and to understand the other party's circumstances. They also consider mediation more educational and useful. Offenders, in a higher degree than victims, would choose mediation again if they needed it, and they would recommend it more than victims.

4. General conclusions

From the statistical data, the characteristics of the offenders involved in a mediation process are:
- A lot or quite a lot participate in the program to avoid family suffering, and to avoid court proceedings.
- At the beginning of mediation, they feel a lot of worry and fear and little calmness.
- At the end, medium of worry, little fear and quite a lot of satisfaction.
- They find the mediator medium comforting, respectful, distant and understanding, but the explanations less impartial and more excessive than the victims.
- They are very satisfied with the agreements, the attitude of the other party and the process.
- The mediation has allowed them to understand the other party quite a lot and to resolve the problem.
- With a similar situation they would very often choose mediation. Their opinion is that the process of justice has been very educational.

The characteristics of the victims who participate in the process of mediation:

- Mediation has allowed them less to resolve a problem and to understand the situation of the other party than the offenders.
- They place the responsibility for crimes on parents, friends, school and the justice system more than victims.
- They would advise mediation to relatives and acquaintances to a high degree. They have achieved their expectations less than the offenders.
- The judicial intervention seemed less useful to them than to the offender and less effective in preventing new offenses.
- At the beginning of mediation they feel a bit or a lot of calmness and indifference and very little fear and worry.

We make some hypotheses to understand these results better. With reference to the information about the process, a high percentage of offenders and victims had not heard about mediation before. Those that had heard about it had been informed by professionals within the penal field. This makes us wonder whether mediation has enough support or dissemination.

When we consider the results about emotions manifested at the beginning and at the end, we can deduce that mediation has had influence on emotions. It has increased the calmness and the satisfaction and it has reduced fear, worry and rage.

We find that the offender's experience of the judicial process is different from the victim's. The consequences will be different for minors, and because of that, they feel more fear and worry than victims. And victims feel calmer and more indifferent. At the end of the process, the differences in the emotions of these two groups are not so marked. Even though all of them have reduced their worry and indifference, the offenders continue feeling more worried and victims more indifferent. We need to state that offenders are still waiting for legal resolution unlike the victims, who consider the process closed.

The attribution of responsibility focuses priority on the minor and on his or her friends. We must remember that during adolescence, friends influence behaviour in a great way. Victims consider the parents, friends and school more responsible than offenders do. If we differentiate among adult and minor victims, we find that the adult victims make the parents and the friends more responsible, and the minor victims make themselves and the police more responsible. Relating to this result, we consider whether there is a previous acquaintance between the victim and the offender when the victim is also a minor. Sometimes we find adolescent conflicts in which victims consider that they have some responsibility for the origin of the conflict. Another outstanding and relevant datum is that female victims make the parents, the justice system and the school more responsible than males. In this sense, we could evaluate the different attributions that the females and the males make in relation to responsibility.

Main motivations for participation in mediation are the resolution of the conflict and to avoid family suffering. The expectation of the avoidance of family suffering has not been accomplished in reality. So, we evaluate the need to work with the family suffering provoked by the facts and its consequences. In conclusion, both parties concluded that mediation is a better alternative than judicial proceedings.

Acknowledgements

We would like to thank Lidia Casadevall, Sheila Moreno and Mª Rosa Vinuesa for reviewing this article.

References

Amat, E.; Delgado, P. (2007) "Reflexions i alternatives sobre la restitució econòmica a les víctimes", presentation at *Gestió del Coneixement. Jornada de Mediadors de Justícia Juvenil*, Centre d'Estudis Jurídics i de Formació Especialitzada, 25 October.

Capdevila, M.; Ferrer, M.; Luque, E. (2005) *La reincidència en el delicte en la Justícia de menors*, working document, Generalitat de Catalunya, Departament de Justícia, Centre d'Estudis Jurídics i de Formació Especialitzada. Available at:
http://www20.gencat.cat/docs/Justicia/Documents/ARXIUS/doc_10245043_1.pdf (accessed 5July 2010)

Castilla del Pino, C. (2001) *Teoría de los sentimientos*, Tusquets editores. ISBN 9788483107980.

Cruz Márquez, B. (2005) "La mediación en la Ley Orgànica 5/2000, reguladora de la responsabilidad penal de los menores: conciliación y reparación del daño", *Revista Electrónica de Ciencia Penal y Criminología*, RECPC 07-14.

Dapena, J.; Martín, J. (2006) *Avaluació de l'aplicació de l'experiència pilot de la mediació i reparació en la jurisdicció penal ordinària,* working document, Generalitat de Catalunya, Departament de Justícia, Centre d'Estudis Jurídics i Formació Especialitzada. Available at:
http://idt.uab.es/llibreblanc/docs_publics/Avaluacio%20de%20l_aplicacio%20de%20l_experiencia%20pilot%20de%20mediacio%20i%20reparacio%20en%20la%20jurisdiccio%20penal%20ordinaria.pdf (accessed 5July 2010)

Díaz, M. et al. (2007) "Les víctimes en el procés de mediació. La reparació econòmica" presentation at *Gestió del Coneixement. Jornada de Mediadors de Justícia Juvenil*, Centre d'Estudis Jurídics i de Formació Especialitzada, 25 October.

Chumillas, Delgado, Díaz, Fuertes, García, Martínez, Melero, Menéndez, Molina, Mora, Rué, Torra

Funes i Artiaga, J. et al. (1994) "Mediació i Justícia Juvenil". Colecció Justícia i Societat, n. 12, Generalitat de Catalunya, Departament de Justícia, Centre d'Estudis Jurídics i Formació Especialitzada. ISBN:84-393-2960-1.

Generalitat de Catalunya (2008) *Informació estadística bàsica. Serveis penitenciaris, rehabilitació i justícia juvenil,* half-yearly publication, July, Departament de Justícia. Available at: http://www20.gencat.cat/docs/Justicia/Documents/ARXIUS/butlleti_serveis_pe nitenciaris_juliol2008.pdf (accessed 5 July 2010)

Larrauri, E. (2004) "Tendencias actuales de la Justicia Restauradora" in Pérez Álvarez, F. *Serta: In Memoriam Alexandri Baratta.* Ediciones Universidad de Salamanca, pp- 439-464.

Martín Rios, P. (2007) "La mediación víctima-menor ofensor en el proceso espanyol de menores", presentation at International Congress "Phenomena in Juvenile Deliquency: New Penal Forms", Seville, 6 – 7 November.

Parkinson, L. (2005) *Mediación familiar. Teoría y pràctica; principios y estrategias operativas*, Editorial Gedisa S.A., Barcelona. ISBN:84-97824-075-5

Romero, F.; Melero, A.; Cánovas, C.; Antolín, M. (2005) "La violència dels joves en la família: Una aproximació als menors denunciats pels seus pares", working document, Generalitat de Catalunya, Departament de Justícia, Centre d'Estudis Jurídics i de Formació Especialitzada. Available at: http://www20.gencat.cat/docs/Justicia/Documents/ARXIUS/doc_15303494_1.p df (accessed 5July 2010)

Rössner, D. et al. (1999) *La mediación penal*, Col·lecció Justícia i Societat n. 19, Generalitat de Catalunya, Departament de Justícia, Centre d'Estudis Jurídics i Formació. ISBN: 84-393-4766-9

Wright, M. (1995) "Alternatives to the criminal justice process" in *Iuris: Quaderns de Política Jurídica*, n. 4, Centre d'Estudis Jurídics i Formació Especialitzada, Generalitat de Catalunya, pp. 47 – 58. ISSN: 1134-8372.

The English Mediation System in Juvenile Criminal Cases

Juan Ramón Liébana Ortiz
Universidad de La Rioja

Abstract. This paper offers an overview of the English mediation system applied to juvenile criminal cases. England has a solid tradition of criminal juvenile mediation, especially if compared to the Spanish judicial system. In this perspective, the English system constitutes a most relevant referent to examine.

Keywords: ADR, Mediation, Young offenders, Victim's reparation, British criminal justice system.

1. Alternative Dispute Resolution in the United Kingdom

In the common law legal systems, the Alternative Dispute Resolution processes —ordinarily known as ADR, acronym used hereinafter — are recognised not only as a distinct system of dispute resolution, but also as a system that interacts interdependently with the legal system. Thus, we can bring up to Cappelleti (1993), who categorises ADR as a third wave in the worldwide access-to-justice movement. Consequently, ADR provides a different approach and a different sort of justice for solving disputes, what the author labels «co-existential justice».

The growing importance of the ADR processes is highlighted both by the legislation and the judiciary statements. As a matter of fact, the Rule 26.4 of the Civil Procedure Rules 1998 enables judges, at their own volition, or if requested by both parties, to stay cases they consider may be amenable to some other more satisfactory form of resolution, such as arbitration or mediation.

On other grounds, a clear message in favour of ADR in the UK is provided by Lord Chancellor Irvine of Lairg who, in his Inaugural Lecture to the Faculty of Mediation and ADR in 1999, pointed out: «ADR is, I believe, entirely consistent with the principle of the better delivery of justice (…) ADR has many supporters. But they too have a responsibility to proceed with care. ADR is not a panacea, nor is it cost-free. But I do believe that it can play a vital part in the opening of access to justice» (Irvine, 1999).

With these premises, the future of the English justice seems to be one of processes that widen the available solutions beyond those based on the traditional punitive way to reach the restorative justice.[1]

2. Mediation in Juvenile Criminal Cases in the United Kingdom

The flexible range of ADR methods is most clearly demonstrated precisely in the context of mediation in criminal cases, which is more and more considered as an effective way to increase access to, participation in and satisfaction with the way legal disputes are resolved.

In terms of legal practice, mediation is the fastest growing form of ADR in the world. The reasons behind its rapid expansion and growing acceptance lay precisely in the widespread belief that mediation offers quantitative and qualitative advantages: the saving of time and money involved in litigating disputes, the need to reduce court case loads,[2] the wish of the parties to have a greater control over the person who will decide their dispute or the higher confidentiality and privacy of the parties, among others studied by Gordillo Santana (2007). However, some authors such as Ashworth (2002), Braithwaite (1999) or Feld (1997) have stressed the need to make a greater emphasis upon procedural safeguards and substantive limits in the pursuit of the apparently beneficent goals of restorative justice.[3]

Precisely because of greater need of the children and young people's intimacy and image protection, mediation in criminal cases has become a dispute resolution method that has experienced a rapid growth worldwide since its origins. Mediation was born in the United States of America back in the 1970s as a reaction against the high cost and long delays of litigating business disputes.

Actually, the development of mediation in criminal cases in the UK began in the early 1980s with the implementation of a series of concrete

---

[1] As Slapper and Kelly (1999) have pointed out.

[2] Indeed, the need to lighten the burden of Courts' case load is common to all the western legal systems. In the Spanish case, there has been a recent attempt to achieve an effective lightening of the Courts' case load in the field of Civil and Commercial Law with the failed proceeding of a project of voluntary Jurisdiction Act, the main innovations of which — correct in my opinion— were to attribute competences to the court secretary and to create a new general proceeding in accordance with today's needs. For a more in depth study on this method of resolution of non-jurisdictional matters, see Liébana Ortiz, J.R. (2006).

[3] In addition, Feld (1997) suggests to formally recognise youthfulness as a mitigating factor in criminal sentencing since, in his opinion, young offenders differ from adults in their breadth of experience, temporal perspective, willingness to take risks, maturity of judgment, and susceptibility to peer influences. Recognising youthfulness as a mitigating factor in criminal sentencing, Feld (1997) seeks to develop a more consistent sentencing policy toward chronic younger offenders.

measures. This initial trend carried out its consolidation without the back of any legislative development, but was characterized by a huge consensus over the principles and objectives pursued. Until recently, there was no concrete regulation about mediation in criminal cases. In fact, it can be noticed that the establishment and defence of the mediation method have spread thanks to a relatively small number of individuals or social workers associations. This traditional legislative emptiness has allowed for mediation to develop in all the stages of the criminal system, both for adults and children and young people alike and for all types of offences.

As we said above, the legal emptiness existing in the English legal system in relation to mediation in criminal cases has changed for the youth justice system, affecting children and teenagers aged between 10 and 17.[4] Nowadays there are two Acts of Parliament that allow and promote mediation. They have changed the practice of criminal justice: on the one hand, these Acts of Parliament have introduced the victim's perspective in the youth justice system; on the other hand, they encourage young offenders to correct their antisocial and illegal behaviours through the reparation of their offences, as Schelkens (1998) has pointed out.

2.1. THE CRIME AND DISORDER ACT 1998

The Crime and Disorder Act 1998 (C&D Act 1998 hereinafter) has four aspects that must be pointed out. Firstly, it establishes that the principal aim of the youth justice system is to prevent offending by children and young persons [Section 37 (1)]. Every action within the youth justice system must tend to this goal. Second, the C&D Act 1998 introduces within the British justice system the Youth Justice Board for England and Wales, and an independent Board —nor a servant or agent of the Crown nor enjoying any status, immunity or privilege of the Crown— consisting of 10, 11 or 12 members appointed by the Secretary of State among persons who have extensive recent experience in the youth justice system. The Youth Justice Board for England and Wales is responsible for monitoring the operation of the youth justice system and the provision of youth justice services [Section 41 (5)]. Third, the local authorities have the legal duty to create Youth Offending Teams with the duties to evacuate the relevant reports to the competent Courts, to supervise the young persons sentenced to a probation order, a community service order or a combination order and to co-ordinate the provision of youth justice services for all those in the authority's area

---

[4] The English legal system establishes some special rules for people under 18 years old, at which you come of age in the UK. Thus, children under 10 years old are considered *doli incapax* and, hence, are exempt *iuris et de iure* of criminal liability in any event. When the children come to the age of 10 they are liable for the offences they may commit because they are entirely responsible of their acts and are liable before the juvenile Courts (argument *a contrario ex* section 34 Crime and Disorder Act 1998).

who need them. Every team must include at least a probation officer; a social worker of a local authority social services department; a police officer; a person nominated by a health authority, any part of whose area lies within the local authority's area and a person nominated by the chief education officer appointed by the local authority. Additionally, a Youth Offending Team may also include other persons if the local authority thinks it is appropriate after consulting the probation committee, the health authority and the Chief Officer of Police (Section 39). And finally, the C&D Act 1998 introduces a series of new orders and reprimands and reforms the existing ones.

Reparation has turned out to be the central topic of the new criminal legislation and, thus, the C&D Act 1998 introduces the reparation order (Sections 67 and 68). It allows the Court by or before which the young offender is convicted to require him to make the reparation specified in the order, either directly to the person identified by the Court as a victim of the offence (or another person otherwise affected by), or generally to the community at large. Before the Court makes this order, it must assess whether the reparation activity takes into account the wishes of both parties. The maximum length the Court may impose with the reparation order is 24 hours during 3 months. The reparation order seeks to confront young offenders with the crime they have committed and challenge them to carry out its reparation.

Nevertheless, it is not a mechanical process based on «an eye for an eye» basis but, on the contrary, the reparation order must reach two main goals: it must help the victims of the offence to agree over the suffered damages and whether they wish to receive any practical compensation for the inconvenient. It must help the young offender to understand the consequences of his actions, accept his responsibility and mend his ways. Thus, it can be said that the wish of the young offender in taking part in the mediation constitutes and act of reparation in itself and, hence, mediation should be voluntary for every party.

The C&D Act 1998 has also introduced the *Action plan order* (Sections 69 and 70) which applies where a child or young person is convicted of an offence other than one for which the sentence is fixed by law. With a maximum length of 3 months, it aims to comply with an action plan, that is to say, a series of restorative activities such as to summit to a curfew or going to school or a resocialization programme. Together with these two new truly restorative orders, the C&D Act 1998 also regulates another type of orders such as supervision orders, detention and training orders (Sections 71 and 79) of which there is no need to expand further.

In addition, the C&D Act 1998 sets up a reprimands and warnings system (Sections 65 and 66). Thus, young offenders may be warned if they have not previously been warned or, if so, the offence was committed more than two years after the date of the previous warning and the constable considers the offence not to be so serious as to require a charge to be brought. However, such a serious offence as to require a warning, or a second warning within two years after the date of the previous warning, will give grounds for the constable to require a reprimand. And any subsequent offence or misdemeanour will require a Court charge to be brought.

2.2. THE YOUTH JUSTICE & CRIMINAL EVIDENCE ACT 1999

This Act of Parliament introduces a compulsory proceeding, trough the referral order (Sections 1 to 5), seen by the British Government as the first restorative justice incursion within the juvenile Courts. This referral order applies to persons under the age of 18 who have pleaded guilty, who have never been convicted by or before a court in the United Kingdom of any offence other than the offence at stake and any associated offence, and the Court is not proposing to impose a custodial sentence on the offender, nor proposing to discharge him absolutely in respect of the offence at stake or any associated offence.

In appliance of this referral order, the Court shall decide what the appropriate extension of the offender binding to fulfil the sentences is, not exceeding 12 months in any event. Once the sentence binding period is decided, the young offender is required to attend meetings of the Youth Offender Panel (Sections 6 and 7) that will decide the material content of the sentence, being mediation one of the possible methods included in the sentence. The Panel will consist of the young offender, his or her parents or guardians, other relatives and/or supporters of the offender, the victim or victims and their supporters and three community members. The aim of this meeting is to facilitate a frank conversation over what happened, how the victims suffered the consequences and what is necessary to correct the situation and prevent future offences. Likewise, the Youth Offender Panel must seek to reach agreement of contract —whose legal regimen is regulated in Sections 8 to 12— with the offender on a programme of behaviour whose aim (or principal aim) is the prevention of re-offending by the offender. If the young offender has complied to date with the terms of the contract at full length, then the offence is immediately considered prescribed with the effect of discharging the referral order, and all his criminal record is suppressed. Thus, the young will not have the duty (and burden) to declare them in the future.

2.3. ORGANISATION OF MEDIATION

For these judicial measures to take place, it is necessary to constitute mediation services to implement them. Mediation UK is the foremost provider of mediation services nationwide between offenders and victims. It gathers and coordinates different regional mediation services, such as Mediation Wales or the Disability Conciliation Service. However, it is absolutely independent from the British Government and, therefore, it does not receive an assignment from the Government Budget. On the contrary, it receives funds from the public and private sector (organisations so disparate as the Big Lottery Fund, the CHK Charities, the Welsh Assembly Government or the Department of Constitutional Affairs). Mediation UK has developed a training system –which is nationally accredited by the British Government—to individuals and organisations wishing to practice as mediators. The accreditation process is based on passing of a series of tests during the different mediation training courses available.

The concrete organisation of the local and regional mediation services is very different. Next, we are going through some units and services in charge of young justice:

- Leeds Victim-Offender Unit. It gets its fund from the Parole Service and nowadays it is devoted to obtain remissions from any agency and whatever the criminal process stage, including the self-remissions of victim-offender. The mediation services are carried out by community members properly trained and quarterly paid. Likewise, there are three full-time members whose function is to coordinate the service.
- Northamptonshire Diversion Unit. It is made up by a staff set up of policemen, social workers, parole officials, social educators and nurses. In this unit they make both direct and indirect mediation plans and, in both methods, victims are contacted to evaluate how the offence has affected them and how it could be mended.
- Thames Valley Police Restorative Conferencing Units. Oddly enough, the Thames Valley Police Units provide the bigger number of criminal mediators of England. Each Police Unit of the Thames Valley has its own Restorative Justice Coordinator, a police official trained in mediation techniques who is responsible for the service.
- Crime Concern Mediation and Reparation Service. Located in Southampton, this service meets mediation needs, both directly and indirectly, through a series of meetings between the young offender and his or her victim in which the former apologizes orally and in written form to the latter. The service is made up by two full time workers. In addition, there is a bunch of qualified voluntary mediators who come into operation when the service is overflowed with work.
- Victim-Offender Mediation Service. This service covers three Northern Districts of London. Its sources of financing are diverse, and thereby it is an absolutely independent body from the London City Council or the District in which it operates. It is made up by a General Director and three area coordinators, corresponding to each of the three London

Districts. In addition, it has a bunch of community volunteers who help in mediation when it is necessary.

From what has been said so far, we can infer a disparate organisation of the English mediation system in juvenile criminal cases. However, we can extract some common points:

1.   Mediation services between young offenders and victims need to tend very good connections with the community organisations in order to obtain the economic and material help. The majority of these services have a local committee which supervises that all the process is carried out in accordance with the good practices code set up by the English Government. As well, almost all of them have a Victim Support Office since it is very important to ensure that the victim's perspective is taken into account throughout the process.

2.   All the mediation services attending juvenile criminal cases are for free, but they have diverse sources of financing. Those services depending on a public body enjoy a more or less stable financing, even though it is subject to reduction as a consequence of a policy change. Voluntary organisations have to invest a great amount of time to seek for financing among charities, local authorities' subsidies, agreements with different private institutions, etc.

3.   In the UK, and particularly in England, there are no independent private mediators. In such events in which there is no a competent mediation service, they will seek for the help from the closer mediation services.

2.4. THE MEDIATION PROCESS

Once identified the young offender, the victim and collected information over the case, a mediator gets in touch with the parties to explain them his reasons and the possibilities of mediation in order to find out if they are interested in the mediation method. The rules about whether the first to be contacted ought to be the young offender or the victim are not so clear. The argument in favour of contacting the victim in the first place is to show respect for his or her situation, while the argument against it is that there is a certain risk to victimise him or her. In any event, the significant point is that none of the parties develop high prospects. This contact and assessment period is the beginning of the indirect mediation process due to the fact that the commentaries and questions done in these initial sessions can be exchanged between both parties, always with prior permission. However, the meeting only will take place if mediators are convinced that none of the parties is exposed to a risk. Parties are entitled to come to the meeting accompanied if they wish so, but in that event companions must be previously interviewed by the mediators.

In England, there are three main direct mediation methods. The first of them is the standard mediation, followed by the majority of the mediation services. The meeting begins when the mediators welcome the parties and remember them the conduct rules they have agreed. Afterwards, parties are given a determined period of time for them to «tell their story» and then are entitled to ask the relevant questions. The aim of this meeting is to create an appropriate atmosphere, opened to dialogue between the parties, within which it can be properly decided whether a reparation activity is necessary or if the young offender must pay any compensation. Subsequently, a summary with the relevant issues and agreements of the meeting must be written down and signed by both parties since it becomes a non binding legal document.

The second direct mediation method is quite similar; the only difference is that after welcoming and remembering the conduct rules, parties are free to say what they wish, without the leading role of the mediator. Likewise, a non binding legal document containing the agreements of the parties is written down.

The last direct mediation method is known as the «restorative conference». It is followed by the Thames Valley Police and is based on the written model developed by the New South Wales Police in Australia. It is a group structure process in which all the participants are asked a series of open questions. In the first instance, the young offender is invited to describe what happened, what he was thinking in those moments, and who he thought it had affected and how. Later the victim is invited to tell what happened and how it affected him or her. Afterwards, both victim and offender's companions, in this order, are allowed to say what they think it happened and how it affected the victim. Dialogue goes on discussing what type of actions should be carried out to repair the offence. At the end of the conference, they prepare a written document that is signed by the offender, the victim and the mediator.

Lastly, the majority of the mediation services visit the parties aiming to assess whether the mediation process has worked out successfully. It also allows the mediation service to control the proper performance of the agreements. Even though the agreement reached out of the mediation process is not legally binding and therefore cannot be fulfilled, if any of the parties is discontent with the mediation's results, from these post-mediation visits, a later meeting can be scheduled to talk about why the agreement has no been fulfilled.

3. Conclusion

The conclusion arising from this brief summary of the mediation system in juvenile criminal cases applicable in the United Kingdom is the strong influence of the local authorities and the founded commitment of the community volunteers towards mediation in juvenile criminal cases. That is possible, in my opinion, due to the British society view where criminal behaviour can be nipped in the bud if dealt with at an early enough stage, since it is well recognised that all children go through a rebellious phase in their teens.

It is true that in the majority of cases the British mediation in juvenile criminal cases system is designed as a diverting method in order to not to apply the adults' laws to young offenders while achieving a dual aim: let the offender understand the real extension of the harm that has caused to his or her victim and additionally allow the victim to obtain a reparation for the offences suffered.

The Spanish mediation in juvenile criminal cases system should follow the common law tradition at least in two points: it should rely upon lay community volunteers and it should seek more for the victim's reparation and the young offender understanding of the bad things done and its negative consequences rather than punishing him or her.

References

Ashworth, A. (2002) "Responsibilities, Rights and Restorative Justice", *The British Journal of Criminology*, vol. 42, pp. 578-595.

Braithwaite, H. (1999) "Assessing an immodest theory and a pessimistic theory", *Crime & Justice*, vol. 25, pp. 1-127.

Cappelletti, M. (1993) "Alternative dispute resolution processes within the framework of the worldwide access-to-justice movement", *Modern Law Review*, vol. 56, pp. 282-296.

Feld. B. C. (1997) "Abolish the juvenile court: Youthfulness, criminal responsibility, and sentencing policy", *Journal of Criminal Law & Criminology*, vol. 88, pp. 68-136.

Gordillo Santana, L. F. (2007) *La justicia restaurativa y la mediación penal*, Iustel, Madrid.

Irvine, D. (1999) *Inaugural Lecture to the Faculty of Mediation and ADR*, available at: http://www.dca.gov.uk/speeches/1999/27-1-99.htm (accessed 25 may 2009).

Liébana Ortiz, J. R. (2006) "Notas sobre el anteproyecto de reforma de la jurisdicción voluntaria de octubre de 2005" in Robles Garzón, J. A.; Ortells Ramos, M. *Problemas actuales del proceso iberoamericano*, vol. II, CEDMA, Málaga, pp. 113-126.

Slapper, G.; Kelly, D. (1999) *The English Legal System*, Cavendish, London.

Schelkens, W. (1998) "Community service and mediation in the juvenile justice legislation in Europe" in Walgrave, L. (ed.) *Restorative Justice for juveniles. Potentialities, Risks and Problems*, Leuven University Press, Leuven, pp. 159-183.

Community Mediation and the Natural Mediators'[1] Programme

Maria Munné, Marc Ros, Maria Granell, Luci Morera, Miguel Bonet, Ana Gómez
Alter, serveis de mediació integrals. Ltd.

Abstract. We present an experience in community mediation that complements professional mediation with non-formal mediation. This project consists of introducing non-professional mediators from the territory into the mediation culture and training them to play a new role in the community: the "natural mediator". This person could improve and help the citizens' communication and improve participation channels. 37 volunteers from the town of Terrassa got involved in the natural mediators programme, and all of them received training in mediation skills. All volunteers usually participate in their territory as conflict workers.

Keywords: Natural mediators, Community mediation, Conflict, Community of citizens.

1. The mediator figure in the citizen's community

There are different mediator figures in the community: some are professionally qualified mediators and the others manage conflicts in a non-formal way. We call the latter non-formal or non-professional mediators. So, we can establish a difference between professional mediators, who have been trained to manage conflicts with the principles of mediation culture, and those who, having not been trained in the same way, use mediation in a non-formal way to deal with interpersonal conflicts. Among these, we can find people who help others in managing conflict situations using their conciliating skills, and workers who are used to dealing with conflicts as a part of their job.

Every city needs spaces for mediation, places for a responsible and autonomous management of conflicts, with respect for differences, some of

---

[1] The natural mediators programme has been developed by the Community Mediation Service of the Àrea de Ciutadania i Drets Civils (Citizenship and Civil Rights Service) of the Terrassa City Council. This Service has been funded by the Secretaría de Estado de Immigración y Emigración (Immigration and Emmigration State Secretary) during 2007 and by the Direcció General de Participació Ciutadana de la Generalitat de Catalunya (General Direction of Citizen Participation of the Catalan Government) during 2008.

them in a professional dimension and some, on the other hand, in a non formal way. Creating and consolidating citizens and entities with mediation skills enriches the social network and enforces links within the community, and it can also encourage responsible citizen participation, increasing respect for interpersonal differences and a peaceful coexistence (Munné and McCragh, 2006).

In such a society, moral structures, which used to become universal guidelines, lose their hegemony, and it is the individual who becomes the moral subject (Bauman, 1992). In this situation, more and more resources are required to facilitate the individual and community responsibility. This would –in J. Deklerck's words[2]— encourage the links among people, with others, with the community –group, society and culture—, and with life in a wide sense.

Mediation is helpful for the creation of links among us, with others and with the community. Fomenting and empowering mediation figures and mediation spaces helps the knowledge of mediation culture and interpersonal meeting. In this same line, Galtung's recommendation is to "increase spaces for the actors not to use violence in conflict" and, at the same time, "to implement an active and non violent training, in mediation skills, and with the aim to learn how to train local citizens" (Galtung, 2003). Galtung states that the world needs a huge number of conflict workers with a low profile and next to general population. He observes how these mediators of the territory are good conflict transformers and he suggests that, in order to make this transformation possible, they need to learn about parties' culture to generate a sincere, non-violent and creative dialogue (Rozemblum de Horowitz, 2007).

The professional mediator must be provided with local resources and, in consequence, needs to work with the mediation figures, natural helpers (Lederach, 1998), who are part of the context where conflicts develop, and who can profit from their knowledge of the territory and people who live there.

Ury introduces the "third side" concept into the community with a youth violence related experience. This was initiated in Boston during the '90s, when Paul Evans from the Boston police commission used figures that he called "community counsellors". These were often ex-gang members who helped the gang members to exchange arms for words in their conflicts' management (Ury, 2000).

We can also find other experiences of mediators who came up from the territory and worked for the community and for the people living in the

---

[2] ¿De una tècnica de mediación a una cultura de la vinculación? Algunas consideraciones sobre los desarrollos de la mediación en Europa [From a mediation technique to a links' culture? Some considerations about the development of mediation in Europe]. Presentation in the First Conference of Community Mediation in el Prat de Llobregat, 21st – 23rd November 2000.

"Community Boards" in San Francisco (USA). There is also the "National Mediation Service" from Norway, where professional mediators and other mediator figures (volunteer mediators) work together in community mediation programmes, offering spaces for dealing with conflicts in several mediation settings. These experiences are based on the participation of the community which has been previously trained in some conflicts' management emerging from it.

In a mediation culture perspective, there are prestigious people, trained in mediation skills, who improve the pre-existing citizen participation and communication channels. These people develop participative procedures, help participation systems and make citizen responsible within a territory become natural mediators. Such figures are an efficacious and necessary tool to work for peace.

2. A project of Community Mediation: Natural Mediators' Training

The Natural Mediators' Training started in the second half of 2007. It was made possible by the interest and support of the Citizenship and Civil Rights Department of the Terrassa City Council (Àrea de Ciutadania i Drets Civils de l'Ajuntament de Terrassa). The project was funded to create a natural mediators' network in the city of Terrassa. The aim of this network was to build new community participation and responsibility channels by managing community conflicts with the culture mediation tools. The natural mediators programme is still alive and it is an important project for the Terrassa City Council.

2.1. PROJECT DEVELOPMENT

This project has been structured in four phases which are repeated for each participating group.

2.1.1. *Stage 1: Participants' choice and proposal*
This stage consists of seeking, detecting and selecting those people who have some previously gained skills requisite to become a natural mediator. First, we interviewed people who know the territory and the city – workers of the city council, district managers and relevant people from entities – with the aim of detecting members for the Natural Mediators Programme. When we have a sufficient number we interview and select them to evaluate their profile and to begin the training. The members of the programme are selected because of their status in their community, because they are interested in the project and finally because they have a profile that

allows the creation of a heterogeneous group in which most of the community groups are represented.

2.1.2. *Stage 2: Natural Mediators' Training*

The Natural Mediators Training is a 32 hour course. It consists of a theoretical comprehension and an interpersonal conflict practice. It also brings to the trainee basic elements of communication, mediator profile and mediation process.

2.1.3. *Stage 3: Mentoring*

When the training is finished, the project continues by offering tutoring to the natural mediators who passed the training. Every natural mediator has a professional mediator mentor who will guide him to formulate and develop a concrete project. The mentor works with the natural mediator for 3 sessions. In the first session, the training and its utility for the natural mediators are evaluated through the design of a little project in and for culture mediation. In the second session, a follow-up process of the project is planned; and in the third and last one, the project is evaluated. At the same time, these newly recruited natural mediators begin to collaborate with the Community Mediation Service, and they become a part of the referring network. They may begin to manage interpersonal conflicts and support the Community Mediation Centre in concrete cases.

2.1.4. *Stage 4: Natural Mediators programme evaluation*

The programme can be evaluated with direct and indirect indicators. The natural mediators' satisfaction with the training and the project is evaluated. Their influence in the territory and the intention to continue in the project are also evaluated. An important issue to evaluate is the number of referred cases that a natural mediator has sent to the Community Mediation Centre, and also the number of cases in which they got involved. We could also qualitatively evaluate the influence of the training in the cases in which they take part. Finally, we look at the number of cases in which they have worked as mediators and all the actions that they have taken to prevent conflict, improve coexistence and expand the mediation culture, e.g. the links that have been created between people beyond their differences.

2.2. PARTICIPANTS PROFILE

37 people have participated in the Natural Mediators' Training. Of those people, 6 did not continue with the project.

We have a heterogeneous and representative group of participants in the Natural Mediators' Project, and we are achieving with every group a significant representation of the city of Terrassa.

Our intention is to represent as many community groups of the city as possible (gender, age, represented groups and influence and territorial distribution).

In Figure 1, we have a pie chart representing the different age-groups of all the participants over the age of 23.

Almost half of the participants in the project were females (18 women and 19 men). The least represented range was the elderly (>65 years old). On the other hand, in Figure 2, we see a culturally heterogeneous natural mediators' group. In these groups, almost all the original nationalities of Terrassa's population are represented.

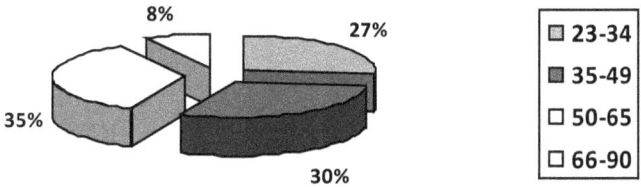

Figure 1. Age-groups

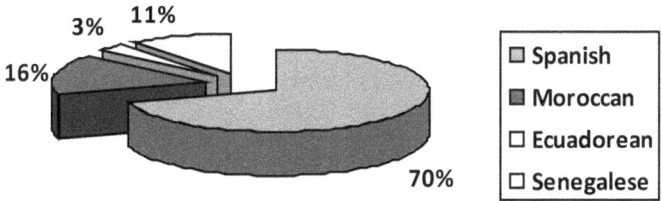

Figure 2. Original nationality

Finally, we tried to keep all the groups that coexist in the city represented amongst the natural mediators because our aim was to reach all the groups, entities and citizens of Terrassa. Figure 3 shows the different settings that we were able to represent. Despite this, we know that there are still groups with no representation.

We observed a high number of cultural associations and other representative entities which work directly for the integration of those people who have newly immigrated to the town of Terrassa. Making these associations take part in our projects helped us to establish a municipal network able to profit from already existing networks. The second most representative group of natural mediators came from organisations which give support to facilitate the integration of immigrants. Another group of natural mediators is formed by youth and women representatives. In the 'others' section, we combined people from the Red Cross, a municipal education centre, the Evangelical Church and, finally, a person who works for the City Council in the Citizens' Advice Bureau.

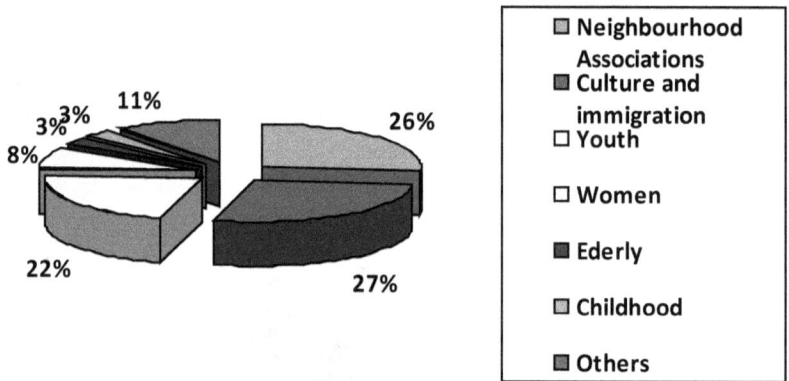

Figure 3. Group representation

Although we consider that we managed to achieve a good representation of the whole territory, there are still some cultural groups and different associations which are not yet included in the Natural Mediators' Programme. As far as the training programme for natural mediators is concerned, we consider those not included previously (because of gender, age, geographical origin and other causes) as an inclusion criterion.

2.3. RESULTS

At the moment, we still do not have enough quantitative and objective data to measure the range and influence of the Natural Mediators' Programme in our territory. Nevertheless, we are able to anticipate some of the effects that the training programme has originated. First of all, we would like to point out the projects that have been proposed by different natural mediators. Nowadays, these projects are in diverse stages of development.

2.3.1. *Mediation divulgation and case referral*
Our first output has been bringing together people with previous knowledge of the mediation service and of mediation as a process. They have been able to facilitate the awareness of the service and of the mediation culture to those collectives where they operate and within which they have established new referring networks. One of the projects that natural

mediators have presented consists of the presentation of the mediation centre and the mediation itself as a tool to manage differences.

2.3.2. *Interventions in conflict situations*
Another very important outcome that has emerged from the new training is the management of conflict situations in their own setting through the mediation culture. Therefore, there are some natural mediators who have already intervened in conflicts, using their new mediation skills, helping people to solve their differences through respect and dialogue.

2.3.3. *Coordinated actions and collaboration with the mediation service*
Natural mediators have been working in cooperation and voluntarily with the Community Mediation Centre, with the aim of becoming a support point between the Centre and the citizen. In the same way, we have also received their support to create consensus in processes amongst neighbours, and to establish complementary actions based on linking people to some sort of collective.

2.3.4. *Training in mediation for the personal autonomy and the respect to differences in the management of conflicts*
One of the natural mediators has initiated a project with youth. The aim of the project is to train the youth in mediation skills. This project is being developed in a community centre of the city. The community centre youth teachers are also being trained in mediation culture.

2.3.5. *"Dialogues in the District"*
This specific project consists of activating "dialogue spaces" for the neighbours of the district. In these spaces, they could explain their own point of view about anything that concerns them and, at the same time, learn to understand different perspectives.

These dialogues are based on the methodology of "public conversations" (Becker, 2000), and their aim is to support the good communication to understand every point of view on one specific topic. Therefore, the main objective is not the achievement of an agreement or a consensus, but the dialogue within differences. The space where the district dialogue takes place is usually the same where the topic discussed might happen.

At the moment, the dialogue about "use of and living in public space" is taking place. This dialogue is being carried out by people from different ages, genders and cultures. They have to speak and listen to each other with the presence of a mediator (in this case of a natural mediator and a professional one).

A district's representative will transcript these dialogues and will present them to the same population in the district. Depending on the results, the natural mediators' aim with this project is to repeat the dialogues along a year, dealing with the neighbours' personal and the district's realities.

2.3.6. *Creating a mediation service located in a neighbourhood association*
One of the natural mediators is nowadays directing a neighbourhood mediation service located in a municipal neighbourhood association. This service manages local conflict situations and also collaborates with the Community Mediation Centre referring cases, as well as helping to extend a culture of mediation in the district where it is located. At this moment, this service has incorporated the figure of a second natural mediator.

3. Final considerations

A community service needs to be integrated in the territory (Munné, 2008), and must be connected and collocated with the lives of the members of the community. Collaborating with non-professional mediators is necessary to the creation of a mediation culture, and to establish a viable network to manage citizens' conflicts on the basis of respect for differences, peaceful dialogue, an autonomous morality and responsible citizenship.

Our experience in Terrassa shows the potential of the cultural work with the citizenship and communities, offered through the mediation process.

The creation of mediation spaces leads to the establishment of participation and responsibility giving spaces which encourage peaceful coexistence. Professional mediators, who are nowadays working in Catalan towns, occupy a great position from which to build, enforce and coordinate these spaces. In the future, when we are in possession of more information about the different experiences of non-formal mediation, we will be in a good position to explain the influence that these programmes have in relation to coexistence and the relationships between citizens in the towns and cities where they are being developed.

Acknowledgements

First of all, we want to thank all the natural mediators for all their voluntary work. We would like to thank Daniel Prieto-Alhambra and Mark Pear for the translation and manuscript review.

Finally, we thank the support given by the team in charge of the White Book, the Terrassa City Council and ALTER Sim S.L.

References

Becker, C.; Chasin, L.; Chasin, R.; Herzig, M.; Roth S. (2000) "Del debate estancado a una nueva conversación sobre los temas controvertidos: el proyecto de conversaciones públicas" in Fried Schnitman, D.; Schnitman, J. (comp.) *Resolución de conflictos. Nuevos diseños, nuevos contextos*. Ediciones Granica, Barcelona.

Galtung, J. (2003) *Paz por medios pacíficos. Paz y conflicto, desarrollo y civilización*. Bakeaz, Gernika.

Lederach, J. P. (1998) *Construyendo la paz. Reconciliación sostenible en sociedades divididas*. Bakeaz, Gernika.

Munné, M.; McCragh, P. (2006) *Els deu principis de la Cultura de la Mediació*. Graó, Barcelona.

Munné, M. (coord.) (2008) *Decàleg de Bones pràctiques de la Mediació Ciutadana i Comunitària*. Programa Compartim. Centre d'Estudis Jurídics de la Generalitat de Catalunya.

Rozemblum de Horowitz, S. (2007) *Mediación: Convivencia y resolución de conflictos en la comunidad*. Graó, Barcelona.

Ury, W. L. (2000) *Alcanzar la paz: Resolución de conflictos y mediación en la familia, el trabajo y el mundo*. Paidós, Barcelona.

Aspects of the Discourse Used for Intra Judicial Family Mediation Informative Session

Núria Villanueva Rey
Catalonia's Family Mediation Centre, Generalitat de Catalunya

Abstract. This paper aims at describing how the Mediation Service of the Catalonia's Family Mediation Centre in Barcelona Family Courts handles the judiciary referrals to intra judicial mediation informative voluntary sessions. In particular, it goes deeply into the actual discourse used by the mediator to inform the parties making an almost literal transcription of the verbal language used. As a conclusion, it is emphasized that the principal purpose of these sessions is to allow the parties involved in a litigious proceeding the opportunity to know about the mediation procedures and values. It is underlined that if both parties consider it suitable, they have the option to ask for a mediator and carry out an intra judicial family mediation.

Keywords: Informative session, Intra judicial family mediation, Judiciary referrals, Mediator's discourse.

1. Introduction

The first intra judicial family mediation experiences in Catalonia were developed along the 90's decade thanks to the initiative of professionals in the Barcelona Family Courts and the Department of Justice of the Catalan Government.

From the approval of the Catalan Family Mediation Act 1/2001, a stage begins where the intra judicial family mediation has little casuistry. But in 2006, a pilot trial in Spain begins led by the General Council of the Judiciary (Ortuño, 2006) which will mean a significant increase of the intra judicial mediation activity as Table I shows.

Table I. Evolution of judicial mediation information sessions in Catalonia

	Year 2004	Year 2005	Year 2006	Year 2007	Year 2008
Judiciary referrals to family mediation informative session from all courts in Catalonia	36	33	244	370	916

The Department of Justice of the Catalan Government has taken part in this pilot trial through the Catalonia's Family Mediation Centre (CFMC hereinafter). Due to this fact, a specific service is established in the judicial premises: the Mediation Service in the Barcelona Family Courts. The Mediation Service allows the CFMC to keep a continuous coordination with operators and judiciary bodies as well as a privileged proximity to citizens involved in litigious proceedings (Villanueva, 2006).

Even though sometimes a debate arises about whether the intra judicial mediation is or is not mediation (Ibáñez, 1999), the Mediation Service in the Barcelona Family Courts (MSBFC hereinafter) considers it essential to offer as well a dialogue chance when the lawsuit is in course (Bolaños, 2003). Furthermore, it is crucial that the intra judicial mediation informative session opens a door to an alternative and complementary mediation space at the same time of the litigious proceeding.

In summary, the referral of cases to the mediation informative session supposes an improvement in the service offered by courts (Hinojal, 2008). This has also given rise to working out a protocol for the intra judicial family mediation introduction designed by judges (Martín Nájera, 2008). In 2008, the Mediation Committee of the Forum for Justice designed another protocol, too.

The Act 15/2009 on mediation in the field of civil law, dated July 22, came into force and it abolishes the Act 1/2001, dated March 15, on family mediation in Catalonia. The Act 15/2009 enlarges the cases of family mediation covered by law and introduces civil mediation for conflicts derived from civic and social coexistence as well as for other private conflicts where parties have to keep a relationship in the future. Article 11 refers to the mediation informative session establishing that, once the judicial process has begun, the judge can provide that the parties attend a mediation informative session.

2. The Mediation Service in the Barcelona Family Courts (MSBFC)

The MSBFC is located at the same premises where all Barcelona Family Courts are located along with the Incapacitation Courts.

The main duties of the mediator in charge of the service are:

1. Carrying out all mediation informative sessions derived from the courts in the judicial premises.
2. Facilitating the process to assign the case to a mediator authorized by the CFMC if the parties request the mediation.
3. Performing, in some cases, some of the requested mediations.

3. The flowchart of judiciary referrals to informative session

3.1. HOW COURTS DERIVE TO THE INFORMATIVE SESSION

At present, five courts have available a specific mediation notebook to appoint informative sessions in an ordinary way and it is the coordination means between the court and the MSBFC. The rest of courts apply to the Mediation Service to set a day and hour for an informative session in the cases they find appropriate for this proposal.

On some occasions, extraordinarily, express informative sessions are carried out the same day the parties are in the courts premises before, during or after the course of a hearing or an appearance.

3.2. JUDICIARY STAGE OF THE REFERRAL TO INFORMATIVE SESSION

In most cases, the parties are derived to a mediation informative session in the ruling where the date of the principal hearing is set. There is an average interval of four weeks between both and, during this time, the mediation takes place.

In this ruling, the court informs the parties about the possibility to attend voluntarily a family mediation informative session free of charge, setting a date and hour, and giving the Mediation Service phone number and the name of the person they will meet.

But there is also a group of cases in which the referral is made in the course of the principal hearing, before the sentence, in the sentence, in execution, and in appeal; as well as before the hearing for previous measures or afterwards in the previous measures writ.

3.3. HOW IS THE INFORMATION HANDED TO THE PARTIES

The solicitors send the judiciary documents to the lawyer and they give the information to the parties. The lawyers usually inform their clients by phone about the trial's date and, at the same time, about the date of the mediation informative session. Occasionally, the lawyer or the parties call the Mediation Service asking for information or for a change of hour or date.

3.4. INFORMATIVE SESSIONS' METHODOLOGY

The Protocol for Developing and Implementing Mediation defines the intra judicial informative session as an individual or joint session aimed at informing the lawyers as well as the parties about the characteristics, requirements, contributions and benefits of mediation (Mediation Commission of the Forum for Justice, 2008). Similarly, the informative session at the MSBFC is thought to inform jointly or individually both parties with or without the presence of the two lawyers. Together or separately, when both parties have been informed about mediation, in 50% of cases, they ask for starting the mediation process.

When only one of the parties comes, it is equally informed and has the opportunity to say what he/she considers it convenient with respect to the service being offered. On some occasions, the other party finally comes to the informative session and mediation begins in the end. There are also cases in which no party comes to the informative session.

4. Description of the intra judicial family mediation informative session

In the following text, there is a description of an approach to the literal general discourse of a joint informative session without the presence of attorneys in a litigious divorce proceeding.

4.1. PRESENTATION OF THE SERVICE AND RECEPTION OF THE PARTS

"Good morning, welcome to the Mediation Service of the Catalonia's Family Mediation Centre in the Barcelona Family Courts. My name is Núria Villanueva and I have the responsibility to inform you about mediation. Here you have documentation with general information that you can take home. You will find there my name and how to contact this service.

Look, the Court has considered it convenient to offer you the possibility to attend a voluntary mediation informative session in order to allow you, once you get the information, to evaluate whether the service offered gives an answer to any need you may have.

Beginning a mediation means that you, if both of you consider it appropriate, decide to seat at a dialogue table just to talk about the differences you have. A professional conflict mediator will help you with the aim of improving the situation in which you and your children may be.

The mediation will take place if you make today or in next days a mediation application, either a joint one or two individual ones, filling out these forms that I am giving you.

In this application form, in addition to your personal data, you should point out, in a general and guiding way, the area or areas where you think differently about how things have to be arranged from now on: the big area of children's custody, the big area of the paternal power exercise including communication between father and mother, the big area of the children's visitation regulation, the big area related to residence, and the big area of economic matters in general related or not to children.

In the form, you should also describe the general reason or reasons to request the mediation. These reasons should be congruous with wishing to seat to talk between you as father and mother of your children in order to try to reach an agreement or some agreements. This is your way to request in your own words a dialogue table that the Mediation Service offers. Therefore, in the form you should not describe the difficulties and the different points of view that you maintain: you will have the opportunity to work these points out in the mediation process helped by the mediator.

To sum up, if you both request the mediation, you need to agree with the number of topics to mediate and the reasons to do so when you meet the mediator to start mediation, so that the outcome is satisfactory for both of you.

The mediation will be free of charge and will take place in hours previously agreed with the mediator, and whenever possible, your time availability will be taken into account".

4.2. IMAGINING HOW THE MEDIATION WOULD BE IN YOUR CASE

"I am going to tell you how the process would be if you chose mediation, so that you can get an idea of the service we are offering. The first day that you meet the mediator, you will sign this "Initial Act" in which a whole of characteristics and commitments are stated. I am going to describe them now.

A mediation will start if you voluntarily ask us for a mediator: the court has not derived you to mediation but to a voluntary mediation informative session so that you, once you have received the information, and if the mediation gives answer to some need you may have, decide to ask for a mediation process or not. Therefore, if the mediator realizes that there is not wilfulness in your request, he / she will ask you to evaluate the situation and what is appropriate at that moment.

The mediator will work for you both in an impartial way and with neutrality, and will not give you any piece of advice, neither legal –as you have your lawyers—, nor social, psychological or therapeutical. You are the owners of your problem and you are the owners of your solution. The mediator is neither an arbitrator proposing a solution from your proposals, nor an expert preparing a report to the court on your characteristics and your children. The mediator will help you so that you can constructively explain the reasons each of you have to raise your issues; will facilitate that you listen to each other; will promote that you put yourselves in the place of the other; will favour that your positions come closer; and finally, if the chance comes up, that you reach agreements that improve the situation in which you and your children could be.

For this reason, the first objective of the intra judicial mediation that we are offering you is that you come to the trial's date, which is not suspended or adjourned, having a minimum of restored communication, trust and harmony between a father and a mother. You are a husband and wife who are divorcing, but who continue to be the father and the mother of your children.

The second objective will be that you also come to the trial's date with some aspect or aspects agreed on between you. Those aspects on which there is no agreement will be treated at the court. In this way, part of the sentence will be yours and the rest of it will be decided by the judge. The third objective will be that you also come to the trial's date with many aspects agreed on between you, and that either you conciliate with the judge before the hearing or agree on during the hearing. And the fourth objective will be that you make a global agreement and therefore do not come to a trial, and bring the litigious proceeding back to a mutual agreement procedure.

In case you reach some agreement, no matter how little it is, this will be very important and will be written in your own words, without juridical technicalities. Before you sign it with the mediator, you will be requested to inform your lawyers about the contents of this agreement to be able to advise you. In this manner, you will never be judicially or legally unprotected. The document of mediation agreements is signed by you and the mediator and it will not be sent to the court. This document may consist of three lines or 3 pages so to speak, and you should give a copy to your lawyer. Both lawyers, in mutual agreement, will respect the spirit of your private agreement, will translate it to a legal language and will write the necessary legal technical document which will be presented to the court so that it has the effects it should have.

Upon ending the mediation, the mediator will present a document to the court in charge of your case informing about the ending date and if there have been agreements or not. If there have been agreements, the court is informed that these are in your hands, and if there have not been agreements, the mediator does not give any type of information about the reasons or any written report. The mediator keeps the confidentiality along the whole process."

4.3. CONCLUSION AND GOODBYE TO THE PARTIES

"If you both, today or in the next days, apply for the mediation, we will assign you a mediator. Any other situation will mean that, at least by now, the mediation does not take place. If one of you says yes and the other one says no, the mediation will not take place because the necessary circumstance is that both of you say yes. The mediation is voluntary and therefore you should ask for a mediator if mediation answers some need that each of you may have. If this is not the case, you should not feel under pressure and you are free to say no.

The CFMC will only inform the court about whether the mediation begins or not and about the number of parties that have been informed. The CFMC will not tell the court the option you have chosen or any other detail. Even when only one party is informed, we do not report which part has come, we report to the court that one party has been informed and that's all.

The most significant moment to try a mediation is now, before the trial is carried out. However, if the conditions to begin it are not given now but they arise in the future, do not doubt to get in touch again with our service. In the same manner that at any time, you can convert the litigious proceeding into one of mutual agreement from the inter negotiation of your lawyers. At any time you can as well decide to seat to talk to reach your own agreements helped by the mediator.

Moreover, sentences usually say "what has to be done" but they do not say "how has to be done". If you have the need to talk about the best way to carry out the sentence pronounced by the court, you continue to have the mediation at your disposal.

The objective of this intra judicial family mediation informative session has been reached as long as we have had the opportunity to inform you both, and now you know how mediation can help you in your situation of difference and difficulty. Tell your lawyers about the decision you take about mediation and about the fact that we are at their disposal to inform them personally or by phone. Particularly, in case that the mediation takes place and you reach agreements, they will be the ones to convert your document containing mediation agreements into the corresponding legal technical document. They will also present it in court in order to get the expected mediation effects.

Finally, your children, you and the rest of relatives around you can enjoy the beneficial effects if a minimum of trust, communication and harmony between you is recovered. And this is the first objective to achieve in the intra judicial mediation we offer you. Have a nice day, we are at your disposal: the mediation door is always open. Thank you very much for your attention."

5. Some reflections as conclusion

The informative session plays a basic role in the extra judicial mediation as well as in the intra judicial one, but it is evident that both take place in different moments and contexts.

The results of the intra judicial mediation pilot experiences have clearly shown the need to give support to the presence of specialised mediation services at courts premises. These services offer intra judicial family mediation informative sessions as part of the mediation implementation with the consensus of all the juridical and social operators on the methodology.

The mediation act defines mediation as a method of conflicts management that seeks to avoid the opening of contentious trials, to put an end to the ones already in course or to reduce their scope. This last aim, reducing the impact through partial agreements, is the one greatly unknown and forgotten. However, it should be developed because of the chain effect toward global future agreements thanks to the work in network of all operators.

A way has been done from the beginnings of family mediation in Spain (Coy et al., 1986) up to now, and it is important to take it into account, to look back and learn from past experiences as well as to look forward and build up new practices and methodologies. The intra judicial mediation is one of them. Both protocols –one to introduce the intra judicial family mediation mentioned above and designed by judges and lawyers along 2008, and the other that is being designed by Catalan judicial mediators in 2009 — are the evidence that mediation has all the professional guarantees and desires of improving the condition of justice in Spain.

References

Bolaños, I. (2003) "Mediación familiar en contextos judiciales" in Poyatos García, A. (coord.) *Mediación familiar y social en diferentes contextos*, Publicacions de la Universitat de València, Nau llibres, pp. 175-212. Available at: http://www.poder-judicial-bc.gob.mx/admonjus/n24/AJ24_005.htm (accessed 11 June 2009)

Coy, A.; Benito, F.; Martin, S. (1986) "Divorcio: ¿Justícia sin juzgados?", Revista Jurídica de la Región de Murcia, n. 3, p. 86-101. Available at: http://www.fundacionmarianoruizfunes.com/ver_articulo.php?articulo=12 (accessed 11 June 2009)

Comisión de Mediación Foro por la Justicia (2008) *Protocolo para el desarrollo e implementación de la mediación familiar.* Available online at http://forojusticia.cgae.es/ejercicio-2009/comision-de-mediacion/foro-protocolo-mediacion-familiar-2008-2.pdf/view (accessed 11 June 2009)

Hinojal, S. et al. (2008) "La mediación en el ámbito de los procesos de familia" in Saez, C. (coord.) *La mediación familiar. La mediación penal y penitenciaria. El estatuto del mediador. Un programa para su regulación*, Aranzadi, pp. 13-45.

Ibáñez Valverde, V. J. (1999) "Mediación familiar intrajudicial", *Papeles del psicólogo,* n. 73, Consejo General de Colegios Oficiales de Psicólogos de España. Available at http://www.papelesdelpsicologo.es/vernumero.asp?id=832 (accessed 11 June 2009)

Martín Nájera, T. et al. (2008) "Protocolo para la implantación de la mediación familiar intrajudical en los juzgadoz y tribunales que conocen de procesos de familia" in *LexFamily.es Revista Digital de Derecho de Familia.* Available at: http://www.lexfamily.es/revista.php?codigo=396 (accessed 11 June 2009)

Ortuño Muñoz, P.; Saez Valcárcel, R. (2006) *Alternativas a la judicialización de los conflictos: la mediación,* Consejo General del Poder Judicial. Estudios de Derecho Judicial. Madrid.

Villanueva Rey, N. (2006) "Mediación familiar intrajudicial en los juzgados de familia de Barcelona" in Ortuño Muñoz, P.; Saez Valcárcel, R. *Alternativas a la judicialización de los conflictos: la mediación*, Consejo General del Poder Judicial. Estudios de Derecho Judicial. Madrid, pp. 451-480

Dynamics and Special Characteristics of the Extrajudicial Information Session

Josep Fité Guarro

Mediation Guidance Service, Catalonia's Private Law Mediation Centre, Generalitat de Catalunya

Abstract. The Legal Guidance Service of the Barcelona Bar Association is the main referral source for directing individual parties towards the family mediation process, which is run by the Barcelona Mediation Guidance Service (SOM) in an extrajudicial context while following procedural protocols. Most users make an appointment simply to request a free legal-aid lawyer, which means that the mediator running the extrajudicial information session often becomes the first point of contact that the disputing parties will have with their own legal proceedings. Even before they meet a lawyer, the mediator will be the first professional they encounter to handle that dispute.

This fact has an influence on the focus, direction and discursive resources at the disposal of the mediator at the Barcelona Mediation Guidance Service (SOM) during the extrajudicial information service. This information session also noticeably differs from one conducted in a judicial context.

In a definitive way, given the personal profile of people being seen in the extrajudicial context and, more significantly, the point in the conflict process at which the session takes place, the mediator is presented with a series of opportunities to openly question the contentious process. The mediator is also to present mediation as a more effective space for dealing with a family conflict, as opposed to the adversarial space which the parties have not chosen yet.

Keywords: Extrajudicial information service, Family mediation, Mediation Guidance Service (SOM), Empowerment, Space for cooperation, Adversarial space.

1. The procedure involved to begin an extrajudicial mediation process at the Barcelona Mediation Guidance Service

A mediator from the Catalonia's Private Law Mediation Centre runs the Barcelona Mediation Guidance Service (SOM), which works in cooperation with the Legal Guidance Service of the Barcelona Bar Association. The centre provides assistance for the parties in a family conflict as well as proposes the beginning of a mediation process. This process will allow the parties to handle their family conflict in a new space intended for dialogue and cooperation under the Catalan Act 15/2009 of 22 July on mediation in private law.[1]

The Legal Guidance Service is the main source of referral, accounting for a clear majority (78% of cases handled in 2008). Nevertheless, an increase has been noted over the course of 2009, although so far it is a limited increase in the referrals coming from other channels, both from the social services and, more importantly, from the current information gathered through mediation.

In virtually all cases referred by the Legal Guidance Service, mediation initially takes the form of two private sessions; joint sessions are the exception.

With this double interview model, if the first party attended wishes to open a mediation process, the SOM mediator will then get in contact with the other party and invite it to a similar private session. Once both parties have accepted, the file can be forwarded to the Private Law Mediation Centre, so a mediator to manage the process can be appointed.

2. The parties to the extrajudicial information service

Since the majority of referrals to the Barcelona Mediation Guidance Service come directly from the Legal Guidance Service, it is mainly people who come to request a free legal-aid lawyer based on their income. The service can then assist them in dealing with their dispute by offering them legal guidance. This guidance will help them in working through a process where they may be unaware of a large part of the legal characteristics and consequences. Quite simply, the parties find themselves at the beginning of a journey that they have hardly begun and, in this context, they see themselves in vulnerable position before the law. They are short of legal information and unaware of the dynamics, stages, duration and the legal and technical characteristics of the process they have just undertaken.

It is something of a paradox that, despite their lack of knowledge and guidance, the parties bring with them their own previously formed ideas about the path that the conflict supposedly must follow. This, 'naturally', has to be adversarial. Therefore, they arrive with a preformed opinion about the outcome: the legal authorities will issue a coercive decision, one that imposes a particular type of custody, visiting rights and maintenance which the other party will undoubtedly comply with.

Ultimately, people come in many cases to the Mediation Guidance Service with overflowing baggage of emotions involved in the conflict and the experience they are going through. This will range from the person who

---

[1] *Llei 15/2009, del 22 de juliol, de mediació en l'àmbit del dret privat*, available at: http://www.gencat.cat/diari/5432/09202029.htm

has taken the decision (and who will reach the Mediation Guidance Service with a more elaborate version of the psycho-emotional aspects of the conflict) to the person affected by it. Lisa Parkinson (Parkinson, 2005) has provided an enlightening diagram in this regard. It maps the diversity between the parties as they go through the different phases of the psycho-emotional separation process:

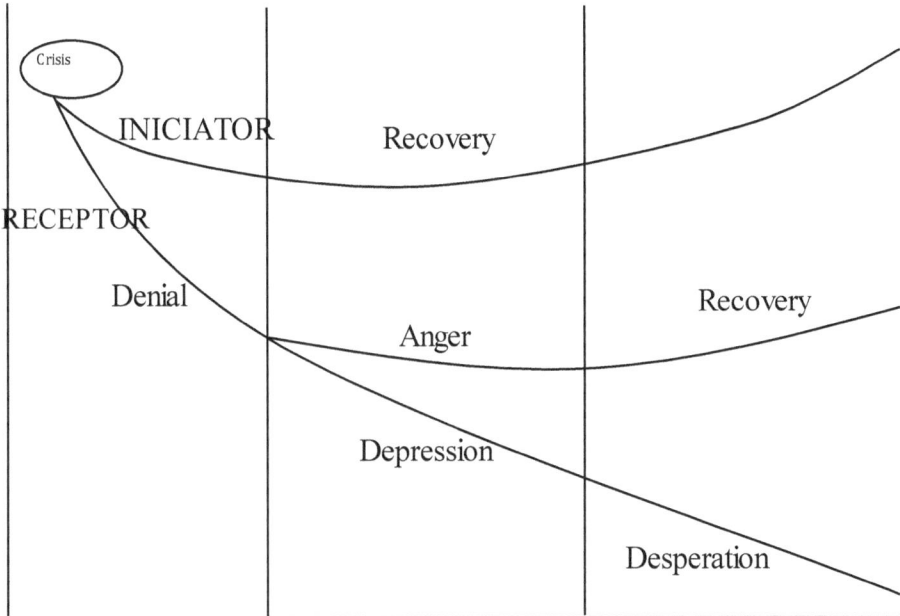

Figure 1. Psyco-emotional Phases of the separation process (Parkinson, 2005)

As a result of our experience, we are able to describe some of the characteristics typically shared by those referred to the Mediation Guidance Service. They tend to feel anxiety about the present, they are overwhelmed because they feel that they have lost control of the conflict; they are worried and uncertain about the future; they experience anger, resentment, and a sense of disorientation; they are lacking in legal information (or indeed they have been directly given incorrect information). Their outlook is hopeless because of their expectations from the dispute, which they perceive inevitable to be by its very nature. And they will have a previously formed idea of the path that the conflict will take, one that they invariably expect to be adversarial in nature.

3. The moment of the extrajudicial information service

One particular aspect that clearly demonstrates the distinctive elements of the extrajudicial information interview is the point at which it takes place.

By and large, citizens gain access to mediation when they come to the Legal Guidance Service. They preliminary seek legal advice and request the appointment of a free legal-aid lawyer that they will need for conducting the legal procedure about to begin. In the event that the legal grounds may be handled through the mediation process, lawyers from the service immediately refer the citizen to the Mediation Guidance Service (SOM) where they will be given the option of the mediation process.

The importance of this referral is rooted in the fact that it takes place before the citizen has the opportunity to speak to his or her court-appointed lawyer. The lawyer will not be available for consultation until the Processing Service, which makes a decision about the matter and approves an application for free legal aid. This process means that the persons concerned have to comply by waiting out a certain period of time.

As a result, the mediator will in all likelihood become the first professional contact for the person concerned in the management of their conflict. This factor places the Barcelona Mediation Guidance Service (SOM) in a different position compared to the legal mediation services. On the one hand, in practice the SOM has to respond to the individual who needs information and guidance, while ensuring that the professional role of mediator does not become confused with that of a lawyer yet to be appointed. At the same time, the moment at which the information session takes place gives the mediator a unique opportunity: he or she is one of the first professionals to have contact with the parties. Consequently, this may positively become a cooperative space for treating the conflict, since the parties have not chosen yet an adversarial space where they may invest their efforts, time, money and emotions.

We regard this as a key factor in understanding the focus of offering mediation from SOM in Barcelona. The mediator effectively has an opportunity to centre the parties and the current conflict in which they are involved within a cooperative space for dealing with their concerns; while directly questioning and looking at the negative aspects of adversarial spaces and directly question their effectiveness in resolving conflicts, when the real aim is to achieve some stable, strong and dependable guidelines for a family following divorce.

Professional praxis at the Barcelona Mediation Guidance Service has shown that one of the core ideas most widely accepted by the people treated is related to the inefficiency and intrinsic weakness of solutions that automatically produce a loser. This becomes the seed for future confrontations and gives rise to a dynamic whereby family guidelines are replaced by legal rules and a chronic dependence on the legal system (Bolaños, 2008).

Information sessions currently being run at the Mediation Guidance Service make the most of this opportunity of being one of the first professionals to reach the individual and to directly propose (despite not in those terms) that there is an alternative model to the adversarial one for dealing with conflicts.

The diverse arguments vary according to the dynamics of the session, yet the following points are typical in all sessions:
- Illustrate the cooperative spaces that exist for dealing with divorce, for example, spaces that by law are given protection and preference.
- Define the dual nature between the conjugal relation that is coming to an end and the parental relationship that continues.
- Set an inviolable and indisputable place for the family nucleus for future relationships.
- Reformulate terms for the process being played out: in this way, "to transform the model of cohabitation and the parent-child bond", rather than "custody and visitation rights"; or "to give you a new system for managing the family finances", rather than "child support or alimony"
- Focus the dilemma: "now that you find yourself at the beginning, you must select between adversity or cooperation, gunshots or dialogue".

4. Core ideas for the extrajudicial information service

The information service given at the Barcelona Mediation Guidance Service is focused around various core ideas that the mediator drives home, using formulations that naturally vary from one session to the next. Without being exhaustive, here we name three of particular importance in the professional practice for the SOM in Barcelona.

4.1. EMPOWERING THE PARTIES

Quite often, this ends up being the centre point for the extrajudicial information service. "The most important for you is not necessarily the most important for the other person, although it remains a significant part of the conflict": this is frequently iterated in the sessions being run at the SOM.

The parties are told that legally speaking they have power and the ability to take whatever decisions they consider most appropriate for their family.

At the same time, it is systematically emphasised that the key to handle the conflict is the possibility to achieve stable, strong and dependable guidelines for organising the family space. These guidelines must be acceptable and feasible to both parties. They only have the genuine capacity to discuss the real needs, expectations, values and emotions at play, so any guidelines must allow this exchange so that all family members concerned can take them on board and comply with them.

As part of the information session, a point is frequently made of the fact that 72% of enforced judgments under civil family arise from conventions reached by mutual agreement (Ortuño, Hernández, 2007). This point of information has great effect in illustrating the weakness of particular conventions: even those reached through mutual agreement, using the model whereby control over the whole process passes to the lawyers and, as a result, the parties do not have the opportunity to go into detail as to the circumstances, real needs and underlying worries for the family (Ortuño, Hernández, 2007).

4.2. ESTABLISHING THE ROLE OF THE MEDIATOR

An essential component of the extrajudicial information service consists of establishing and defining the role of the mediator as a professional who guides the mediation process without influencing either directly or indirectly any decisions taken. Here we highlight, for the practical effect we have noted, some of the core ideas that help in establishing the role of the mediator:

- He or she will create or reconstruct the conditions for establishing an effective dialogue between the parties. The role is often compared with that of a lamp, as part of a metaphor that has been shown to be extraordinarily clear and which helps the parties to properly understand the professional available to them. As a plumber, mediators professionally work on the communication line between the parties concerned. They unblock the line, and wherever necessary repair it, and keep it clear so that information can flow once again in both directions, in a clear and precise way, unencumbered by outside interference.
- He or she will guarantees two essential needs for people who come for mediation:
  - Each party concerned can explain to the other whatever they consider important to say, being given as much time as necessary to express it in their own words, in a respectful way and with clarity. Then all the information needed by the other party to understand – although this does not necessarily mean accept – their point of view is naturally provided.
  - When expressing themselves, each of the parties concerned feels that they are being heard out in silence and shown due respect as well as they are being listened to in an attentive way and without interruption.

- He or she will establish the key ideas that the parties concerned bring and will help to identify and define the central aspects of the problem, while organising them into a working agenda.
- He or she will organise the exploration and creation of opinions while helping the parties concerned to make decisions on the basis of mutual acceptability and a readiness of complying with them.

4.3. REAFIRMING THE IDENTITY OF FAMILY MEDIATION

We borrow the expression used by Lisa Parkinson (Parkinson, 2005) in identifying one of the points of particular emphasis in the information sessions taking place at the SOM.

Individuals who come to the SOM generally have an overall plan for handling the family conflict which inevitably takes the path of the direct intervention – or, direct, coercive intervention – of a third party wielding some legal or scientific authority over the parties. This authority may be a lawyer, a judge or a psychologist who is being consulted in order to impose some guidelines for their governing agreement. From this conception, from the user's point of view, the figure of the mediator has no reason to separate from. So, he or she will serve as an oracle that reveals the right solution or as a hypnotist who will ensure that the other party rectifies, accepts and follows to the letter whatever comes stipulated in the agreement. And the first comments and queries that people have for the mediator at the Barcelona Mediation Guidance Service invariably take this path.

This places an obligation on the mediator during the information session to establish a separate identity for family mediation as a process of conflict management as opposed to other forms of legal, therapeutic or social intervention.

In this respect, the clear distinction between the mediator and the lawyer (and in a similar way, but in fewer cases, the psychologist) is systematically explained during the sessions. His or full compatibility is noted and, moreover, a direct recommendation from the mediations is made so that the parties can advise one another in tandem with the dialogue process.

The non-directive role of the mediator is clearly established. He or she will not make decisions, give advice, act as consultant or make value judgements. The figure of the lawyer is unequivocally recognised: this is compulsory prior to the mediation and necessary during it so that the parties can take their own decisions not only in a free, conscious and mutually acceptable way, but also in a fully informed way.

5. The power of the metaphor

In the dynamic used in the extrajudicial information sessions that take place, metaphors have been used with noted success when it comes to address any complex issue such as:
 – changing the space for handling the family conflict; or
 – when making explicitly clear that once the space is stated on the day following the divorce, there will still be room where to coexist and a bond between the parties who today find themselves in confrontation with one another.
A change of model is needed to deal with this situation. Here we lay out four of the most widely used models commonly used during the information sessions, purely for the purpose of explanation.

5.1. TRENCH WARFARE

This is one of the most powerful images: "imagine two armies, one trench facing the other, both lined with soldiers about to go over the top and fight for values they consider right. And yet, on the last minute, someone raises a white flag and offers a truce and a table in no-man's land where through negotiation they can resolve the conflict that has led them to the battlefield. The truce can produce varied results: if they fail to reach an agreement, no problem, they simply return to the trenches and get ready to fight. However, if they achieve a solution, they can all go home without suffering any of the harm that ensues from combat. We –the mediators— are the third party that proposes a truce and ensures safe dialogue".

5.2. THE PUBLIC SQUARE

This metaphor makes the association between the common family space which remains on a square, with two neighbours – the parents – who can continue to play there with their child. The square will ever cease to exist; it will always be there every time they open the door of the house. Yet the parents retain the right to decide how they wish to continue, or even to opt for the mayor who will dictate matters. Which one do they prefer?

5.3. THE ICEBERG

Well known to mediators, yet surprisingly effective in explaining the difference between:
 – a stalled negotiation through the use of positions; and

– the power to unblock which lies in incorporating into the conflict legitimate interests, underlying needs and future expectations together with the values, emotions and experiences of each party to the conflict.

5.4. SAILING ON A CALM SEA

The parties are like two seafarers on a boat sailing the high seas. They have to decide which direction to take and which island they wish to land on. If they wish to touch land, they will have no other choice but to reach a decision by consensus, since the only alternative is to become seafarers adrift on the high sea. While the mediator cannot make a decision which must be made by themselves, if he or she has the capacity, so long as the parties accept, he or she can calm the trouble waters so they can better navigate.

References

Bolaños Cartujo, I. (2008) *Hijos alineados y padres alienados. Mediación Familiar en rupturas conflictivas,* Reus Ed., Madrid.

Ortuño Muñoz, P. et al (2007) *Sistemas alternativos a la resolución de conflictos (ADR): La mediación en las jurisdicciones civil y penal,* Fundación Alternativas, Madrid.

Parkinson, L. (2005) *Mediación Familiar. Teoría y práctica: principios y estrategias operativas,* Gedisa, Barcelona.

Spaces for Conflict Management in Healthcare Organisations: from Theory to Practice

Judith Esparrica[1], Carles Cervera[2], Immacualada Armadans[3]
[1]Consorci Santiari Integral
[2]Institut de Seguretat Pública de Catalunya
[3]Facultat de Psicologia, Universitat de Barcelona

Abstract. In the context of a complex and changing society, healthcare organisations have to face conflict situations. Spaces for conflict management constitute a better way of managing people in terms of organisational dynamics. This paper presents a review of the theoretical background and a case study. The situation is presented as a new opportunity to transform healthcare organisations by focusing on the human resources department and/or the management of the added value of people.

Keywords: Healthcare organisations, Conflict, Human resources, Space for conflict management.

1. Introduction

Western societies are undergoing a social and historical transition of major importance. Ulrick Beck, Anthony Giddens, Manuel Castells or Zygmunt Bauman and other social scientists have stated that the industrial society constructed during the 19th and 20th centuries is moving towards a post-industrial society that is characterised by economic globalisation, the domain of information technology and new knowledge, and the individualisation of rights (Giddens, 1995). This context generates new opportunities and threats. Economic, cultural and technological globalisation has led to:
- economic and interdependent markets;
- work becoming highly flexible and also increasingly deregulated;
- bigger social inequalities;
- more economic migrants; and
- many people feeling vulnerable and experiencing various forms and degrees of social exclusion due to of their group ethnicity, origin, sex, social class, age, health, sexual orientation or having limited access to education and citizenship.

In the new society, traditional institutions such as family, education, health, religion and security forces that comprised industrial society and the welfare state have become much more complex. This new society not only requires new networks and economic and social structures, but also new forms of highly complex interpersonal and intercultural relationships. The consequences of this situation are more problems, personal suffering and conflict.

The social change process that institutions must face is evident in healthcare organisations. This dynamic and constant evolving process is linked to the numerous interrelated situations found in these organisations. Notable aspects of healthcare situations include the following: the nature of healthcare organisations; the diversity and number of elements of which they are composed; the number and kind of people who interact with them; and the relationships that exist with the environment and between the different actors in the organisation (Novel, 2009). Illness and its treatment can cause tension. In general, healthcare professionals have to work under pressure and healthcare users and their relatives frequently experience emotional shock as a result of illness. Adequate management of these situations usually overwhelms the available healthcare and health resources (Armadans, Mola, Igual, 2009; Armadans, Aneas, Soria, Bosch, 2009).

Therefore, healthcare organisations are under constant pressure and there is a high potential for the development of conflicts. Conflicts may arise with the healthcare users or exist within the organisation. The systemic nature of health organisations means that there is interrelation between multiple levels, functions and actors that usually make it a highly difficult system to manage. Consequently, conflict management is of strategic importance, as it can help such organisations to be productive and efficient in response to the challenges they face.

2. Conflict Management in healthcare organisations

A variety of approaches to conflicts is required to face the situations that arise in complex healthcare organisations and to ensure health services. Healthcare organisations use several methods to manage their conflicts. Trials were common in the past, while mediation has been introduced recently (Stoller, 2008). Mediation can be described in several ways, according to the various existing models. In general, it is a process in which a third person intervenes to help in the management of a conflict between people or groups, using language and influence over the interpersonal relationship (De Diego and Guillén, 2006).

Although mediation is gaining ground in conflict management in healthcare organisations, there is still strong resistance to this technique (Mayer, 2008). This resistance to mediation, as well as the limitations that trials entail, indicates that there is a strong need to address conflicts using another conflict management approach. This approach should include several conflict management tools which can then be selected according to the conflict situation. The approach should be in line with the organisation and consider it from a systemic perspective. Due to the complexity of health organisations, conflicts must be addressed using an integrated model of resolution and management that incorporates a systemic perspective (Constantino and Merchant, 1997).

Professionals who already use systemic methods in healthcare organisations emphasize that productive conflict management leads to higher quality services (Blanch, 2000).

Conflict prevention and management programs that are based on an integrated and systemic perspective have the following characteristics (Hayes, Hetzler, Morrison, Gerardi, 2006):

1. Promotion of justice, equality, empowerment and control
2. Provision of tools to improve communication, collaboration and confidence
3. Obtainment of more creative solutions
4. Maintenance and promotion of relationships
5. Efficiency in terms of time and economic cost

The diversity of variables involved in a healthcare organisation creates an environment that is affected by numerous problems and conflict situations. More tools are required to manage the variety and types of conflicts that occur in these organisations.

Mediation systems offer a number of processes, techniques and tools that improve individual skills and enable people in an organisation to work together in a culturally competent way. The conflict resolution systems that are currently used in healthcare organisations have some limitations and experience some resistance. Consequently, other techniques must be incorporated, in addition to those that are already in use.

Conflict situations are diverse. Trials are not always appropriate and entail high temporary and financial costs for healthcare organisations. Negotiations are hard, extensive and usually competitive. Finally, healthcare workers and professionals have to manage difficult situations with users and their respective families. Therefore, different conflict management tools need to be incorporated into the system. For example, facilitation and mediation have been used to manage conflicts and to make agreements in healthcare organisations, in particular when there is a loss of confidence in the system and perceived differences which prevent the actors from taking decisions and solving problems.

A space for dialogue needs to be created. Dialogue should be understood as a process that enables people and groups to achieve their common objectives by working in a collaborative manner and considering the differences among the actors. For example, coaching, appreciative dialogues or organisational constellations provide tools for managing personal relationships positively. In this respect, people and groups are more willing to move forward, and to leave daily conflicts in the organisation aside (Gerardi and Font-Guzman, 2006).

A conflict management method that incorporates the potential of different conflict management approaches (trials, mediation, coaching, appreciative dialogues, etc.) and uses them according to needs represents an opportunity for organisations and actors to grow, transform and learn.

2.1. MEDIATION SYSTEMS' APPROACH IN HEALTHCARE ORGANISATIONS

Some healthcare organisations are beginning to incorporate alternative conflict management tools, for example mediation. The presence of an inside mediator-expert in alternative conflict management, who works with the actors of the organisation and is familiar with the organisational dynamics and culture, ensures that conflict management is treated in a natural way by the organisation.

However, one person cannot manage all of the conflict demands. Different conflicts require different management methods. Likewise, the ability to change must come from a mediation system that incorporates varied professional profiles (Hayes, Hetzler; Morrison, Gerardi, 2006). A working team made up of people with different backgrounds in the organisation makes conflict management highly flexible. Consequently, actions and responses to a conflict can be more accurate and precise in different conflict situations. In this respect, organisations require an internal system that periodically interacts with healthcare workers and the mediation space, and takes into account the organisation's values and conflicts. Moreover, many organisations do not want conflicts to be managed by external consultants; they prefer to rely on internal programs (Schnitman and Schnitman, 2000).

There are several advantages to a mediation system with these characteristics, such as the system described at the end of this paper. A mediation system can manage change through a transformative conception of the conflict (the conflict as an opportunity) and of the meaning, work and social environment in the organisations (Vinyamata, 1999). We consider that mediation systems should be part of health organisations' human resources departments for several reasons. Human resources departments safeguard the career development and welfare of the organisation's healthcare professionals and employees. The organisation itself should be considered a systemic network.

Human resources departments are of strategic importance to organisations. Aspects related to people and their value are important and represent one of the main factors of success for organisations. In fact, some of the main strategies of organisations include concepts that are implemented and managed by the human resources department, for example:

- the capacity to attract and retain qualified staff;
- changes in organisational culture and employees' attitudes;
- changes in managerial and executive teams; and
- improvements in staff efficiency.

This strategic importance can be seen in the significant increase concerning investment in human resources in recent years. Although few changes can be observed in Europe, in the United States there has been approximately a 22% increase in spending since 2000.

Organisations that consider that people are their main asset also give more importance to the human resources department in their strategic plans. Such organisations tend to have a high number of employees (like healthcare organisations), and also need to constantly select new staff, negotiate collective agreements, train staff, take care of organisational health and prevent work hazards (Sarries and Casares, 2008).

Human resources departments increasingly need to understand people's problems. There has been a rise in professional participation in several areas and people are specifically trained to manage human resources in an organisation. So the main function of the human resources department in large organisations is to attain an environment in which confrontations are reduced and collaboration and transformation are progressively incorporated. Therefore, the traditional administrative responsibilities of human resources departments are changing (Sarries and Casares 2008).

With regard to this new conception of human resources departments, a mediation system that is based on the aforementioned characteristics should be an integral part of this department's strategy. The focus of human resources departments and the characteristics of their employees make them a perfect place for managing conflict and social change.

3. Space for prevention and alternative conflict management (E-PRAC)

To manage conflict and social change in healthcare organisations, a space is needed for conflict prevention and alternative conflict management. This space must be legitimate and effective for its users, in accordance with the main E-PRAC objectives established by the Integral Health Consortium (CSI).[1]

---

[1] The CSI was created to provide quality health and social services based on the expectations and needs of citizens, scientific evidence, continuity and care through the

The CSI is defined as a model organisation of people for people. For its development, a human resources model based on specific values is used. The corporate values of the CSI are: professional quality, team work, development and commitment.

However, a series of intense conflicts arose in the organisation, as shown by the results of different studies and the 2005 report (absenteeism indicators, disagreements and environmental work surveys). Consequently, the CSI management set up a conflict prevention and alternative management service: the mediation E-PRAC service, which is based in the human resources department. The aim of this service is to address conflicts in the organisation.

The E-PRAC service offers conflict prevention and alternative conflict management to solve internal (workers) and external (users, suppliers) conflicts that appear in CSI centres, and to establish operative procedures and the tools required to manage the service successfully.

The main functions of the E-PRAC model are:
- To train managers, supervisors and other people in the organisation in conflict management procedures so that they can become experts in their respective work areas.
- To create a network of natural voluntary mediators through a process of selection (any member of the organisation can ask to become a natural mediator; including members of the organisation's board, collaborators, supervisors, etc.) to manage, prevent and intervene in conflicts in the CSI.
- To provide mediation tools and skills for the mediation process.
- To teach healthcare professionals and workers specific strategies for conflict management.
- To foster a positive approach to conflicts through dialogue, in order to promote coexistence and personal and professional well-being.
- To create a culture of mediation in the area of healthcare.

The main characteristics of the E-PRAC model are:
- Internal service.
- Part of human resources management.
- Required by CSI professionals and employees (general management, company board, supervisors, departments, collaborators, conflicting parties, even when only one party requests the services).
- Required by CSI users.
- Focused on the process.
- Therapeutic, legal and educational interventions, when necessary.
- Aimed at people (employees, professionals and users) in the organisation who are involved in a conflict.

---

efficient use of the resources and with competent, committed and satisfied healthcare professionals.

− Interactive work with multidisciplinary contents.
− Protection of basic labour rights and equal opportunities.
− Advice, design, evaluation, strategic plans, training, etc.
− Systemic approach to conflicts.
− Involvement, responsibility and commitment of the mediator for each
    part of the conflict.
− Direct request made to the mediator by e-mail or telephone.
The main advantages of the E-PRAC model are:
− Workers feel that they are listened by the organisation.
− Fast and flexible service.
− Any natural mediator, professional or employee can be chosen freely by
    the person who is involved in a conflict.
− Conflict management during working hours.
The E-PRAC model brings knowledge, tools and skills to all the actors in the healthcare organisation (Mayer, 2008). In this respect, the theoretical model described here demonstrates that it can be possible for the parties involved in a conflict to recognise their responsibility in the development of the conflict as well as that of the other party. On many occasions, this enables an agreement to be reached because it represents the consequence of a change produced in the relationships between participants. This change is possible because the mediation process stresses the revaluation and recognition of others. However, we should assess the empirical results of these interventions to confirm the value of these conflict management spaces.

4. Conclusions

Healthcare organisations, which are defined by their complexity, clearly reflect the social change that has occurred over the last few decades. As a result of this change, conflict management has now an evident strategic role in the improvement of organisations and the development of the professionals who work in them.

In the future, the management of conflict situations in healthcare organisations could involve the creation of new spaces for alternative conflict management from a systemic perspective. An important role could be played by human resources departments or any other integrated systems in the organisation that are responsible for managing people and their values. Our decisions will affect our future and our welfare in healthcare organisations.

References

Armadans, I.; Mola, B.; Igual, B. (2009) "La mediació en l'àmbit de la salut: una nova opció alternativa de gestió de conflictes", *Materials del Llibre Blanc de la Mediació a Catalunya,* Col·lecció Justicia i Societat n. 32, Generalitat de Catalunya, Departament de Justicia, Centre d'Estudis Jurídics i Formació Especialitzada, pp. 119-127.

Armadans, I.; Aneas, A.; Soria, M. A.; Bosch, Ll. (2009) "La mediación en el ámbito de la salud", *Medicina Clínica*, vol. 133, pp. 187-192.

Blanch, A (2000) "Mental Health Systems Try New Approaches to Conflict Resolution", *Networks: Practical Tools for a Changing Environment,* National Technical Assistance Center for State Mental Health Planning, available at: http://www.nasmhpd.org/general_files/publications/ntac_pubs/networks/fallmai n.pdf (accessed 1 July 2010)

Constantino, C.; Merchant, C. (1997) *Diseños de sistemas para enfrentar conflictos,* Ediciones Juan Granica, Barcelona.

De Diego, R.; Guillén, C. (2006) *Mediación; Proceso, tácticas y técnicas*, Editorial Pirámide, Madrid.

Gerardi, D; Font-Guzman, J. (2006) *Conflict at End of Live. A growing need for dispute resolution practices,* Creghton Lawyer.

Hayes, L.; Hetzler, D.; Morrison, V.; Gerardi, D. (2004) "Curing conflict: a prescription for ADR in healthcare", *Dispute Resolution Magazine-Journal of American Bar Association, Dispute Resolution Section*, pp. 5-7.

Luis, S.; Casares, E. (2002) *Buenas prácticas de recursos humanos,* Ed. ESIC, Madrid.

Mayer, B. (2008) *Más allá de la neutralidad, cómo superar la crisis de la resolución de conflictos,* Editorial Gedisa, Barcelona

Novel, G. (2009) "Sistemes de mediació en organitzacions complexes: el cas de la salut", *Materials del Llibre Blanc de la Mediació a Catalunya*, Col·lecció Justicia i Societat n. 32, Generalitat de Catalunya, Departament de Justicia, Centre d'Estudis Jurídics i Formació Especialitzada, pp. 263-272.

Ritzer, G. (2001) *Teoría Sociológica Moderna*, Mc Graw Hill, 5th edition.

Schnitman, D.; Schnitman, J. (2000) *Resolución de conflictos. Nuevos diseños, nuevos contextos,* Editorial Granica, Buenos Aires, Argentina.

Stoller, S. (2008) *Mediation in the Healthcare Context: Challanges and Responses,* Center for Mediation Services, City of New York, available at: http://www.nyc.gov/html/oath/pdf/Stoller.pdf (accessed 1 July 2010)

Vinyamata, E. (1999) *Manual de prevención y resolución de conflictos: Conciliación, mediación, negociación*, Editorial Ariel, Barcelona.

Mediators and the Catalan Health System

Blanca Igual Ayerbe[1], Bruna Mola Sanna[2], Eva M. Monge Baciero[3]
[1]*Fundació Carles Pi i Sunyer*
[2]*Universitat de Barcelona*
[3]*Institut Català de la Salut*

Abstract. The aim of this paper is to analyse the types of mediators who work in the health sector. Firstly, we link definitions of mediation to a categorisation of types of mediation and mediators that is based on two variables: the mediation as a structured process and the mediator's level of training or specialisation. Secondly, we analyse the characteristics of the Catalan health system, health organisations in general and the conflicts that arise in these organisations in order to define the specific features of mediation in the health sector. This is an entirely conceptual attempt, and is therefore just a starting point, as little work has been carried out in this area up to date.

Keywords: Professional mediation, Natural mediation, Informal mediation, Culture of Peace, Conflicts, Health sector.

> Perhaps the most simple and significant reason why people argue is the lack of an alternative.
> William L. Ury (2005)

1. Categorisation of types of mediation and mediator profiles

There are many and varied definitions of mediation. The practice of mediation covers such a broad field that a strict definition is not possible (Folberg and Taylor, 1992).

Some authors describe mediation as a method and, consequently, as a structured process with particular emphasis on its stages. For example, Vinyamata (2003) defines mediation as a communication process between conflicting parties that is assisted by an impartial mediator, who tries to get those involved in the dispute to reach an agreement by themselves. The agreement should enable good relations to be reestablished and put an end to, or at least mitigate, the conflict. Such action is preventative and leads to improved coexistence. Taylor (1981; cited in Folberg & Taylor, 1992) considers that the realistic goal of mediation is to resolve disagreements or handle conflicts. In this case, mediation involves a series of defined stages and the use of techniques to attain the required objectives. Both definitions indicate that time is required to complete all the stages, which have a certain continuity and lead to a result.

Other definitions refer to mediation as a tool or an instrument for intervening in order to resolve conflicts. Of particular note are definitions that refer to mediation as a strategy or a set of basic communication techniques for positively managing or transforming a conflict (open questions, active listening, positive paraphrasing, positive summary and positive reframing, among others). Mediation can also be seen as intervention, mainly through the use of language, in interpersonal or intergroup relationships to help to resolve a conflict (De Diego and Guillén, 2006).

If we consider mediation as a structured process, then specific, specialised training is required. In this training, mediators must learn the stages and the necessary skills for each stage. Such skills are related to rational, psycho-emotional and identity aspects of conflicts. This definition of mediation could be associated with the figure of a professional, institutional or formal mediator. In the health sector, this kind of mediator will carry out a specific task for an institution or health organisation and its clients. These are expert professionals who have been trained to resolve well-defined conflicts. Thus, they must have basic and specialised training. In France, for example, Article 1 of the Code of Mediation used by the National Centre for Mediation states that:

"Mediation is an optional procedure that requires the voluntary and explicit agreement of the parties involved to commit themselves to an action (mediation) with the assistance of a independent and neutral third party (the mediator), who is specially trained in this field" (cited in Six, 1997).

However, if mediation is considered a tool or intervention instrument, the approach is broader and more flexible. It takes into account aspects of the culture of mediation that go beyond the strict application of a process of conflict resolution in defined and successive stages. These stages can only be undertaken by a professional with highly specific knowledge. Thus, natural mediation and informal mediation also have their place. Natural mediation does not require the level of training and specialisation found in professional mediation, and informal mediation does not require any specific kind of training, according to our approach.

In reference to mediation in family companies, De Federico and Villanueva (in Vinyamata, 2004) distinguish between formal and informal mediation. They define formal mediation as that which is undertaken by a professional mediator, who is not linked in any way to the family company and applies a structured conflict management process. Manso (2001) considers that such mediators should be highly qualified, technically educated and specialised, with deep knowledge of mediation techniques and of commercial, legal and corporate aspects. Villanueva (1999) adds that a flexible approach to conflicts is essential, as is experience in family relationships from the perspective of psychology, sociology and family law. In contrast, informal mediation is defined as that which is undertaken by a person who is not part of the family company and who uses mediation techniques to generate informal spaces for managing and resolving conflicts. Informal mediators act as facilitators, due to their prestige and the respect that they are given by members of the family. According to these authors, the main difference between formal and informal mediation lies in the structure of the process. De Federico and Villanueva (in Vinyamata, 2004) also distinguish between formal mediation intervention (the process of mediation is partially structured) and informal mediation intervention (there is no mediation process as such).

Another document that discusses types of mediators is the ten good practices for citizen and community mediation (family mediation 2008), which was drawn up as part of the knowledge management program, *Programa Compartim*, promoted by the Catalan Department of Justice. This document defines three types of mediation that correspond with three types of mediators:

1. *Informal mediation:* this is undertaken by professionals for members of the family, etc. to bring the parties closer together. In this case, mediation is not the main objective of the profession or task. In fact, the function of the mediator is often undertaken without any expressed intention, as it is just another aspect of the individual's professional role, for example, that of municipal police, social workers, community educators, intercultural mediators, etc.

2. *Urban mediation:* this is undertaken by natural and voluntary mediators.
   a) Natural mediators are people who can influence a social group and choose to devote some of their time to resolve conflicts in the community that they represent.
   b) Voluntary mediators periodically devote some time to help to resolve conflicts between citizens.

3. *Formal mediation*: this is a profession. The aim is to undertake tasks according to the principles of mediation and to receive a professional fee for this activity.

To highlight the importance of non-professional mediators, Faget (2001; cited in Villagrasa, 2004) defined mediation as a new method and process for resolving conflicts in western societies that involves the creation of a culture that promotes responsibility and dialogue as an innovative way of attaining social understanding. According to Ury (2005), we all have the opportunity to mediate informally on a daily basis. Supervisors can mediate for their subordinates, employees for their heads, colleagues for their peers and managers for their team members. People may not even be aware of the fact that they are mediating. However, mediation is definitely involved when an individual listens attentively to the people who are arguing, asks them what they really want, suggests potential approaches and urges them to consider the cost of not reaching an agreement. The mediator does not aim to determine who is right and who is wrong, instead, he/she tries to get to the heart of the dispute and to determine the interests of each party, their needs, concerns, desires, fears and aspirations.

However, other authors, such as Six (1997), do not agree with those who consider that mediation requires a kind of innate state or those who see mediation as an art that is difficult to transmit. Six (1997) considers that the identity of the mediator is acquired, rather than innate. Although some people are drawn to mediation by their natural inclinations or temperament, it is a practice that must be worked on, updated and perfected. Therefore, it requires a training process and constant retraining. The identity of a mediator is not obtained once and for always, but must constantly be constructed. Thus, mediators must change their perspectives and their way of conceiving their relationships with each party. This approach can help us to understand that to act as a mediator, an individual must attain an essential level of maturity. In addition, natural and informal mediators have a different function from professional mediators.

2. The Catalan health system and mediation in health organisations

Mediators who work in the different areas of the Catalan health system find an environment with highly specific characteristics. Knowledge of these characteristics helps to improve understanding of the conflicts that can arise and ensures that the mediators are better trained to manage such conflicts effectively.

The Spanish state covers the health needs of all its citizens through the National Health System, which is funded by taxes. The General Health Act (LGS)[1], established under Article 149.1.16 of the Spanish Constitution, states that the health system shall focus on promoting health and preventing diseases, and that public health care shall be available for the entire Spanish population.

The National Health System is made up of a network of services in each autonomous community. In the framework of this model, the Health Care Organisation in Catalonia Act (LOSC)[2] was drawn up. The aim of this Act

---

[1] General Health Act 14/25 April 1986.

[2] Health Care Organisation in Catalonia Act 15/9 July 1990.

was to organise the public health system in accordance with some significant principles, including the following:

– *Universal* provision of individual and group health services for all residents of Catalonia.
– *Integration of services*: the creation of a mixed model in which all health resources are part of one public network, regardless of whether or not they are publicly owed. This network includes all the organisations that have traditionally been dedicated to health care (mutual benefit associations, foundations, consortiums, church centres).

The Catalan health service is a publically funded system which provides universal cover for all residents of Catalonia. The agency responsible for public health insurance is the Catalan Health Service (CatSalut), which is a public organisation attached to the Catalan Department of Health. CatSalut[3] ensures that all Catalan citizens have access to comprehensive, quality health care and guarantees the provision of public health cover. It offers

– primary health care, which is the first level of access to health care and is mainly provided in primary health care centres (CAPs); and
– specialised health care, which is the second level of access to public health and includes hospital, social health, psychiatric and mental health care, as well as drug dependency services and other specialised resources.

An alternative to the public health system is private health care or private health insurance organisations. There are two options:

– joining private organisations that offer health care services to members who pay a monthly fee for one of several types of policies (including packages that guarantee access to almost all health care services, and policies for outpatient services and hospitalisation only); or
– requesting and paying for services or private health care when needed.

---

[3] www10.gencat.net/catsalut/cat

Catalan Health Model

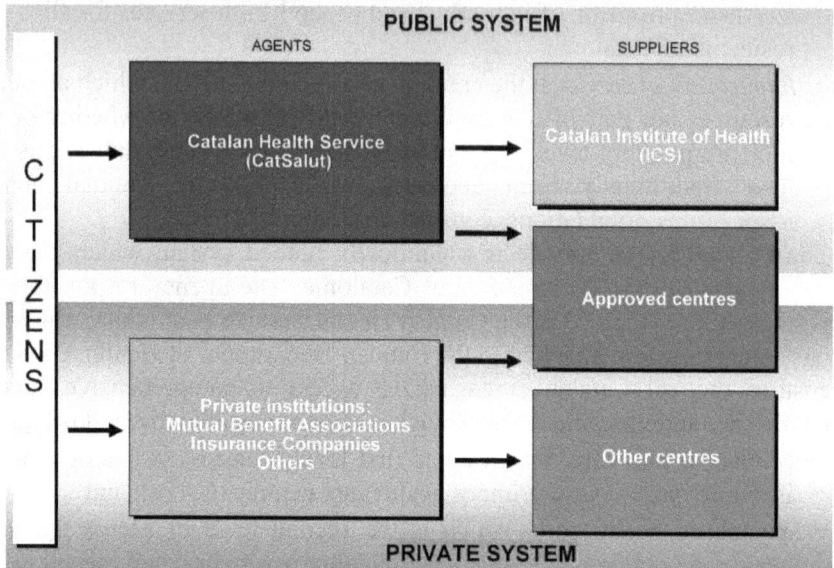

Figure 1. Health care System in Catalonia

Therefore, the Catalan Health System is complex and made up of various agents:

- Citizens, who are at the heart of the system and are the users of the health services. They participate increasingly actively and take even more responsibility for health care processes and clinical decisions.
- Health care professionals, who are in charge of meeting the population's health care expectations. They provide their services in multidisciplinary and interdisciplinary teams in various health care centres and establishments (CAPs, hospitals, social health centres, residential centres, etc.).
- Health care organisations, whose missions, visions and values are aimed at providing quality health services.

In addition to this diverse system, a very high emotional component is one of the factors that spark conflicts. This factor is related to the vulnerability of users, due to their health care experiences, the pressures on the health care system under which professionals work, and the expectations and demands of society, among others.

Conflicts that require the assistance of health care mediators emerge in the relationships between the agents listed above. Such conflicts can be defined by classifying them as internal or external, depending on the parties involved. Internal conflicts are those that are managed within a health institution. They may be between the organisation and its employees (group conflicts) or between employees (interprofessional conflicts, which could involve individuals or groups). External conflicts include those in which one of the parties is a health organisation or its members and the other party is external, either another institution or users of health care services.

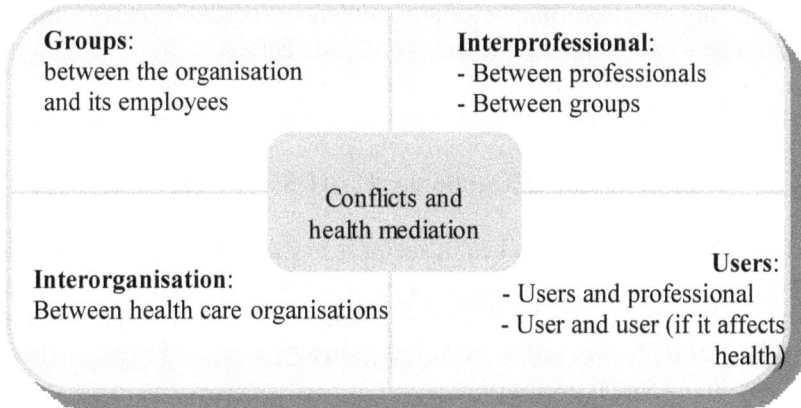

Groups:
between the organisation
and its employees

Interprofessional:
- Between professionals
- Between groups

Conflicts and
health mediation

Interorganisation:
Between health care organisations

Users:
- Users and professional
- User and user (if it affects health)

Figure 2. Conflicts categorization at Health Organizations

All of the above indicates that the figure of mediator in any of its forms (professional, natural or informal) has its place within the system. The common aim of all these mediators is to disseminate the culture of peace within this sector, and to raise users' and professionals' awareness of the use of dialogue instead of confrontation. However, in addition to this common aim, each type of mediator manages conflicts and tries to stop them from escalating through the use of their skills and knowledge.

Thus, the informal mediator, who has no specific training in mediation, uses his/her innate communication skills, often unconsciously, to promote coexistence and to participate in managing conflicts. An informal mediator could be any team member who is recognised for his/her conciliation skills, for example the mediator-manager cited by Floyer (2004). Natural mediators do have certain specific training in conflict resolution and an influence over their organisations. They act to promote understanding between people through dialogue, and also undertake conflict management. However, unlike informal mediators, they undertake this process deliberately on the basis of their training. Natural mediators include directors or customer service professionals who have been trained in mediation skills. Although they do not engage in a structured mediation process, they facilitate conflict management. Finally, professional mediators use the mediation process to help the parties involved in a conflict to find the best solution to their problem.

According to to Ury (2005), the success of a company depends on the ability of its employees to resolve the numerous conflicts that arise within it. Nevertheless, for employees to gain such abilities, the organizational culture must favour and promote values related to the culture of peace. In this respect, Farré (2004) states that an organisational culture can implicitly or explicitly protect and justify behaviour, attitudes and structural elements of the organisation that produce violence. In such cases, mediation activities will not attain the expected satisfactory results. Therefore, the values of mediation and of the organisation must be in line.

3. Experiences in Catalonia: UMICS and MEDIMAYOR

Although mediation in the health sector is in its initial stages, we consider it appropriate to describe two specific examples of the activities that are being undertaken: the Mediation Department of the Catalan Institute of Health (UMICS) in relation to primary health care; and the "Medimayor" project in the social health field.

3.1. MEDIATION DEPARTMENT OF THE CATALAN INSTITUTE OF HEALTH (UMICS)

From November 2006 to January 2009, a project was undertaken to establish an ICS mediation service in the primary care sector. This project was based on the idea that major health organisations should employ professionals who are trained in Alternative Dispute Resolution (ADR). The development of a culture of mediation within an institution can have many benefits:
− Promote civic coexistence between professionals and give them the opportunity to participate and be jointly responsible for managing their differences.
− Increase acceptance of different perceptions and opinions, based on respect for others.
− Increase participation, which reduces apathy and disillusionment.
− Improve the dialogue between people/groups.
− Enable the conflict to be positively accepted.
Team of professional mediators: in order to start up this project, six professionals were selected from different job categories (doctors, nurses, managers, etc.). All members of the team took the Master's Degree in Mediation in Health Organisations at the University of Barcelona (IL3).
   Action areas: the activities undertaken during this pilot test were focused on three areas:

- Training and dissemination: managers' awareness of mediation was raised and they were trained in conflict resolution. In addition, tasks of dissemination were undertaken to inform staff in each primary health care teams (EAPs) about mediation.
- Advice on the prevention and management of conflicts was given to members of the institution that requested this service.
- Formal mediation processes were undertaken.

3.2. "MEDIMAYOR" PILOT PROGRAM

Research funded by the Spanish Institute for the Elderly and Social Services (IMSERSO) was carried out between the months of January and December 2007. Participants included the University of Barcelona, the Ramón Llull University and the University of the Basque Country. This research was based on a consideration of the importance of social transformation in the aging population. It involved a theoretical and empirical reflection on scientific and social evidence of the utility and future of mediation as an intervention tool in conflict situations involving dependent and independent elderly. One of its aims was to examine in depth the opportunities for using mediation in an intervention program for the elderly.

To achieve the aforementioned objective, the team developed a basic program focused on working on conflicts and relationships of coexistence to develop strategies that enabled an atmosphere of trust to be created, decisions to be taken by consensus and work to be undertaken on cooperation, analysis and negotiation. This multifaceted intervention was aimed at users, professionals and families and helped latent conflicts to emerge in social health centres. These conflicts could then be managed by a professional mediator.

4. Conclusions

On the basis of the definitions analysed throughout this paper and the authors' knowledge of the health sector, we reached the following conclusions.

If we only consider definitions that refer to mediation as a structured process, then we are supporting the idea of health mediation that is carried out exclusively by professional mediators.

However, if we are more flexible and consider a wider range of definitions that describe mediation as an intervention tool or a culture of dialogue to promote peaceful coexistence, then we can include the figures of natural and informal mediators, as they play a role within health institutions.

– In the health sector, natural mediators emerge in their own group to meet its needs. Their function is to facilitate communication between the conflicting parties so that they can manage their differences and improve their bad relationship. They are members of the community in which they act and have moral authority and a certain influence over the other members.

– Although informal mediators have not been specifically trained to manage conflicts, they use their innate qualities and skills that predispose them to mediation (a conciliatory attitude, empathy, generosity, respect, patience, serenity, listening skills and the ability to generate trust). They can be essential to prevent a conflict or in managing a conflict when it is in an early stage.

– Formal mediators are those individuals who have received basic academic training as well as specific training in mediation and who also have wide knowledge of the specific sector in which they will work, which in this case is the health sector. As a high level of competence is required of formal mediators, this professional category needs to be regulated.

– Health organisations need to include a culture of peace within their values in order to increase awareness of positive conflict management.

References

Armadans, I. et al. *La mediación como instrumento de gestión del conflicto en el ámbito de las personas mayores y autonómas*, research report, available at: http://www.publicacions.ub.es/doi/documents/236.pdf (accessed 5 July 2010)

De Diego, R.; Guillén, C. (2006) *Mediación. Procesos, tácticas y técnicas*, Pirámide, Madrid.

Farré, S. (2004) *Gestión de conflictos: taller de mediación. Un enfoque socioafectivo*, Ariel Social, Barcelona.

Floyer, A. (2004) *Como utilizar la mediación para resolver conflictos en las organizaciones*, Paidos, Barcelona.

Folger, J.; Taylor, A. (1992) *Mediación. Resolución de conflictos sin Litigio*, Ed. Limusa, México.

Manso Díaz-Laviada (2001) *Mediación y empresa familiar. Jornadas sobre mediación en la familia y en la empresa familiar*, Valencia, 26th -27th October 2001.

Six, J.F. (1997) *Dinámica de la mediación*, Paidos, Buenos Aires.

Ury, W. (2005). *Alcanzar la paz. Resolución de conflictos y mediación en la familia, el trabajo y el mundo*, Paidos, Barcelona.

Villagrasa, C. (coord.) (2004) *La mediació. L'alternativa multidisciplinària a la resolució dels conflictos*, Ed. Pòrtic, Universitat de Barcelona, Barcelona.

Vinyamata, E. (2003) *Aprender Mediación*. Paidós Aprender, Barcelona.
Vinyamata, E. (2004) *Guerra y paz en el trabajo: conflictos y conflictología en las organizaciones*. Tirant lo Blanc, Valencia.
Villanueva, N. (1999) "De naranjas, pasteles, juegos de cartas, puzzles... y otras definiciones de conflicto en mediación familiar" in *Actas del Congreso Internacional de Mediación Familiar*. Ed. Aranzadi, Barcelona.

Mediation Systems in Complex Organisations: The Case of Healthcare

Glòria Novel Martí
Mediation Observatory, University of Barcelona

Abstract. This chapter starts with a description of the concept of complexity in organisations, and develops a series of elements which are generally valid for any organisation that can be defined as complex. Based on the conviction that healthcare organisations are extremely complex and can thus be used as a paradigmatic case to study the topic of organisational mediation, we hereby present the results of a healthcare mediation project after three years of research (2004-2008). This project was carried out in Catalonia and implemented by the University of Barcelona in close partnership with the Department of Health of the Catalan Government and other partner healthcare institutions, which we would like to thank for their support and involvement during those years. Likewise, we would like to specifically acknowledge all the people who have participated enthusiastically in the project from the beginning up to now and who are making the dream to create a "third side health organisation" come true.

Keywords: Promotion of relational healthcare, Complex organisations, Conflict management, Conflict prevention, Mediation process, Mediation systems, Mediation units.

1. Complex organisations

The concept of complex organisation is related to a specific type of company and the relationships that are established therein, as well as the current social context where needs, requirements and expectations are constantly changing.

On the one hand, the complexity of an organisation stems from various elements which should be considered, such as: the type of company in question, the diversity of elements which make up the organisation, the number and type of persons who interact, the relationships established between the various actors within the organisational system and their relationship with their immediate environment.

In this type of organisations, there are a large number of highly interrelated variables that are linked to certain prevalent dynamics and which make it impossible to consider simple decision-making processes when faced with issues, and even less in situations of conflict.

On the other hand, the context we have to cope with today implies that there are certain characteristics related to the existence of multiple relational networks, requirements for quick feedback, synchronisation of activities, interdependence to achieve objectives, high specialisation level, need to reduce costs and consequently make the most of resources, possibility of short cycles to innovate, obligation to keep up the pace under pressure, etc.

1.1. HEALTHCARE ORGANISATIONS: ARE THEY THE MOST COMPLEX ORGANISATIONS?

When we analyze healthcare organisations, we see that they are – compared to any others – the most complex ones since, on top of all the previously mentioned elements, we must add other characteristics which increase those aspects of complexity and affect the general organisation, especially the relationships established therein. We can mention the following main elements:
- *The type of service provided:* aimed at the care of people facing illness, loss or death, which means that these institutions are places with a high emotional content.
- *The type of personnel who work there*: there are personnel with the same professional category, but different types of contracts, some with a certain number of years of service with the institution and a high level of turnover between the various departments or services.
- *The level of interdependence in the work which is carried out*: there are services with a high interdependence level, in which teams must negotiate objectives, practice or procedure so that independent and/or common results are achieved though increasing the risk of conflict (Floyer, 1993).
- *The requirement for specialisation:* this type of organisations requires a high level of specialisation both in the organisation itself and for the people who work there, which may lead to discrepancies in team objectives in relation to the overall organisation (Burton, 1991).
- *The requirement for team work:* in organisations with such a level of interdependence, teams must work in a systematic and multidisciplinary way. This increases the quantity and quality of interpersonal interactions as well as the confrontation of differences which appear and with which they have to coexist in an inclusive and collaborative manner.
- *The type of decisions:* there are certain types of decisions at management level that are similar to any other organisation. However, at individual and group level there is a wide array of situations where, with deficient resources and life-threatening factors for the people involved, decisions about treatment or care must be made urgently.

– *The type of relationships that are created:* Given the highly emotional content of healthcare centres and the type of services that are provided, relationships are the major element around which daily life revolves. In fact, the therapeutic relationship itself that is established between healthcare professionals and users of the system is a decisive element in achieving confidence in the health teams. This, in turn, facilitates, or not, that the medical treatment and orders of nursing, or other professional staff, are followed. On the other hand, given the intense and close contact that is typical of the work carried out by healthcare teams, with distinct and complementary roles, cultural issues that affect beliefs and decision making systems, gender elements, etc., we can assert that these teams can be defined as *"human families"*[1] with relational components typical of the family system. That is to say, in the long term there is a high level of interaction, meaningfulness and need to coexist and deal with differences.

All those elements enable us to define healthcare organisations as being particularly complex, where relationships and networks are multiplied, and whose transformation into "third side organisations", as Ury calls them, is highly recommended by implementing a system to manage differences and build approval though peaceful dialogue and by means of mediation systems (Ury, 2000).

This type of "third side" organisations are successful in the way they provide means to promote relational healthcare, prevent conflicts from the start and deal with differences through mediation by restoring the organisational structure and thus creating added value in a way described in the following table:

Table I. "Third side" organisations: creating value

PROMOTING relational healthcare:
  ✓ Revitalizes hospitals
  ✓ Boosts synergies of the teams and best practices
  ✓ Creates shared satisfaction
 	
PREVENTING conflicts and related costs:
  ✓ Brings support to leaders, managers, groups and people
  ✓ Improves work atmosphere
  ✓ Induces expected changes
 	
DEALING with conflicts:
  ✓ Is useful to manage conflicts
  ✓ Restores confidence

---

[1] This term is used reformulating Ury's concept which defines humanity in general as a "big human family" (Ury, 2000)

> ✓ Reduces personnel and organisational costs
>
> RESTORING the organisational structure:
>   ✓ Promotes an appreciative and cooperative spirit
>   ✓ Increases individual and group potential
>   ✓ Enables direct action on improvement areas

GENERATING PRACTICES TO BUILD ORGANISATIONAL PEACE

Finally, we would add that mediators who work in this type of organisations should have a wide experience as consultants in conflict management as well as a specific mediator profile, all of which is gained from experience in inclusive, multidisciplinary and stable teams. They should also provide a model of behaviour for people in these organisations. Some of the characteristics that mediators who work with organisations should have are shown in the following table:

Table II. Profile of mediators' teams

CONSULTANT PROFILE:	MEDIATOR PROFILE:
✓ Initiative	✓ In-depth mediation knowledge
✓ Vision	✓ Mediator qualities
✓ Ability to analyze	✓ Communication skills
✓ Handle pressure	✓ Creativity
✓ Imagination	✓ Ability to adapt to change
✓ Experience	✓ Appreciative vision
✓ Communication	✓ Disposition to reflection and continuous learning
✓ Abstraction	✓ Teamwork
✓ Commitment	✓ Extensive and complementary abilities and knowledge
✓ Strategic thinking	
✓ Ability to motivate	

MULTIDISCIPLINARY, INCLUSIVE, COMPLEMENTARY AND STABLE TEAMS

2. An innovative project: Mediation in Healthcare Organisations

In the next sections, we present the results of research that started in Catalonia in 2004 and in which a strategic design was carried out to promote organisational change and the implementation of a mediation culture in the Catalan healthcare system. The aim was to teach mediation to healthcare professionals and open units in healthcare mediation (UMS).

1.2. INITIAL PERCEPTION

Initially, and based on the knowledge of the public health system through direct observation, information provided by professionals in active service and managers, as well as from press information about the occurrence of conflicts and aggressiveness in healthcare services, we concluded that there were various elements that made healthy work relationships difficult and generated undesired costs for healthcare organisations, such as:

- Conflicts which were either unaddressed or solved in an unsustainable manner.
- Dissatisfaction of professionals and users, loss in faith in the system, rising number of complaints or signs of discontent, fear of demands or aggressions, etc.
- Costs for organisations due to unsolved conflicts between workers or between workers and management, such as productivity loss (Folberg & Taylor, 1992), loss of managerial time, difficulty to make decisions, incorrect use of installations, lack of commitment, etc. (Femenia in Ganaropciones.com, 2006).
- Ignorance of mediation as an alternative and pacific method to settle conflict.
- Lack of an institutional model which would take alternative methods, specifically mediation, into consideration to prevent and manage organisational conflict.

1.3. SET OBJECTIVES

We designed a project in relation to the detected issues with the following *general objectives*:

- Create an innovative system within the public healthcare system with regard to settle conflicts and mediation.
- Disseminate mediation, as a movement belonging to the culture of peace, by creating spaces for dialogue within the Catalan healthcare system.

We can mention the following *specific objectives*:

- Start the Healthcare Mediation Project with pilot units in healthcare mediation (UMS),[2] and plan the continuity and expansion of the project in the various healthcare areas.
- Create a distinctive identity so that the healthcare institution is associated with a philosophy of quality and relationships based on negotiated agreements.

---

[2] UMS stands for *Unidades Pilotos de Mediación Sanitaria* in Spanish

- Improve the quality of medical care using creative ways to prevent increased costs.
- Use the system's own resources in order to create a mediation space with health professionals who are trained as mediators, thus helping to revitalize healthcare institutions.
- Take advantage of the "added value" generated by the implementation of a mediation project: Medical care is more human-oriented and teamwork becomes a reality.
- Create stable links of collaboration in healthcare institutions.

1.4. TRAINING PLAN

In accordance with those objectives, a training program was created – by the University – on two levels:
- A post-graduate course in *"Consulting and management of conflicts in healthcare organisations"*, with 250 training hours (theory 200h - practical 50h), aimed at people wishing to improve their skills in conflict management.
- A Master in *"Mediation in healthcare organisations. Consulting in conflict management"*, with 550 training hours (theory 250h - practical 300h), to train healthcare professionals to become mediators.

1.5. ACTION PLAN IMPLEMENTED THROUGH UMS

In October 2005, four units in healthcare mediation (UMS) were opened, both in hospitals and community healthcare centres, where second year Master students carried out 250 hours of practice in mediation systems. The following units opened the first year, all located in the Barcelona area:
- *Hospital Universitario Vall D´Hebron*
- *Consorci Sanitari de Terrasa*
- *Ámbito de Atención Primaria "Costa de Ponent"* [3]
- *Ámbito de Atención Primaria "Centre"*

The UMS were defined as "cross-department spaces for conflict management" and the type of conflicts that could be addressed were both internal (between professionals) and external (with users and their families).

The array of services offered was part of the "Mediation Systems". This concept goes beyond "mediation processes" and refers to a series of actions used – in a systemic way – to prevent and manage conflict as well as to

---

[3] As from the second year, this Unit and the *Atención Primaria "Centre"* Unit were both taken on and directly managed by the *Instituto Catalán de la Salud* (ICS – Catalonia National Health Service). The other two Units remained as part of the initial Project.

create mediation spaces in general. Consequently, the preventive actions deployed include *"training, counselling, managerial and group coaching, and groups of approval",* [4] and curative actions refer to *"Mediation"* processes.

Likewise, in order to guarantee the quality of services and training of students who were carrying out the practical part of their course, the following documents and guidelines were designed, for example: Guidelines for Case Management, Rules for Case Management in Mediation Units and a Mediator Code of Ethics.

This way, a series of register systems were designed to facilitate work in the UMS as well as the *assessment* which was planned in detail and carried out in order to present final results to teaching and healthcare authorities. These results included process, structure and result indicators.

1.6. CURRENT RESULTS

Presently, there are a total of 91 health professionals who are trained in mediation:
- 31 experts in conflict management
- 60 health specialist mediators.

As for data from the three years the UMS were running (2005-2008), a total of 142 actions were carried out with the following characteristics:
- 77 solved cases of active conflict involving 232 users or parties, with curative-type actions:
  - 34 Counselling actions
  - 34 Mediation actions
  - 9 Approval group techniques
- 65 preventive-type actions: training workshops on conflict management and mediation skills

We assessed both the direct impact (based on training actions) and the indirect impact (based on media actions). The result was a total of 5.554 users who received, one way or another, information about mediation and services that were opened for conflict management.

There are other results from this Project that are worth mentioning, such as:
1. The creation of a Mediation Observatory at the University of Barcelona (Spain), dedicated to innovation and research on organisational conflict management and mediation, in September 2008.
2. The settlement of the Project thanks to annual agreements with the various healthcare institutions in Catalonia (collaborative centres,

---

[4] Although we generally consider those actions as being preventive, we sometimes use them in situations of active conflict, where they are then considered as "curative", as presented in the results section.

CatSalut and the Department of Healthcare of the Catalan Government) from 2006 to date.
3. Availability of an annual innovation system and continuous training for healthcare mediators in the form of "Mediation Laboratories" which have already taken place four times, from 2005 to date.

3. Conclusions

From the data obtained and subsequent qualitative and quantitative analysis, we can confirm that there are factors that underlie, generate or activate conflict in this kind of organisations. They are basically what we call the *"Coexistence effect"*, which happens in specific departments and the *"Accumulative effect"* due to joint work year after year, whether in the same department or in the same organisation.[5]

Knowing these "effects" enables us to design preventive systems to tackle conflict and systems which promote healthy relationships for the people and groups involved. On the other hand, early action is a must to improve negotiation spaces in healthcare institutions. Anyhow, UMS have strengthened and they now offer high quality services in situations of conflict which can be complex, highly intense and, in certain cases, chronic.

This is why we recommend a series of actions which are necessary to build a socially responsible organisation that "cares" in the widest possible sense of the term:
1. A comprehensive and systematic training of people who work in healthcare. This improves the relational culture of organisations and enables conflict prevention and self-management in the workplace itself. It also increases the real penetration of the mediation culture while making UMS more cost efficient.
2. Authorizing a "primary healthcare system for conflict" which would facilitate the management of discrepancies and conflicts where they happen, by peer mediators who are specifically trained for that purpose.
3. Create a second level or "special care system for conflict", which would imply the existence of Mediation Units where high-level conflicts or difficult to solve conflicts would be addressed and where more complex actions could take place, for instance mediation in those cases or the application of group approval techniques.[6]

---

[5] Data extracted from the doctoral thesis of the author presented in September 2008, at the *Universidad Complutense de Madrid* (pending publication)
[6] This systemic approach is being implemented from 2009 in Catalonia thanks to agreements between The Mediation Observatory of the University of Barcelona, *CatSalut* and the Department of Health of the Catalan Government, as an annual innovation and with the aim of organizing a conflict management system from a mediation viewpoint within the

4. These Mediation Units should be opened in a sufficient but not excessive number, as specialized services dedicated to dealing with conflict and where people who need a professional mediator could go. This recommendation arises from one of the mediation principles which refers to "giving back responsibility to concerned parties". That is to say, we should help to improve their skills to prevent and manage conflict, but not cause them to become dependent with regard to handle conflict on a daily basis. For that purpose, training is obviously a pillar on which any approach for change and improvement in healthcare institutions that is oriented towards "the culture of peace" and "building third side organisations", also called third way organisations, should be based.

Finally, we think that it is necessary to add that the decision to create this type of services represents an added value for the Public Administration to consider, given that the presented approach can be extrapolated, with the required adjustments, to any type of complex organisation.

An organisation which not only develops whatever it was created for, but which is also capable of going beyond what is expected by trying to make the working space more useful and "caring" is an intelligent organisation, a learning organisation, which uses criteria of social corporative responsibility and can define itself and picture itself with this distinctive positive mark.

In such an organisation, "leaders are designers, stewards, and teachers. They are responsible for building organisations where people continually expand their capabilities to understand complexity, clarify vision, and improve shared mental models – that is, they are responsible for learning" (Senge, 1993). Similarly, people who work and make contacts there learn to collaborate, develop their skills and creativity, work with excellence and participate in a negotiated and pacifying way, seeking the common interests and the satisfaction of everyone's needs.

References

Abrevaya S, Basz V. (2005) *Facilitación en Políticas Públicas. Una experiencia Interhospitalaria*, HL Librería Editorial Histórica, Buenos Aires.

Ambrojo, J. C. (2006) "Apoyo a la fiscalía por pedir la cárcel para los agresores de profesores y personal sanitario", *El País*, 16 November, available at: http://www.elpais.com/articulo/Comunidad/Valenciana/Fiscalia/plantea/tratami entos/ambulatorios/lugar/internar/enfermos/psiquiatricos/elpepuespval/2007012 9elpval_13/Tes (accessed 20 November 2006)

Bertrand, LL. (2005) "El Síndic de Greuges investiga la tardanza de salud en resolver quejas por errores médicos", *El País*, 7 November.

Catalan healthcare system.

Burton, J. (2000) *La Resolución de Conflictos como Sistema Político*, Instituto de Análisis y Resolución de Conflictos, George Mason University, Fairfax, Virginia.

Cabezalí, J. M. (2001) "¿Cómo se manifiestan los conflictos en el ámbito sanitario?", *Revista de Conflictología. Una herramienta para la paz*. Edimurtra, n. 3, pp. 41-45.

Farré, S. (2004) *Gestión de Conflictos: Taller de mediación. Un enfoque socioafectivo*, Ariel, Barcelona.

Floyer A. (1993) *Como utilizar la mediación para resolver conflictos en las organizaciones,* Paidos, Barcelona.

Femenia, N. "Costos y Consecuencias de los conflictos" in *Ganaroposiciones.com*, Florida, available at: www.ganaropciones.com/conflicto.htm (accessed 20 August 2006).

Novel, G. (2009) *Los programas educativos en la resolución de conflictos en el ámbito sanitario: propuesta de un modelo*, doctoral thesis presented at the Universidad Complutense de Madrid, Madrid (pending publication)

Prats, A.; Pons, G. (2004) "Prevención de conflictos empresa/sociedad. La responsabilidad social corporativa" in Vinyamata, E. *Guerra y paz en el trabajo: Conflictos y Conflictología en las organizaciones,* Tirant lo Blanc, Universitat de València, Valencia, pp. 81-100.

Sancho, F. (2006) "El creciente malestar de la sanidad catalana" in *Diario Médico.com*, Tribuna, available at: http://www.diariomedico.com/edicion/diario_medico/profesion/es/desarrollo/6 45080.html (accessed 17 July 2006), Tribuna.

Schnitman, D. F.; Schnitman, J. (eds.) (2000) *Resolución de conflictos. Nuevos diseños, nuevos contextos,* Granica, Buenos Aires.

Senge, P. (1993) *La Quinta Disciplina,* Granica, Buenos Aires.

Ury, W. L. (2000) *Alcanzar la paz: Diez caminos para resolver conflictos, en la casa, el trabajo y el mundo,* Paidós: Barcelona.

Vall, A. (2004) "Los conflictos en las Organizaciones" in Vinyamata, E. *Guerra y paz en el trabajo: Conflictos y Conflictología en las organizaciones,* Tirant lo Blanc, Universitat de Valencia, Valencia, pp. 175-201.

www.ingramcontent.com/pod-product-compliance
Lightning Source LLC
Chambersburg PA
CBHW070717220326
41598CB00024BA/3192